Becoming a Teacher of Language and Literacy

Becoming a Teacher of Language and Literacy explores what it means to be a literacy educator in the 21st century. It promotes a reflective and inquiry-based approach to literacy teaching and examines three central questions:

1. How do teachers approach the teaching of reading and writing, speaking and listening within a digital age?
2. How do teachers approach the standardisation of literacy, including high-stakes testing?
3. How do teachers work within the framework of the Australian Curriculum: English?

The book covers a range of contemporary topics in language and literacy education, including reading and creating digital texts, supporting intercultural engagement in literacy education, and developing community partnerships. Each chapter features teacher narratives, current theoretical perspectives, examples of practice and reflective questions.

The narratives are designed to prompt reflection about teachers' professional practice within local school settings. They convey the voices of teachers as they grapple with the challenges of their professional practice.

Written by a team of experts, *Becoming a Teacher of Language and Literacy* is a valuable resource for teachers as they make the transition from pre-service education to their first years of teaching.

Additional resources for students are available online at www.cambridge.edu.au/academic/languageandliteracy.

Becoming a Teacher of Language and Literacy

Edited by
Brenton Doecke, Glenn Auld and
Muriel Wells

CAMBRIDGE
UNIVERSITY PRESS

477 Williamstown Road, Port Melbourne, VIC 3207, Australia

Cambridge University Press is part of the University of Cambridge.

It furthers the University's mission by disseminating knowledge in the pursuit of education, learning and research at the highest international levels of excellence.

www.cambridge.org

Information on this title: www.cambridge.org/9781107662865

© Cambridge University Press 2014

This publication is copyright. Subject to statutory exception
and to the provisions of relevant collective licensing agreements,
no reproduction of any part may take place without the written
permission of Cambridge University Press.

First published 2014

Cover designed by Studio Pounce
Typeset by Aptara Corp.
Printed in Singapore by C.O.S Printers Pte Ltd

A catalogue record for this publication is available from the British Library

*A Cataloguing-in-Publication entry is available from the catalogue
of the National Library of Australia at* www.nla.gov.au

ISBN 978-1-107-66286-5 Paperback

Additional resources for this publication at www.cambridge.edu.au/academic/languageandliteracy.

Reproduction and communication for educational purposes

The Australian *Copyright Act 1968* (the Act) allows a maximum of
one chapter or 10% of the pages of this work, whichever is the greater,
to be reproduced and/or communicated by any educational institution
for its educational purposes provided that the educational institution
(or the body that administers it) has given a remuneration notice to
Copyright Agency Limited (CAL) under the Act.

For details of the CAL licence for educational institutions contact:

Copyright Agency Limited
Level 15, 233 Castlereagh Street
Sydney NSW 2000
Telephone: (02) 9394 7600
Facsimile: (02) 9394 7601
E-mail: info@copyright.com.au

Cambridge University Press has no responsibility for the persistence or
accuracy of URLs for external or third-party internet websites referred to in
this publication and does not guarantee that any content on such
websites is, or will remain, accurate or appropriate.

*Please be aware that this publication may contain several variations of Aboriginal and Torres
Strait Islander terms and spellings; no disrespect is intended. Please note that the terms
'Indigenous Australians' and 'Aboriginal and Torres Strait Islander peoples' may be used
interchangeably in this publication.*

Contents

Contents

About the authors

Brenton Doecke   Brenton Doecke is a professor in the School of Education, Deakin University. He was the editor of *English in Australia*, the journal of the Australian Association for the Teaching of English (AATE), as well as the co-editor (with Jennifer Rennie and Annette Patterson) of *The Australian Journal of Language and Literacy*. He played a leading role, with Margaret Gill, in developing the Standards for Teachers of English Language and Literacy in Australia (STELLA), a joint project involving both the AATE and the Australian Literacy Educators Association (ALEA). His most recent publications include *Literary Praxis: A Conversational Inquiry into the Teaching of Literature* 2011, Sense, Rotterdam, co-edited with Piet-Hein van de Ven and *Confronting Practice: Classroom Investigations into Language and Learning* 2011, Phoenix Education, Putney NSW, co-authored with Douglas McClenaghan.

Glenn Auld   Glenn Auld is a senior lecturer in Education specialising in language and literacy at Deakin University in Melboure. He teaches and researches in the areas of new media, ethics and Aboriginal and Torres Strait Islander Education. Glenn was the inaugural winner of the Betty Watts Award for research in Indigenous Education from the Australian Association of Researchers in Education. Glenn has recently explored the ethical dilemmas of using social media in the classroom. He is interested in how teachers connect the standardised curriculum with the sociocultural interests of the students.

Muriel Wells   Muriel Wells is a senior lecturer at Deakin University in Geelong. Muriel's research is focused on the teaching of literacy in primary schools, on the use of emerging technologies in education generally, how mobile technologies might be used to enhance learning in primary schools, the flipped classroom, social media and remixing learning. Muriel also teaches about, and conducts research into, the pedagogies of online teaching and learning and teacher professional learning. She has worked closely with a range of schools across educational sectors to support the work of teachers as researchers, particularly in regard to the infusion of emerging technologies into teaching and learning, and conducted research partnerships that have investigated sustainable models of teacher professional learning and capacity building in schools.

Anne Cloonan   Anne Cloonan is coordinator of Language and Literacy Education at Deakin University. Her teaching and research explore the complexities surrounding contemporary literacy education. With a preference for working in partnerships of collaborative inquiry with teachers, students and parents, her projects include 'The impact of professional learning on literacy teachers and learners' (Catholic Education Office), 'Literacy education in innovative learning environments' (Department of Education and Early Childhood Development/Organisation for Economic Cooperation and Development), 'Asia literate teaching' (Asia Education Foundation/Australian Institute for Teaching and School Leadership), 'Intercultural understanding in primary and secondary schools' (Australian Research Council) and 'Creative, critical, digital: connecting home and school learning' (Catholic Education Office).

Gaelene Hope-Rowe   Gaelene Hope-Rowe is a lecturer in Pedagogy and Curriculum and her teaching intersects with her research through her continued teaching practice in rural and regional school settings. Gaelene's research interests are in middle years classrooms, interdisciplinary and community-based curricula, and perspectives on teaching students with diverse cultural and linguistic resources. She is interested in pedagogies that promote positively diverse classrooms and the role of withdrawal programs in providing literacy support for older 'at-risk' learners. Gaelene works with teachers from predominantly monocultural communities to reflect on their personal resources in preparing to teach diverse learners and is writing a self-study for an international publication on rural teacher education (in press, Springer 2014).

Kirsten Hutchison   Kirsten Hutchison is a senior lecturer in Language and Literacy at Deakin University and teaches in undergraduate, masters and higher degree by research programs, with a focus on early and middle years language and literacy teaching, new and traditional literacies and community literacies. Her research and teaching interests are centred on language and literacy and the nexus between education and social justice. Several of her current research projects involve working with teachers and academics to develop digital and culturally responsive pedagogies, work-integrated learning and internationalised curriculum. She coordinates a mentoring program at Deakin University which involves pre-service teachers collaboratively researching their literacy and teaching practices in culturally diverse secondary school communities. Her research experience also includes major projects funded by the Australian Research Council, the Department of Education and Early Childhood Development, Victoria and collaborations with the Centre for Multicultural Youth and the Catholic Education Office.

Rachel MacGilp   Rachel MacGilp is a primary school teacher in Melbourne. In her teaching in rural, remote and metropolitan schools she has fostered a reflective teaching practice that informs her teaching and maintains a professional dialogue with her teaching peers. Through these reflections on her practice she has developed a strong professional understanding of the challenges and rewards that come from teaching students from diverse backgrounds. Rachel has a strong understanding of literacy pedagogy grounded in her role as a teacher linguist in a remote Indigenous Australian community. Rachel is a PhD candidate, researching how teachers work with and around the standardised curriculum.

Maria Nicholas   Maria Nicholas is a lecturer at Deakin University in Geelong. Maria is an early career researcher with interests in literacy engagement and development in the pre-school years, and digital literacies. Maria's research interests also include literacy development in the early years of schooling, diverse educational needs in the middle years, school curriculum design and planning, assessment and feedback and teacher education. Maria's teaching interests include early and middle years language and literacy teaching, and teachers as reflective practitioners. Maria began her career as a primary school teacher and has worked for the Department of Education and Early Childhood Development, offering literacy and numeracy education consultancy to primary and secondary schools in Victoria, Australia.

Sarah Ohi Sarah Ohi is a lecturer at Deakin University in Melbourne. Sarah believes that all children have the right to become literate as being literate empowers people and changes their lives. Sarah's teaching, research and publications are nested in three main areas, Literacy, Teacher Learning and Policy. Her main emphasis is on the power of words and the impact of discourse and the development of concepts in education settings (e.g. recent work on building intercultural understanding through literature). Her research on teacher learning investigates the affordances that technology offers for professional learning and involves her designing and delivering professional learning for pre-service and in-service teachers to ensure they establish firm foundational knowledge of children's literacy development. She also focuses on literacy policy and the way in which it is subject to periodic change and is continually evolving. Sarah's research interests have resulted in the development of rich partnerships with early childhood centres, schools and the winning of government research tenders.

Joanne O'Mara Joanne O'Mara is a senior lecturer in Language and Literacy at Deakin University in Melbourne. Her current research investigates mobile touch screen devices in the literacy classroom, digital games and literacy and aesthetics and arts of the English curriculum. Joanne's previous research has also focused on advancing understandings of contemporary language and literacy practices, innovative pedagogical approaches to language and literacy education and ways in which educational stakeholders might improve student language and literacy learning in the future. She is particularly interested in the ways in which drama pedagogy and the uses of digital games and tools might contribute to literacy learning. Joanne teaches in the areas of English Curriculum Studies, creativity in the curriculum, language and literacy development through drama and new technologies and drama pedagogy.

Louise Paatsch Louise Paatsch is a senior lecturer at Deakin University in Geelong. Louise is currently involved in a number of research projects in the areas of early childhood and primary-aged language literacy, multimodal literacies and teaching literacy pedagogy. Her research uses a mixed-methods approach. Other research includes investigation of the following areas: pragmatic and narrative skills of children and adolescents with hearing loss, oral language skills of young school-aged children within play-based programs, connecting creative and critical thinking within digital literacies in and out of school, teacher strategies that scaffold children's language and literacy learning and home literacy practices and language skills of pre-school children.

Acknowledgements

This book draws on a range of research projects in which the authors have been involved, and they are mentioned here. None of these projects would have been possible without the participation of teachers, parents and students, as well as paraprofessionals who work with students in inclusive classrooms. We thank all these people for the support they have given us in our research. Some of these projects have involved industry support, for which we are also grateful.

Mandated literacy assessment and the reorganisation of teachers' work

Australian Research Council (ARC) Discovery Project (no. DP0986449) involving the University of South Australia, Queensland University of Technology and Deakin University in Australia and York and Victoria Universities in Canada. Chief investigators (2009–11): Barbara Comber, Philip Cormack, Helen Nixon, Alex Kostogriz and Brenton Doecke. Partner investigators in Canada: Dorothy Smith and Alison Griffith.

Studying the effectiveness of teacher education (SETE <http://www.setearc.com.au/>)

ARC Linkage Project (no. LP110100003) involving the Victorian Institute of Teaching (VIT), the Queensland College of Teachers (QCT) the Victorian Department of Education and Early Childhood Development (DEECD), the Queensland Department of Education, Training and Employment (QDETE), Deakin University's School of Education in Victoria and Griffith University's Faculty of Education in Queensland. Researchers (2011–14): Diane Mayer (Victoria University), Andrea Allard (Deakin University), Richard Bates (Deakin University), Mary Dixon (Deakin University), Brenton Doecke (Deakin University), Alex Kostogriz (Deakin University), Bernadette Walker-Gibbs (Deakin University), Simone White (Monash University), Leonie Rowan (Griffith University), Jodie Kline (Deakin University) and Phillipa Hodder (Deakin University).

Doing diversity differently: intercultural understanding in primary and secondary schools

ARC Linkage Project (no. LP120200319). Researchers (2012–15): Christine Halse, Fethi Mansouri, Ruth Arber, Claire Charles, Anne Cloonan, Julianne Moss, Sarah Ohi, Jo O'Mara, Yin Paradis (all from Deakin University), with Colin Arrowsmith (RMIT University), Nida Densen (University of Western Sydney) and Naomi Priest (The University of Melbourne). Partner organisations include Together for Humanity (TFH), the Department of Education and Early Childhood Development (DEECD) Victoria, Victoria Curriculum and Assessment Authority (VCAA) and Pukunui Technology (Moodle).

A comparative investigation of pedagogical possibilities of digital tools for family and school early literacy education

Insight Grant Social Science, Humanities Research Council, Canada (award no. 435-2013-0590). Researchers (2013–16): Linda Laidlaw (University of Alberta), Jill

Acknowledgements

Blackmore (Deakin University), Joanne O'Mara (Deakin University), Dennis Sumara (University of Calgary).

Multiageing: one Australian school story
A project resulting in a short film about inclusion in the Australian primary school context, working with the Royal Children's Hospital (Melbourne) film crew. Julianne Moss and Joanne O'Mara (2013–14).

STAR – Supporting teachers as action researchers
STAR was a three year-long partnership with the Catholic Education Office, Western region of the Department of Education and Early Childhood development (DEECD) and Deakin University. The STAR project explored how teachers' professional learning may be enhanced by positioning teachers as practitioner researchers and professionals who are capable of generating change from within their local contexts. The project looked at how schools might develop and sustain curriculum and pedagogical initiatives by combining the principles of action research and communities of practice, and how teachers' professional learning can be enhanced through regional and university support for teachers as action researchers. Researchers: Muriel Wells and Damian Blake (2008–10).

Principal-led school improvement and teacher capacity building in the Barwon South Network
This local regional network research project followed on from a Victorian statewide approach to school improvement that used evidence-based and data-informed decision-making processes based on an explicit theory of action that underpinned changes and reform linking leadership to school improvement. It was designed to provide a better understanding of the impact the introduction of a new model of school improvement might have on leaders in schools, on teaching practices and student learning. It looked at how the use of data can inform teaching, how policy changes are translated into changed classroom practices and the impact of various leadership styles and the associated decision-making processes. Researchers (2011–12): Russell Tytler, Shaun Rawolle, Coral Campbell, Louise Paatsch and Muriel Wells.

Investigating the impact of professional learning for teachers and their students' learning
Funded by the Catholic Education Office, Melbourne. Researcher (2011): Anne Cloonan.

Evaluating student use of technology in a 1 : 1 computing program
Funded by the Department of Education and Early Childhood Development, Victoria. Researchers (2010): Anne Cloonan, Kirsten Hutchison and Louise Paatsch.

Using mobile phones to improve children's learning outcomes in remote Indigenous communities
Monash University Seeding Grant. Chief Investigators (2010): Glenn Auld, Ilana Snyder and Michael Henderson.

The Australian Curriculum: and now what?
Small grant for the Centre for Research on Futures and Educational Innovation, Deakin University. Chief researchers (2013): Maria Nicholas and Brenton Doecke.

We also wish to acknowledge the contributions that the following teachers, schools and systems made to particular chapters:

Steven Clacher, Chinese International School, Hong Kong
Thomas Fraser, Warrnambool Primary School
Teresa Higgins, Moriac Primary School
Moriac Primary School
Rachel Thomas, Maningrida College
Jade Collier, St Mary's Primary School
Kristina Marinovic, St Mary's Primary School
St Mary's Primary School
Catholic Education Office, Western Region of Victoria.

Chapter 1

How to read this book

Brenton Doecke, Glenn Auld
and Muriel Wells

This is not a 'how-to' book. The following pages are not filled with tips and tricks about how to best teach language and literacy. We believe that the work of language and literacy educators is deeply embedded within the school communities where they are teaching: what works in one setting might not work in another; what works with one child (e.g. drilling and skilling in phonics) might not be appropriate for another child. Language and literacy are complex, as we shall affirm repeatedly in the following chapters, and we are very sceptical of anyone who claims to have found the best method to teach reading, writing or any other dimension of a child's growth as a literate human being, given the unique contexts in which teachers work.

Nor does this book pretend to give you 'all-you-ever-needed-to-know' about language and literacy. Throughout the book you will find references to current research, and sometimes you will be given summary accounts of what that research has found, such as the discussion of Shirley Brice Heath's work in Chapter 2. Several other chapters use the work of researchers such as Luis Moll and Pat Thomson. But by and large, what we have chosen to do is to point you in the direction of research that you might like to follow up, rather than giving you potted versions of what researchers are saying.

What this book aims to do is to support you in your efforts to think critically about your work as a language and literacy educator. In the following chapters you will find plenty of examples of how to investigate, reflect on and better understand your teaching of language and literacy. This is to enable you to become a professional who not only responds to but shapes decisions relating to policy and practice within your school community. Chapter 3, for example, argues the desirability of professional learning that is ongoing, collaborative and embedded in the day-to-day work of teachers. This is also to suppose that you are engaging in ongoing professional reading that enables you to think about your practice differently.

Continuing reading

Teachers who are reflective practitioners can never be fully satisfied with second-hand accounts of current research. No doubt it is difficult for busy classroom teachers to find time to do independent reading. You would certainly find it hard to work through (say) Shirley Brice Heath's *Ways with Words* (1983/1994) after a long day at school, but it is still important to maintain a reading habit of some kind in order to engage critically in your work as a language and literacy educator.

Unfortunately, much of the material about instruction on Departmental websites (e.g. the information about the E5 instructional model on the Victorian Education website or about C2C in Queensland) has the character of 'truths' being delivered through a funnel, to use a metaphor that Jean Clandinin and Michael Connelly (1995, pp. 7–8) employ to characterise the way knowledge is typically passed on to teachers by experts and other authorities, without any recognition of the knowledge that teachers themselves have developed both through their independent reading and (crucially) through their ongoing interactions with children. Curiously enough, such formulae are also abstracted from the research that might underpin them. Stripped of their 'inquiry origins' (to borrow again from Jean Clandinin and Michael Connelly, p. 8), they are reduced to the level of glossy logos or advertising slogans, as though teachers should not be concerned about whether they have any validity. Although it is difficult for a teacher to find the time to read, we are nonetheless thinking of you as someone who does not simply accept what you are told but as someone who continually seeks to maintain a critical perspective on your professional practice by engaging in independent professional reading as a component of your professional learning.

Such reading is important, not only as a source of information about teaching strategies that might be effective, but as a way of re-envisioning your practice as a language and literacy teacher. Reading can open up dimensions of your professional practice that you have not seen or thought about before (to which you have been 'blind', as we shall explain in Chapter 2). Brice Heath's study does not translate directly into strategies that you might use to engage socially disadvantaged students in their learning. What it does is sensitise you to the values and beliefs that shape your work as a teacher, encouraging you to learn more about your students, including getting to know what they believe and value, in order to establish a supportive and productive dialogue with them. Many of the researchers who you might follow as part of your professional reading have spent many years teaching in classrooms. By reading their work you are displaying respect and intellectual generosity towards their approach to language and literacy, with a view to seeing whether their experiences might provide a perspective on your own professional practice. In becoming a teacher of language and literacy you are joining a huge conversation in which teachers and researchers from around the world are engaged, sharing their experiences and trying to learn from one another.

> Information about E5 can be found at <http://www.education.vic.gov.au/school/teachers/support/pages/e5.aspx>.
>
> Information about C2 cam be found at <http://education.qld.gov.au/c2c/>.

Teachers of language and literacy in Australia can gain access to this conversation by becoming members of the Australian Literacy Educators' Association (ALEA) or the Australian Association for the Teaching of English (AATE) (or by joining both). The former has traditionally catered for primary educators, while the latter tends to focus on the work of secondary English teachers. Both professional associations publish highly respected journals, namely *The Australian Journal of Language and Literacy* (ALEA) and *English in Australia* (AATE). Language and Literacy teachers in other countries belong to similar subject associations in order to be part of a larger professional network that sustains their continuing professional learning and professional commitment.

Reading about the work of other teachers enables you to engage in issues beyond your own immediate experience and context. This book features the work of many experienced teachers as they grapple with questions that have emerged for them in the course of their day-to-day practice. These teachers may be able to exercise more professional autonomy than early career teachers, who are typically on contract. The initiatives they take may therefore appear to be outside your realm of possibilities at the current moment. Yet even teachers in ongoing positions continue to grapple with institutional constraints that sometimes conflict with their professional knowledge and beliefs. The chapters in this book show them negotiating the complexities of their professional practice within their particular institutional settings, always with the interests of their students at the forefront of their minds, and thus we hope that their stories will be instructive for you. In response to reading the following accounts of their practice, we hope that you can make informed choices about your own professional practice as you pursue your career.

Reflection and discussion

When early career teachers are asked to recall the parts of their initial teacher education programs that were most effective, they almost invariably nominate their teaching experience or fieldwork as having provided them with the practical experience they needed in order to begin operating in a classroom. This is understandable – it is, after all, vital that you gain experience in negotiating the social relationships that comprise any classroom, learning how to manage children's expectations and gradually developing a wisdom of practice that enables you to handle situations as they emerge. But far from developing 'naturally', such wisdom is the product of continually reflecting on your practice in an effort to understand the complexities of teaching and learning. Early career teachers, in fact, often nominate as the other most valuable part of their initial teacher education programs the fact that they were taught how to be reflective and to learn from their experiences. This is where reading (or 'theory') becomes very important, because it provides you with concepts and a language – 'curriculum', 'pedagogy', 'assessment', 'evaluation', to name the most obvious – that allow you to begin to make sense of the complexities of the social world of the classroom.

How has your reading helped you to understand your experiences as a teacher? Can you think of a book or an idea that gave you particularly compelling insights into the complexities of your professional practice? What, in your view, is the relationship between 'theory' and 'practice'?

These observations derive from a major research project in which researchers at Deakin University have been involved, namely Studying the Effectiveness of Teacher Education (SETE), a longitudinal study that surveyed early career teachers about their initial teacher education programs and their experiences in schools.

For details about SETE see <http://www.setearc.com.au>. See also Allard and Doecke (2014) for an account of the experiences of one group of early career teachers who were interviewed for this project.

Reading stories

Our recognition of the importance of practice is shown by the stories that comprise much of this volume. All are stories about teachers grappling with the challenges they face in their teaching and the kinds of initiatives they take in order to support their students' language and learning. These stories provide examples of the work of committed language and literacy educators, without any of them pretending to be a model of best practice. Rather than being illustrative of best practice, they show teachers working within their school communities, drawing on the knowledge and experience available to them in order to enhance the educational opportunities of their students. Some teachers have told their own stories (see especially Rachael MacGilp's account of her work in Chapter 2). Others take the form of cases constructed by the authors of the chapters on the basis of interviews with teachers with whom they have worked.

Some of these cases are examples of what Timothy Hopper, Kathy Sanford and Sarah Bonsor-Kurki (2012) call 'a creative non-fiction ethnographic genre', whereby the researchers 'tell a story on behalf of participants by creating representative characters and replacing names and places to protect anonymity. The focus of this genre is to engage the reader's emotions using a dramatization of real events that are spliced together to create a believable account.' We should also add that in exercising this kind of creative licence the authors attempt to respect the voice and perspective of teachers and to foreground the complexity of the situations in which they work.

When reading these stories you are not being invited to agree with the rationales that the teachers give for their actions, as though each story contains a lesson that can directly be applied to your own situation. You should feel free to critically (but respectfully) interrogate what these teachers say and do and to consider the applicability of their initiatives to your own situation.

Along with our scepticism of pedagogical bandwagons that herald the best way to teach literacy, we are also sceptical of claims by people that they are able to make judgments about quality teaching, as though it is all about an individual teacher's performance, without regard to the social relationships and school contexts in which teachers operate, or the infrastructure that underpins any teacher's work. This issue is emerging with increasing frequency as governments try to introduce initiatives such as performance pay, turning a blind eye to the fact that teachers are crucially dependent on each other when it comes to implementing curriculum and pedagogy responsive to the needs of the children with whom they are working.

All the teachers whose professional practice is represented in this volume would say that working collaboratively with colleagues is one of the most rewarding aspects of their professional lives (all the stories reflect this kind of professional stance, but you could look at Chapter 6 and Chapter 8 for especially compelling examples of collaborative practice). Along with a disposition to continually reflect on their professional practice (or what Alan Reid [2004] calls an 'inquiry stance'), they would say that a vital dimension of their work is a capacity to collaborate with colleagues, sharing experiences and learning from and with them. That is why they have been generous enough to open up their classroom doors, letting us observe and talk with them about what they are doing. Teaching is at its heart collaborative work, and any attempt to improve the quality of teaching in schools must likewise be collaborative in nature, rather than 'obsessing', as Michael Fullan and Andy Hargreaves (2012) have argued, about 'celebrating the stars and dismissing the duds'.

> Michael Fullan and Andy Hargreaves (2012) suggest there is a 'need to concentrate on moving the entire profession forward instead of obsessing about the extremes in the field by celebrating the stars and dismissing the duds.'

You will find that each story is usually accompanied by prompts that invite you to reflect critically on what you have read. As we have just said, you are not being asked to agree with what the teachers say about their work. You may reach a judgement, for example, that the initiative being described is simply not one that would work in your setting. But whatever judgement you make, you should try to express it in a provisional way. Language and literacy teaching is far too complex to lend itself to simplistic comments about whether any example of teaching is good or bad. Ultimately, you might sense an ideological difference between your stance and that of the teachers whose voices you hear in this volume, but such a judgment should always foreground the deeply situated nature of teaching, and the fact that the circumstances being described are specific to the teacher concerned and the context in which they work.

What occurs in classrooms is always subject to interpretation. There are at least as many versions of what occurs in a classroom as there are people within it. What you need to do when engaging with the stories in this book is to read them reflexively, trying to be mindful of the values and beliefs that might be shaping your own reaction to the people and incidents described, rather than making a hard and fast judgement about the example of professional practice that has been presented to you.

See Brenton Doecke (2013) and Brenton Doecke and Douglas McClenaghan (2011) for arguments about the need for educators to reflexively engage in their professional practice.

The teachers you read about are themselves acting reflexively, critically monitoring the initiatives they are taking. Chapter 4 provides a good example of teachers working reflexively when negotiating curriculum changes in their school, specifically with respect to the need to develop their practice with emerging technologies.

Debating literacy

Another reason why this is not a 'how to' book is that all aspects of language and literacy education have unfortunately been politicised. Just about every week in the media, you'll find someone lamenting declining literacy standards and blaming it all on teachers. 'Back to the basics', 'Direct instruction', 'Explicit teaching', 'Explicit learning' – quick-fix solutions abound in public debates about education, and it is necessary, as a professional, to step back from such claims and quietly insist that there are no easy remedies or instructional manuals that match the complexity of what you do.

In becoming a teacher of language and literacy, you are doing something far more complicated than learning how to drive a car or operate a computer, activities for which instructional manuals may very well be useful. As we have just stated, what you are doing requires a disposition to continually reflect on your teaching, to 'gladly learn and teach' (to borrow a famous line from Geoffrey Chaucer's *The Canterbury Tales*). This involves cultivating an ability to recognise the difference between what you set out to achieve in a lesson and what you actually accomplish. There is always a difference between teaching and learning. One does not simply fold into the other, as in simplistic talk about so-called 'explicit' teaching leading to 'explicit' learning. Classrooms are places where people interact with one another, each bringing something unique to the exchanges that occur there. They are not places where you can apply a 'means-end' mentality, as though a set of inputs will necessarily produce the required outputs.

Far from being a bad thing, this is a condition for rich learning to occur. As Douglas Barnes, a famous English educator, has written about the planning teachers do in advance of instruction:

When people talk about 'the school curriculum' they often mean 'what teachers plan in advance for their pupils to learn'. But a curriculum made only of a teacher's intentions would be an insubstantial thing from which nobody would learn much. To become meaningful, a curriculum has to be enacted by pupils as well as teachers, all of whom have their private lives outside school. By 'enact' I mean come together in a meaningful communication – talk, write, read books, collaborate, become angry with one another, learn what to say and do, and how to interpret what others say and do. A curriculum as soon as it becomes more than intentions is embodied in the communicative life of an institution, the talk and gestures by which pupils and teachers exchange meanings even when they quarrel or cannot agree. In this sense curriculum is a form of communication. (Douglas Barnes 1992, p. 14)

> Douglas Barnes's book, *From Communication to Curriculum*, was originally published in 1975, but you may still find it worthwhile to familiarise yourself with Barnes's work and the key concepts that underpin it, especially these days when a problematical notion of teaching as simply transmission of knowledge to pupils, as though they can be treated as empty vessels to be filled, is once again becoming influential. For a similar understanding of the interactive nature of classroom exchanges, you might also find it worthwhile to read Garth Boomer's (1992) ideas about negotiating the curriculum.

Barnes's description of classroom exchanges gets close, we think, to capturing the complexities of teaching and learning and the professional learning that can occur when teachers reflect on the difference between the intended and the enacted curriculum. Yet, you can hardly detect a trace of those complexities whenever newspapers or television current affairs shows feature debates about literacy and schooling. Everyone, it seems, has an opinion about literacy, often drawing on their own experience of schooling, as though that somehow gives them authority to say whatever they like and impose their views on the entire profession. Politicians and the media are not slow to voice their opinions about the best way to teach reading or writing. You should always ask whether their opinions reflect any substantial knowledge of research on language and literacy.

Reflection and discussion

How do you feel about the way literacy issues are reported in the popular media? Do you feel that the reporting is always accurate? Why is literacy such a hotly debated topic? What, from your reading of newspapers and other popular media, do people appear to think learning to read or write is all about? How does what they say compare with your knowledge of current research? What do they understand by the word 'literacy'? How does this compare with your own understanding of this word? What, as a teacher, do you think you might be able to do in order to show to people outside the profession the complexities of the work you do?

Affirming your professional knowledge

A few years ago groups of primary literacy educators and secondary English teachers came together under the auspices of the Australian Association for the Teaching of English (AATE) and the Australian Literacy Educators' Association (ALEA) to discuss the knowledge and values that unite them as a profession. The project eventually became known as the STELLA project (i.e. Standards for Teachers of English Language and Literacy in Australia), involving the development of a website that comprises statements and stories about the complexities of English teaching.

Visit <http://www.stella.org.au> to read these stories.

This was in an effort to show what AD Hope, the famous poet and critic, had said many years before, namely that for English teachers to truly be a profession, they needed to be 'recognised in the community as the body responsible for expert advice and for saying what ought and ought not to be done by those who administer education in this country'. (Hope, 1967, p. 5)

Given the number of regulatory authorities, such as the Australian Institute of Teaching and School Leadership (AITSL), and the Australian Curriculum and Assessment Authority (ACARA) that have been set up over the past decade, it is a moot point as to whether literacy educators in this country have improved their professional status since Hope gave the address from which we have taken his statement about professionalism.

For the Australian Institute for Teaching and School Leadership (AITSL) go to <http://www.aitsl.edu.au>.

For the Australian Curriculum, Assessment and Reporting Authority (ACARA) see <http://www.acara.edu.au/default.asp>.

Rather than trusting teachers as possessing the authority of knowledge and experience to advise governments as to 'what ought and ought not to be done' when it comes to providing all students in Australian schools with rich learning experiences, teachers are increasingly being told what to do by outside authorities who are operating at a remove from the specific school communities in which teachers are working. This is a disturbing trend that is also evident in other parts of the world, as Michael Fullan and Andy Hargreaves (2012) make plain.

Yet the STELLA website remains a valuable resource for teachers' stories and other texts about language and literacy teaching, and you would find it worthwhile to visit the website, not least because of the statements these teachers developed about the language modes: listening, speaking, writing and reading. The opening sentence of the 'listening and speaking', for example, goes like this:

For accomplished teachers, talk is at the centre of English curriculum and pedagogy.

Their classrooms are rich linguistic communities in which all students participate. They give focused attention to various aspects of listening and speaking, teaching their students to listen actively and to share their ideas and experiences. Crucial in this respect is the establishment of a classroom environment that supports productive interaction between students in both small group situations and whole class activities. Accomplished teachers know how to structure such activities so that their students are able to jointly construct knowledge through talk.

This attempt by a group of language and literacy educators to conceptualise classrooms as spaces for social interaction reflects the same standpoint as the statement by Douglas Barnes that we have already quoted. Along with the other statements about the language modes on the STELLA website, these teachers are acknowledging the agency of students as they come together to engage in communication within classroom settings.

You will find that this recognition of the way students actively participate in classrooms is also a feature of the chapters that follow. Indeed, Chapter 9 focuses specifically on how to ensure that students have agency rather than allowing classroom interactions to be structured predominantly by a hierarchical relationship between the teacher and his or her pupils. This chapter investigates teacher engagement with students' funds of knowledge through classroom-based research and pedagogies that help promote student agency and collaboration in literacy learning. The authors of Chapter 7 have used the concept of funds of knowledge to conceptualise the out of school spaces where students are learning literacy.

For the National Assessment Program – Literacy and Numeracy (NAPLAN) see <http://www.nap.edu.au/naplan/naplan.html>.

But, as we have indicated, time has marched on since the first decade of the 21st century when the teachers originally involved in the STELLA project came together to share their experiences and write stories about their work. Nowadays, when language and literacy educators talk about their teaching, they are obliged to grapple with the effect that standardised testing (such as the National Assessment Program – Literacy and Numeracy [NAPLAN]) is having on their work, as well as the way their teaching is viewed by regulatory authorities such as AITSL.

The following statement by a state primary school teacher in the northern suburbs of Melbourne – let's call her 'May' – conveys some of the tensions that she is experiencing, as she tries to implement a writing program in her school. She is contrasting the assumptions about writing that appear to underpin the standardised literacy tests that her students are obliged to do, when the whole school goes through the NAPLAN ritual, with the kinds of writing her children produce in the course of the year:

The following quotation is taken from Brenton Doecke, Alex Kostogriz and Bella Illesca (2010). This essay is based on interviews that took place as part of a research project on the effects standardised testing (such as NAPLAN) was having on how language and literacy teachers perceived their work.

See also Alex Kostogriz and Brenton Doecke (2013) for further discussion of findings arising from this research project. The whole of this issue, of the *Australian Journal of Language and Literacy* is devoted to the question of the impact of high-stakes literacy testing on teachers' work. See the editorial to this edition by Barbara Comber and Peter Freebody (2013).

When we come to our assessments for writing, it's not the one test we give. It's the whole year. It's not just one snapshot. It's a whole year of observing, listening to these kids, getting them to read their stories, and once in a while you see it and you think, 'Oh my God, I didn't know that this kid could write like that.' And why can that kid write like that? Because you just gave a topic, for example, that they really, really loved. And something has just happened. Like, I've got a boy who is dyslexic, and his father came and saw me a week ago. He said, 'May, I don't know what has happened, but my kid is up to his 20th page of writing.' And I said, 'I saw it the moment that question went out.' It just happened. We read the stories and stuff like that. I said, 'How about if we write stories about a dragon?' And that kid just loved it. So after that, it's just on and on and on and he wants to publish it and make a book. So maybe I wouldn't have been lucky enough to see that in this kid this year, and I would have gone on thinking that this kid, nothing. But I saw it and I thought, 'Wow!' And of course he's got his words back to front and whatever, but who cares! He's writing. And what is he going to get back from the NAPLAN? Nothing. He's going to get nothing. Whereas, from me, at least I can say, 'Look, he did this fantastic story this year.'

May also remarks later in this interview about the way that the children in her class 'just love the sharing and listening to each other'. She continues:

And sometimes when I think the stories are a little bit silly or not really good, the way that they respond to each other, the way that they like each other's stories, I think, you know, I'm two or three generations older than them, so I don't get the same interpretation. So it's good for me to listen to what they have to say about each other's stories, because it teaches me something. It teaches me quite a bit about, they are nine years old after all, and that's what they're interested in and that's what is meaningful for them. And I'm judging it as an adult, not as a kid. That's what is really meaningful to them. So that comes out through a discussion. So assessing kids, you've got to be their teacher to assess kids. You cannot be somebody else.

Reflection and discussion

You might care to pause at this point and identify the principles that appear to shape May's approach to the teaching of writing. Her comment about her surprise at what the young boy accomplished by writing a 'dragon story' may at first sight seem disarming, as though things just happen by accident in her classroom. But she also emphasises the importance of the sustained observations in which teachers engage – 'a whole year of observing, listening to these kids, getting them to read their stories' – as a necessary condition for such moments of insights to occur. A lot of planning, in other words, has gone into organising her classroom and supporting her students to engage in writing.

What do you imagine May would say if she were asked to describe the necessary conditions to engage children in writing? Have a look at the writing component of the NAPLAN test. What assumptions about writing pedagogy appear to underpin this test? How do they compare with what May is doing? May is affirming the importance of teachers listening to and learning from the children they teach, something that is affirmed by many of the educators whose voices you will hear in the following chapters. Do you think that this is a defensible position for a teacher of language and literacy to take?

New literacies and communication practices within classrooms

The impact that standardised testing has had on the way children engage in speaking, writing and reading in classroom settings remains very contentious. In becoming a language and literacy educator you will need to find your own pathway between conflicting claims. Yet it is not as though mandated literacy testing is the only force for change in schools. Another trend has been the attention that teachers and researchers in the field of language and literacy education have been giving to the new modes of communication in out-of-school lives, most notably the increasing use of digital literacies. This can sharpen the tension between teachers' developing knowledge of the meaning-making practices in which young people engage and the way standardised literacy testing constructs literacy. Many of the chapters that follow invite you to reflect on the differences between the way literacy is constructed by tests and the literacy practices in which young people engage in their out-of-school lives. Whereas standardised testing conceptualises literacy as an individual ability that can be measured by a child's capacity to read and write outside the context of meaningful social interactions with others, digital literacies are typically something that young people engage in together.

It is also interesting to reflect on the differences between the genres that young people employ when they are making meaning through digital technologies. When teachers open up opportunities in their classrooms for their pupils to create multimodal texts they invariably find themselves engaging with texts that do not fit the neat generic text types that are tested by NAPLAN.

A key impulse behind the chapters in this book is to affirm the importance of providing students with opportunities in which they can engage in authentic meaning-making activities, given they are using digital technologies and more traditional forms of communication in classrooms. 'Authentic' is a loaded word, and some educators have questioned whether it has a romantic ring to it, which limits its applicability to classroom settings.

> This is the criticism levelled by genre theorists, such as Frances Christie (2013), against advocates of whole language or process writing. See Chapter 8 for an account of how one educator grappled with these competing educational paradigms.

Yet it remains the case that when children read and write and talk and listen in classrooms they are engaging in important forms of identity work, as is shown in Chapter 5, which looks at the importance of facilitating intercultural communication. It is important to recognise that the meaning-making practices in which children engage in school are communicative activities grounded in the social world of their classrooms, not simply dummy runs or simulated activities in preparation for 'real' communication that will occur elsewhere later in their lives.

So ... who does this book think you are?

We have already said a great deal about how we imagine you will engage with this book. We are presupposing that you do not need to have everything handed to you on a platter – that would be an example of the very kind of direct instruction or transmission teaching that we have been criticising. This is why we have included references in each chapter that you might care to chase up in order to extend your understanding of an aspect of language and literacy that especially interests you.

Much of your learning as you read this book will be shaped by the institutional setting in which you find yourself and the opportunities that it opens up for you to engage in reflective practice. We want this book to help you to engage reflectively in your teaching practice, whatever your teaching opportunities might be. We imagine that most of our readers will be students in teacher education programs who are continually crossing the institutional boundaries between university and school, as they complete the fieldwork required for them to qualify as teachers. Are you one of these people? Or perhaps you have already picked up a teaching position or you are an early career teacher who has just completed your teaching qualification.

Whatever the exact nature of your current setting, we are imagining that, along with every other teacher education student or early career teacher, you are spending a lot of time thinking about who you are, about what you might be able to contribute to the profession, and about the kind of teacher you would like to become. The title of this book, *Becoming a Teacher of Language and Literacy*, is intended to acknowledge this process of becoming, of projecting yourself into a future that has yet to unfold.

You might like to reflect on what Steven, a mid-career teacher had to say about his first year of teaching:

Graduating teachers usually have built up an image of the 'teacher that they want to be' but this is quite often lost in the first year of teaching under pressure of administrator demands, assessment and reporting, parent difficulties and lack of support from colleagues.

In my first professional work as an educator I set myself up as a 'lifelong learner' who was willing to learn and grow from the experience and knowledge of those around me. This was a relatively easy identity to adopt in the school where I am working, where teacher identity as 'lifelong learners' is encouraged and desired as a model for students. My colleagues, though mostly young and inexperienced themselves, were a great source of information and learning.

I also set about making a significant contribution to the school community. I originally envisaged this as contributing to the students by running extra-curricular activities through sport. But as Catherine Beauchamp and Lynn Thomas (2011) suggest (an article I remember reading as part of my teacher education program) I found myself surprised by the fact that I ended up engaging in 'community building' which involved interacting with colleagues just as much as students. I achieved this by sharing professional development experiences, taking on leadership roles and sharing successful classroom experiences at staff meetings.

In my first few months I found it incredibly difficult to build a sense of agency and confidence. The 'tension between stable and unstable identities' referred to by Beauchamp and Thomas certainly had some negative manifestations for me. I had thought my classroom life would be easier than what it was and was surprised by my inability to teach, motivate and change the learning behaviours of some of my students. I remember it as often a demoralising time, when I questioned my ability to teach. I was aware of my inadequacies but was at times too embarrassed, too tired or too confused to address the problem. That lack of agency has been addressed with time, experience and further learning through experienced and talented colleagues.

In my current working life I have established an identity as a teacher who cares deeply about students and uses that ethic of care as a foundation for teaching. I also experiment widely with different ideas and continue to be a 'lifelong learner' who is keen to get professional development and apply it as much as possible. Through this I maintain a strong sense of professional identity and satisfaction.

We imagine that, like Steven, you are also experiencing a tension between who you are and who you might be. This is not necessarily a bad thing – every moment of our lives involves a play between past, present and future, as we weigh up where we have been and where we are going.

We hope that the chapters in this book help you to understand better your experiences as a teacher, enabling you to become the teacher you wish to become.

What follows

We have reached a point where we want to hand over to the other contributors to this book in order for them to continue the conversation we have begun with you. We will conclude this opening chapter with a brief outline of what you can expect in the following chapters.

Chapter 2: Engaging with tensions: tensions are the norm

Teachers encounter tensions everyday in their classrooms. Good teachers are trying to work through these tensions with their students in order to develop strong social relationships and show respect for the knowledge their students bring into the classroom. Four teachers tell their stories in this chapter about how they became teachers and the challenges they faced in their professional journeys.

Chapter 3: Teachers researching their practice: learning through practitioner inquiry

Meaningful professional learning, unlike one-off professional development sessions, is responsive to teachers' needs and contexts. It involves participation in ongoing, work-embedded, collaborative inquiry. When teachers investigate and reflect on their language and literacy teaching practices, they are positioning themselves as professionals who not only respond to what is happening around them, but who are able to influence decisions related to whole school policies and practices. This chapter draws on research projects in which teachers worked in collaborative relationships to improve the teaching and learning of language and literacy in their classrooms and schools. It explores approaches to professional learning and presents narratives of teachers' work as they actively inquire into their classroom literacy practices and critique and create knowledge to support their own and their students' learning.

Chapter 4: Literacy teaching and learning in digital times: tales of classroom interactions

The wider community has embraced multimodal texts in a variety of forms. Newspapers, books and other texts are now available in digital form, and so it follows that school-based literacy learning should reflect this cultural shift. Although print-based texts still play an integral role in teaching reading and writing, classroom literacy learning needs to thoughtfully integrate a wider variety of text types in order to support students who live in a multimodal world. This chapter presents teachers' stories about their use of emerging technologies in their literacy classrooms and how they take on the role of teacher researchers to reimagine their literacy teaching practices. The teachers' stories highlight the importance of understanding the diversity of texts in contemporary societies, including how these texts are read, viewed and created.

Chapter 5: Supporting intercultural engagement in literacy education

Unheralded movements of the world's people due to changes in trade, education, business, civil unrest, family reunion and other causes mean that Australia's school population is more diverse than at any point in history. Increasingly, educational policy (including the new Australian Curriculum that has recently been developed) and practice acknowledges the diversity of students as a resource for intercultural engagement and citizenship in a globalised context. This chapter contains school case studies that prompt reflection on how teachers can promote intercultural understanding through critical engagement with texts in their language and literacy classrooms. The teachers develop pedagogies that recognise cultural diversity and promote respect and empathy for others.

Chapter 6: Inclusive literacy education

Australian schools are inclusive environments where all students regardless of ability have a right to participate. This chapter is grounded in the belief that every classroom teacher is working with students with multiple abilities and that every teacher faces the challenge of negotiating strategies that allow them to engage all their students in meaningful learning. The chapter brings together case studies of teachers and the strategies they use for inclusive teaching practices that include multiple entry points for learning, scaffolded literacy learning for all students and the importance of teachers knowing the specific needs of all students in their classrooms.

Chapter 7: Homework: a window into community literacies

Through case studies of culturally diverse learners, this chapter explores how parents interact with their children around homework and literacy learning. The chapter looks at the ways in which literacy practices circulate between home, school and social and community spaces. The case studies involve a homework club in a culturally diverse metropolitan setting and a parent explaining concepts to a child in an Aboriginal community.

Chapter 8: Planning for teaching / planning for learning

Two academics with recent experience as teachers in schools share their experiences of how they planned their teaching of reading, writing, speaking and listening within their literacy programs. These experiences produce a contemporary vision of literacy teaching, showing how teachers can benefit by using assessment data, inquiring into their own teaching and getting to know their students. The chapter shows how the conversations that teachers have with other teachers, members of the school leadership team, as well as students and parents, provide an invaluable resource for planning for the teaching of literacy.

Chapter 9: Teacher and student agency in contemporary literacy classrooms

This chapter draws on research into student and teacher perspectives to consider productive ways of engaging contemporary students in their literacy learning. Through exploring multiple forms of communication within the learning community, the teachers were able to move towards more collaborative, egalitarian and trusting relationships with their students. Teachers and students demonstrated their willingness to share doubt and uncertainty in this ever-changing, fluid learning environment, and together opened up the possibility for developing innovative solutions and sophisticated opportunities for learning.

Professional associations that will be of interest to you as a literacy educator

Australian Literacy Educators Association <http://www.alea.edu.au>

Australian Association for the Teaching of English <http://www.aate.org.au>

Primary English Teachers Association Australia <http://www.petaa.edu.au>

References

Allard, A & Doecke, B 2014 (forthcoming), 'Professional knowledge and standards-based reforms: Learning from the experiences of early career teachers', English Teaching: Practice and Critique, vol. 13, no. 1, May. <http://edlinked.soe.waikato.ac.n2/research/journal/index.php?id=1)>

Barnes, D 1992, *From Communication to Curriculum,* 2nd edn, Boynton/Cook, Portsmouth, NH.

Beauchamp, C & Thomas, L 2011, 'New teachers' identity shifts at the boundary of teacher education and initial practice', *International Journal of Educational Research,* vol 50., pp. 6–13.

Boomer, G 1992, 'Negotiating the curriculum' in G Boomer, N Lester, C Onore & J Cook (eds), *Negotiating the Curriculum: Educating for the 21st century,* Falmer Press, London, pp. 4–14.

Buckingham, D 2007, 'Digital Media Literacies: rethinking media education in the age of the Internet'. *Research in Comparative and International Education*, vol. 2 no. 1, pp. 43–55.

Bulfin, S & Koutsogiannis, D 2012, 'New literacies as multiply placed practices: expanding perspectives on young people's literacies across home and school', *Language and Education*, vol. 26 no. 4, pp. 331–46. doi: 10.1080/09500782.2012.691515

Christie, F 2013, 'Genres and genre theory: a response to Michael Rosen', *Changing English*, vol. 20, no. 1, pp. 11–22.

Clandinin, DJ & Connelly, FM 1995, *Teachers' Professional Knowledge Landscapes*, Teachers College Press, New York and London.

Comber, B & Freebody, P 2013, 'Literacy education in a changing policy environment: an introduction (editorial)', *Australian Journal of Language and Literacy*, vol. 36, no. 2, pp. 65–6.

Doecke, B 2013, 'Storytelling and professional learning', *English in Australia*, vol. 48, no. 2, pp. 11–21.

Doecke, B, Kostogriz, A & Illesca, B 2010, 'Seeing "things" differently: recognition, ethics, praxis", *English Teaching: Practice & Critique*, vol. 9 no. 2, pp. 81–98.

Doecke, B & McClenaghan, D 2011, *Confronting Practice: Classroom Investigations into Language and Learning*, Phoenix Education, Putney Australia.

Dyson, AH 1997, *Writing Superheroes: Contemporary Childhood, Popular Culture, and Classroom Literacy*, Teachers College Press, New York.

Fullan, M & Hargreaves, A 2012, Reviving teaching with "professional capital"'. *Education Week*, vol. 31 no. 33, pp. 30–6.

Heath, SB 1983/1994, *Ways with Words: Language, Life and Work in Communities and Classrooms*, Cambridge University Press, Cambridge.

Hope, AD 1967, 'Presidential address' in *English in Australia*, no. 5, August, pp. 3–10.

Hopper, T, Sanford, K & Bonsor-Kurki, S 2012, 'E–learning and digital media', *E–Learning and Digital Media*, vol. 9, no. 1, pp. 29–42.

Kostogriz, A & Doecke, B 2013, 'The ethical practice of teaching literacy: accountability or responsibility', *Australian Journal of Language and Literacy*, vol. 36, no. 2, pp. 90–8.

Marsh, J 2009, 'Writing and popular culture' in R Beard, D Myhill, RJ & M Nystrand (eds), *The Sage Handbook of Writing Development*, Sage, London, pp. 313–24.

Reid, A 2004, 'Towards a culture of inquiry in DECS', Occasional paper no. 1, Department of Education and Children's Services, Government of South Australia. <http://www.decd.sa.gov.au/learnerwellbeing/files/links/link_72576.pdf>.

Simpson, A & Walsh, M 2013, 'Teaching reading in a digital age: towards an understanding of pedagogic practice' in A Goodwyn, L Reid & C Durrant (eds), *International Perspectives on Teaching English in a Globalised World*, Routledge, London.

Chapter 2

Engaging with tensions

tensions are the norm

Glenn Auld, Brenton Doecke
and Rachel MacGilp

Unlike humans, cephalopods don't have blind spots, that is they don't have an absence of photoreceptor cells in the retina. Humans usually don't notice their blind spot because the other eye helps the brain fill in the missing information.

Chris Bigum & Leonnie Rowan (2012, p. 1)

Chris Bigum and Leonnie Rowan speculate about coming back as cephalopods. That way they wouldn't have any blind spots with respect to their professional practice as educators. This metaphor is a good way to begin thinking about the complexities of your professional practice as a literacy educator in a primary classroom. Teachers often feel that there is something they could do better or that there is a 'blind spot' in their professional knowledge and practice they need to address.

This is not just something that applies to early career teachers. Experienced teachers also feel the need to engage in ongoing professional learning. They might have become aware of a new understanding about the relationship between print and visual media, or perhaps a new program that is being implemented in a neighbouring school that uses popular social media to engage children in their learning. Or, it could be a moment when they have gained insight into the values of the school community in which they are teaching, which helps to explain the children's attitude towards schooling. Good teachers are always trying to fill the gaps in their knowledge in the process of interacting with their students, other teachers and the school administration. This is in order to develop their professional practice in a way that supports the literacy learning of all the students in their class and the school as a whole.

In this chapter we will be introducing you to Rachel, a teacher who is currently working in a primary classroom of a large metropolitan school and tapping into the way she reflects on her teaching and tries to learn from it. Throughout this chapter we will use Rachel's stories from her primary classroom as a jumping-off point to explore some of the themes in this book. You will be able to identify 'the work of the other eye' which is seeking to identify and address her blind spots as she negotiates her practice. Rachel has been at her school for just over six months, and although she is an experienced teacher, having worked in a Northern Territory school for a few years, she still feels the need to continue learning about her teaching. Rachel is also trying to get to know the children in her class at her new school and the community from which they come.

Literacy is complex

In my class I value giving children the time to talk. In a discussion we were having the other day about writing, one child, Benny, said: 'I did this science experiment with my Dad and we wrote it up'. I immediately wondered how much of the literacy success I have in the classroom is due to home or to me. But I also thought how much you can learn from the children in your class if you give them a chance to tell you about their lives, what they do with their friends on weekends, and the kinds of things they do with their families. These interactions provide an invaluable context for supporting their literacy learning. I reflect on the different spoken responses I get from the children and I know these are far more developed than those I could get from a worksheet that might try to establish the background knowledge they have before commencing any new topic. I can see how the discussions refer back to the texts we have read and also foreground the work we are doing in our writing. In the discussions I have with the students they are all listening to each other's responses and this really helps them to think in different ways.

Literacy is an increasingly complex and contested concept. Rachel's reflections highlight the fact that literacy is not only something that children learn at school. The language and literacy they experience at home also needs to be acknowledged, if we are truly to appreciate and support their growth as people. And this is not simply a matter of understanding the knowledge they are bringing to school – in this case, Benny's understanding of scientific experiments – but the social relationships in which they have acquired this knowledge. We need to understand the cultures of our students, and treat those cultures as a resource that supports the learning they do at school. Pat Thomson (2002) uses the term 'virtual schoolbag' to refer to the 'things they have already learned at home, with their friends, and in and from the world in which they live' (Thomson 2002, p. 1).

You might also like to read Luis Moll's (1992) ideas on funds of knowledge that is closely related to Pat Thomson's (2002) work.

Heath's (1983) seminal study on literacy provides a useful framework for understanding the complexity of Rachel's work. Heath identified the diverse range of literacy practices in which people from different communities engage in their everyday lives, exploring how those practices vary from community to community. She famously named the two communities at the heart of her study Trackton and Roadville, detailing the 'ways with words' of each community. Trackton was a close-knit African-American community, whose residents did not consider themselves to be poor, but whose neighbourhood had a 'run-down' quality (Trackton & Roadville, pp. 53–4). The people of Roadville depended for their livelihood on the mill, as well as any other jobs that might be available; they valued 'church-going, respecting authority, the experience of having to work hard, and knowing how to "keep a clean nose" (or to stay out of trouble)' (Trackton & Roadville, pp. 41–2). Heath focused on how the children in each community learned to talk through interacting with each other and with adults, and how they came to appreciate the uses of reading and writing in everyday life. Although her study provides abundant evidence of the richness and complexity of the literacy practices of each community, those practices did not match what children are typically expected to do in school when they are taught how to read and write and to speak and to listen. She thereby raised important questions about how schools can be more responsive to the cultures and literacy practices of the children who attend them. It is easy to slip into what Barbara Comber (1997) and other researchers have called 'deficit' constructions of children whose language and literacy do not match what school expects of them, and it is worth stopping to consider whether labelling children in this way actually involves a built-in 'blind spot' that stops you from seeing the language and literacy practices in which they actually engage, which can sometimes be extraordinarily rich and multifaceted.

For a stimulating account of what teachers can learn from the literacy practices in which students engage outside school, see Barbara Comber and Barbara Kamler's (2005) edited book *Turn-around Pedagogies: Literacy Interventions for At-risk Students*.

Lisa Delpit (1988) has worthwhile reading in her article about power and pedagogy.

This kind of 'blind spot' is not the issue with Benny, whose enthusiasm for 'writing up' the science experiments he does with his dad fits perfectly with the language and literacy that schools typically expect of children. The 'blind spot' that Rachel really seems keen to address in her anecdote concerns the way some teachers get into the habit of requiring their children to do worksheets, imagining that a quiet class is a hard-working class. Rachel's hunch is that the interactions in which children engage when they talk with one another provide a far more generative context for developing their language and literacy than when they do a worksheet. Rather than learning about language, they are actively engaging in language, adopting the role of active participants in their own learning, instead of being positioned as passive 'spectators', as James Britton, another famous language educator, put it (Britton, 1975). Listening to children's talk provides you with not only a sense of their backgrounds and interests, but also insights into their awareness of language and literacy. Rather than treating them as empty vessels to be filled with knowledge about language, and then expecting them to dutifully apply that knowledge in simulated activities that we design for them, we can begin from 'where they are' (another statement made by James Britton, 1975, p. 134), acknowledging that they already know a great deal about language, and build on that.

Reflection and discussion

On the basis of your classroom experience so far:

What do you feel might be the blind spots in your own professional practice as a teacher? How did you become aware of these blind spots? How would you explain their existence? How are you planning to overcome them?

Are those blind spots all of the same kind? Or do they prompt significantly different types of professional learning? What are the multiple sources of knowledge that you need to draw on as a language and literacy teacher? What do you need to learn in order to teach?

Literacy learners are increasingly diverse

We shall now consider an account by Rachel of her previous experiences as a teacher, when she worked at a school in an Indigenous community in the Northern Territory.

It was like any other day in my primary classroom in the Northern Territory. The students all walked in after eating their morning tea, talking to each other in Burarra, their preferred language of communication. Burarra is an Aboriginal language spoken by about 500 people in this community. Each child in the room had 10 years of listening and speaking Burarra through growing up there. The children sat on the mat as I began reading the book, *Big Rain Coming*, to them. During the reading of this printed text, most children struggled to understand the print, but they were able to use the visuals to make meaning from the story. While they were struggling with print literacy, I was likewise struggling to comprehend the linguistic and cultural diversity in this classroom. As a teacher new to this community, I was learning my students' language in sessions, through informal talks with their parents and formal sessions at school. I was aware of how little I knew about the linguistic and cultural backgrounds of my students. I did not know the clan, 'skin' and moiety names of my students, as they did. My students knew a myriad of relational names for themselves and classmates that located them ontologically as a member of this community, while I was struggling simply to comprehend my adopted 'skin' name. My students also knew ways of communicating that I had never experienced, using a complex sign language that would often transcend the silences of my classroom. One student, for instance, could pat his stomach indicating that he was communicating about his mother, or the mother of the person he was looking at. I had only just begun my learning journey about my students' complex social systems that involved mathematical understandings, linguistic and cultural knowledge and knowledge of place that was communicated in multilingual and multimodal ways. Interestingly I could not find this kind of learning in the curriculum that I was obliged to teach them.

Graduates from teacher education programs are expected to be able to address the needs of students from 'diverse linguistic, cultural, religious and socioeconomic backgrounds'. This is to borrow the language of the professional standards for teachers developed by the Australian Institute for Teaching and Secondary School Leadership (AITSL), which are similar to standards that have been developed for teachers around the world. All these standards claim to map the dimensions of what teachers 'should know and be able to do'. Although the AITSL standards have the authority of an 'official' document, you might like to consider whether there seems to be any 'blind spots'. Do you feel that the AITSL standards adequately represent the knowledge and experience you bring to the teaching of literacy?

To access the standards developed by the Australian Institute for Teaching and School Leadership, go to <http://www.teacherstandards.aitsl.edu.au/>

For a thought-provoking critique of professional standards, including the AITSL standards, read Susanne Gannon's (2012) article about the standardisation of teachers' work.

The AITSL standards say that 'Graduate' teachers should be able to '*Demonstrate knowledge of teaching strategies that are responsive* to the learning strengths and needs of students from diverse linguistic, cultural, religious and socioeconomic backgrounds' (Professional Knowledge, 1.3 [our italics]). When you move from being a 'Graduate' to a 'Proficient' teacher, you should, according to AITSL, be able to '*Design and implement teaching strategies that are responsive* to the learning strengths and needs of students from diverse linguistic, cultural, religious and socioeconomic backgrounds'. The key distinction between your knowledge as a 'Graduate' and your knowledge as a 'Proficient' teacher seems to be in a growing capacity on your part to apply your knowledge of cultural diversity through developing teaching strategies that connect with children from a range of backgrounds.

Reflection and discussion

What is involved in being responsive to the diverse communities you might encounter as a primary school teacher? How responsive do you think you are to people from communities that differ from your own? Is this something that you can learn by reading a book? Or is this kind of responsiveness crucially bound up with the extent of your experience of other languages and cultures? How do your upbringing and life experiences shape your interactions with people from diverse backgrounds?

A good way to appreciate cultural diversity is to work in schools that cater for different communities. One of the benefits of initial teacher education programs is when pre-service teachers have an opportunity to go to a diverse range of schools for practicum or teaching/professional experience placements. They might be state schools, Catholic schools, or independent schools, and they might be in urban or rural settings.

Reflection and discussion

What kind of school did you go to when you were a student? How did it differ from the schools that you worked in during your initial teacher education program?

Early career teaching these days often involves beginning with a contract teaching position. When contracts come to an end, teachers sometimes find themselves having to apply to teach at a different school in another region. Some teachers, on the other hand, manage to stay at the same school for a number of years, which means that they become very knowledgeable about the culture of the school community in which they work. Changing schools can throw all that knowledge into relief, when they have to start all over again, getting to know the patterns of life in the new school.

As we indicated, Rachel has only been at her current metropolitan school for around six months, having worked in an Indigenous community prior to that. You have just read her account of the time when she began teaching at this school. Now that she is at a new school, she often reflects on what she learnt at her previous school, how these experiences provide a perspective on her current experience, and what she is able to transfer from her old school to her new one. She is still getting used to the way things are done at her new school.

Effective literacy teachers experience a variety of tensions

These days, for all the emphasis on catering for diversity in documents like the AITSL standards, teachers are required to implement standardised literacy and numeracy tests (what in Australia is known as the National Assessment Program – Literacy and Numeracy, or NAPLAN) in all schools, wherever they are located and whatever the social and cultural differences between them.

A confronting experience for many early career teachers in their first year of teaching in Australia is being obliged to administer the NAPLAN tests, which are unlike anything that they have experienced before as school students. Even very experienced teachers worry about the impact that NAPLAN is having on their professional practice, especially with respect to their capacity to be responsive to the needs of the children in their classrooms. Administering such texts seems to reflect a 'one-size-fits-all' mentality that may conflict with your ethical commitment to be responsive to the child in front of you. This presents teachers with a balancing act that is at times difficult and professionally challenging. Sally, a primary school principal, suggests NAPLAN translates the work of teaching into numbers:

> For information about NAPLAN and examples of the tests go to <http://www.nap.edu.au/naplan/naplan.html>.
>
> For the 2014 Senate Inquiry into NAPLAN go to <http://www.aph.gov.au/Parliamentary_Business/Committees/Senate/Education_and_Employment/Naplan13/Report/Report>.

And I think that the child is being a bit lost in this. It's supposed to be about the child, and the child is not numbers. They're feelings, they're emotions. They've got aspirations, they've got joy and beauty, and they're not just scores. And I think we just focus right in on the scores all the time at the moment, and not enough about the whole child. (Doecke et al. 2010, p. 93)

This comment is taken from work on professional ethics by Brenton Doecke, Alex Kostogriz and Bella Illesca (2010). This article also contains other reflections by experienced teachers on the effects of standardised testing on their professional practice.

Such pressures towards standardisation are not only evident in the form of administering standardised tests. As a literacy educator, Rachel writes about feeling pressured by a range of school and community expectations as she goes about working in her new primary school.

Sometimes I don't cope with the tensions and sometimes I just do what I am supposed to do. Sometimes I think I am doing what I am supposed to be doing, but I am not really doing what is required because I don't understand the expectations necessarily. For example, in our section we do collaborative planning. I was planning literacy for everyone in the section, and I was not explicit enough in my planning for the other staff to understand and they said 'I don't understand that'. This is because the literacy planning I did was a bit different, deriving from what we used to do at my previous school, and it is not what they have done at this school. At this school, the planning is supposed to look the same, down to the same heading, with the same font and whatever, and it has to look the same all the time. But after the planning meeting one teacher said to me: 'Rachel you just plan whatever, and then once we go into our own classroom and close the door, we just do whatever we like.'

The experiences of teaching literacy and curriculum development that Rachel has brought with her from her old school don't seem to be particularly relevant to her new school, where a lot of emphasis is placed on preparing students to do the NAPLAN tests. Her many years working in an Indigenous community and making stories with community elders in a threatened Aboriginal language have put her strangely at odds with the expectations of staff at her new school. Rachel is experiencing tensions in the way she goes about planning, teaching and assessing literacy in the more regulated setting of a suburban primary school in Melbourne. She still likes to draw on her past practices of negotiating the literacy curriculum, where she uses her professional judgement about how to engage students in their learning.

Garth Boomer, a famous Australian educator, has some valuable insights into negotiating the literacy curriculum, when he highlights the danger of teachers teaching 'according to a planned curriculum, without engaging the interests of the students'. He argues that it is vital that teachers invite students 'to contribute to, and to modify, the educational program, so that they will have a real investment both in the learning journey and in the outcomes. Negotiating also means making explicit, and the confronting of the constraints of the learning context and the non-negotiable requirements that apply' (Boomer 1992, p. 14).

In her story, Rachel identifies a tension between compliance with the expectations of the standardised literacy curriculum enacted at her school and her desire to resist the practice of attempting to make teaching literacy the same in all classes. Even though Rachel is an experienced teacher, she admits to not having the power or tenacity to resist the standardisation of literacy teaching all the time. She also identifies a tension involving group and co-operative planning for literacy. Many primary schools have a practice of group planning for literacy in sections or year levels in order for experienced teachers and graduates to work together on their planning. As we shall see later in this chapter and throughout this book, teachers of literacy work both individually and collaboratively as part of their professional practice. Where there is a strong respect for the work of teaching literacy, there is a supportive dialogue between the teachers that enables them to draw on the strengths of each teacher so that each child benefits from the abilities of everyone in the team.

Reflection and discussion

What kinds of tensions have you experienced in your own practice as a teacher of literacy? Why have these tensions occurred? How do you imagine these tensions might be resolved?

How do you react to the principal's statement that a child is 'not numbers'? How do you feel about standardised literacy testing?

Like many teachers, Rachel subtly resists the pressures of a standardised literacy curriculum. This is in order to maintain her sense of integrity as a teacher. She tries to do this without antagonising the school administration or causing friction with other teachers who hold different views from her own. She is also conscious of the expectations of the whole school community, especially the views of those parents who do not see anything wrong with standardised testing.

When I do resist the top down pressures, I don't directly challenge these practices. I engage the children in lots of conversation. I find the learning outcomes they achieve still meet the requirements set by the school, but the process I take is different to what others plan. For example, when staff in my section were planning procedural texts, the staff each took turns in planning something. I planned to use a different kind of media each day, such as a YouTube clip or a book or an image to make the kids think about what they were writing. In the group planning document, there were lots of watching things and reading things and writing about it rather than actually experiencing things. When we did an experiment, the class initially watched a YouTube video I saw at a previous school. We then unpacked the idea of thinking scientifically before doing the experiment. So we formed a hypothesis and they could understand about the different parts of an experiment and why you had to set up your lab or whatever and why you might need a diagram for it and why you need a hypothesis and why you predict what is going to happen ... This was far more effective than just reading something, because they felt like they were scientists through the shared experience of knowing how to do the experiment from the talk we did before, during and after the experience of doing the experiment. In my approach the end result was the same, they produced a scientific report, but they got there by a different route, one that included much more dialogue and modelling of scientific concepts.

You can see that Rachel has the capacity to resist the standardised practices that are expected by the school leadership and yet still fulfil their requirements, albeit by taking a slightly different pathway. Not all teachers are in a position to work in this way. If you are on a contract, you would no doubt feel much less inclined to challenge the school's established practices than you would if you had obtained a permanent position. Yet it still seems important to recognise what individual teachers bring to the process of planning and implementing curriculum, depending on their backgrounds and interests. A major advantage of collaborating with others, as we have observed above, is to draw on the diverse range of knowledge, skills and experiences that individual teachers have developed. A whole school approach to curriculum is important, but a common approach should not mean a standardised approach, which requires everyone to do exactly the same thing at the same time (or indeed to think in exactly the same way). What is your view?

Why have you decided to become a literacy teacher?

Becoming a literacy educator is now very different from the ways in which teachers have previously been socialised into the profession. Rather than getting professional satisfaction from working collaboratively with colleagues in order to achieve the best for the children at your school, sometimes the amount of regulation that exists today can rob you of a sense of professional autonomy. It is therefore worthwhile to periodically revisit your reasons for becoming a literacy educator, and to share your thoughts with colleagues. This can provide a very valuable perspective on your work.

This is exactly what the primary and secondary teachers who participated in the STELLA project did. They wanted to arrive at a sense of the values they shared and to remind themselves of the things that mattered to them as language and literacy educators.

STELLA stands for Standards for Teachers of English Language and Literacy in Australia. The project was a significant attempt by language and literacy teachers to formulate their own professional standards, rather than having those standards imposed on them by an external authority.

See the STELLA website <http://www.stella.org.au> for more details. STELLA is discussed in Chapter 1.

Brenton Doecke and Margaret Gill (2004) have provided a thought-provoking account of the research involved in the STELLA project. This involved teachers coming together and writing stories about their experiences as literacy educators, some of which can still be found on the internet.

Some of the teachers involved in STELLA also wrote autobiographical accounts of why they had become literacy educators. Here are excerpts from three of those accounts found in Doecke, Homer and Nixon (2003).

Poor and female – born to be a teacher

By Robyn Perkins

My teaching is a product of my past.

As a girl growing up in a working-class suburb of Melbourne my career choices were pretty much made for me. I could either become a hairdresser, typist/clerk (with the possibility of ascending to the heights of secretary), a nurse or a teacher …

My mother always went without so that we could have what we needed to stay at school. She had gone to Year 8 herself and worked in factories. She didn't want that for us. To her, hairdressing was out of the question. If there is a hierarchy of occupations hairdressing was pretty close to the bottom. An office job was OK but didn't really offer much in the way of a career or pay. For some reason Mum never saw me as a nurse. This career was reserved for my younger sister.

My mother saw teaching as the practical option. I can still hear her words now. 'If you take up teaching you can always go back to it after you have your family.' She was right.

I guess the path to teaching had been laid out for me long before I was conscious of it myself …

No one in our family had ever been to university, and so when a place was offered to me at the end of Year 12, I was faced with a dilemma. Accepting it would mean leaving home and supporting myself. Mum had made it pretty clear that she couldn't continue to 'keep' me while I studied. University would see me in an Arts course that in reality meant becoming a teacher …

Speaking as 'Other'

By Bella Illesca

As a Chilean-born Australian, September the 11th holds significance for me that is perhaps different to the significance that is currently a part of the media created collective consciousness. It was on this date in 1973 that the world's first democratically elected socialist government was toppled in a bloody coup. These events set in train processes that eventually led to the murder and displacement of hundreds of thousands of Chilean citizens. My family was amongst those sent into exile …

I was too young to understand the implications of the bombing of *La Moneda* – the Presidential Palace – and the murder of Allende. I was also too young to realise the daily terror that people were experiencing as a result of the military's repressive tactics of torture, fear, inflation and shortages. However, although I was too young to 'know', I wasn't too young to feel hunger and experience my mother's shame when she caught me stealing an orange from a neighbour. Nor was I too young to sense my father's long absences and my mother's struggle to feed three children. My experiences are a part of the Chilean people's struggle to claim their voices and to choose their own destiny. This history is a part of who I am in my personal and public life …

Our arrival in Australia in 1974 signalled the beginning of a different kind of struggle … As a child of Chilean migrants I have always felt a strong affinity with the displaced and vulnerable. It would be as difficult to change this as it would be to change my place of birth for this is my inheritance. By this I mean the physics of who I am – woman, non-white, Chilean born; the social milieu and economic conditions that I was born into – Catholic and working class; and the politics that I have adopted – a commitment to social and political reform. The way that these social forces have intersected over the years has shaped my personal and professional identity. However, none has played as significant a role in determining who I am and my sense of self and community as language.

Teaching changes: that constant state of grace

By John Davidson

In the year of Australia's Bicentennial, 1988, I started teaching rounds at an inner-city primary school. The supervising teacher's name was Grace and what I remember best was her marvellous relationship with the children. She would sit in an armchair with the class gathered around her, speaking softly as they waited patiently to show their work. They called her by her name, Grace, and treated each other with the same gentle respect that she modelled.

Grace rarely took on an explicitly didactic role – she had an informal style that could be described as holistic pedagogy. Students worked on projects independently or in small groups, coming to her for a conference when necessary. They collaborated to solve problems, shared their pencils and rulers, sat on the floor or in Grace's chair when she was wandering the room to talk with children. The school had various texts in Greek and Turkish and it was quite acceptable to read and write in the home language, at least some of the time …

I was in the classroom one day a week. As a mature-age student, I was completing an accelerated Diploma of Primary Teaching and all my teaching rounds had to be fitted into one year. Before going back to study I had spent thirteen years in the railways, the last six as a train driver, and had turned to teaching after watching my own children begin to read – watching the process of learning had sparked my interest in teaching.

I thought I was contributing to simply the best classroom in the world. Until one day just after Easter when Grace told me she was leaving for another job. She gave me a box of journals and papers that formed the basis of my own professional library. Took the class one last time, and walked out of all our lives.

The next week when I arrived at the school, the assistant principal called me into the office to tell me the kids had gone nuts and the new teacher was not coping well. He suggested I would be a settling influence on the class because I'd worked with Grace and they would identify me with her. This was my introduction to the sad fact that school administrators don't always know what's happening in classrooms.

The kids took only marginally more notice of me than they did of Elizabeth, as I shall call the replacement teacher. They shouted at each other and threw things around the room. They stole the pencils and broke the rulers. They fought over Grace's chair, as if whoever sat in it might recapture some slight memory of her.

Things went from bad to worse. The assistant principal had to come into the class regularly to remove difficult students, and even the principal made an appearance. The informal classroom was re-organised into rows of tables and children forbidden from walking around or moving seats. Elizabeth, realising eventually that I couldn't save her, treated me like the student teacher I was rather than the mature-age practitioner she'd been promised. She brought back handwriting books and told me to teach cursive script. She might have brought back the strap if that were possible …

Rachel read the foregoing autobiographical narratives, and then had a go at writing her own autobiography. Here is what she wrote:

Working with the tensions

By Rachel MacGilp

I really wanted to be an archaeologist but my father, who was born during the Great Depression and the son of a single mother, thought that I needed a job where I could make a steady income. After a three-year teaching diploma we all had interviews for registration. During the interviews all students were told that yes we would be registered but no, sorry, there will be no jobs. This was 1986. In fact it wasn't strictly true: one person was employed. So my entry into the profession was not smooth. I worked as a relief teacher for two years and then joined the nation of Australian backpackers in Europe for a further two years. During this time my mother rang to inform me that the Northern Territory Department of Education had offered me a primary position in Tennant Creek in the Northern Territory.

This was my first full-time teaching job and it was an ordinary class of upper primary school children in an extraordinary setting. I had not begun teaching in this town by choice, I went there to do what I was qualified to do and this was where I had to go to get started. After three years of living in the desert I moved to Maningrida on the coast in the Arnhem Land in Northern Australia. It was in this teaching context that I realised the process of becoming a teacher of literacy required me to be continually reflexive, always interrogating my practices and beliefs.

The children came to school spasmodically. Sometimes I did not teach the same children on consecutive days. The children came to school learning English as a fourth language. I used to teach lots of phonics but the purposes of speaking in English and the use of symbols to create words had limited use outside of school. I found the purposes for teaching reading were made easier when it was done in their own language, Burarra. They could realise what was written on the page was what they orally communicated. We did lots of language experiences on their own country and then made them into books in the classroom with the help of elders using the images from these experiences as a basis for literacy teaching. With English it was harder to make connections between the words and the text, but we could go to the shop for similar language experience.

Although I was making connections with their cultural understanding, I felt that I was stealing or undermining their identity. Even when I was trying to do maths in Burarra and making connections to the handful of turtle eggs as a numbering system I felt I was doing the wrong thing. I thought that the students would have been better off having stronger connections to meaningful learning in the context of their country.

I became the teacher linguist to develop books and resources to teach literacy through Burarra. In this role I could see how literacy was used to develop a communal construction of knowledge. Knowledge was not an individual endeavour; it was linked to a community of experts, prior knowledge of all the students, shared experiences, connections to land and spiritual identities. I respected the importance of dialogue with the wider community as a way to negotiate ideas for the Burarra texts and how to approach making and checking the accuracy of the information in the texts. I made lots of teaching resources that supported the professional development with the Aboriginal education workers and then lots of lesson plans to go with these resources. I recognised that language would lose status if there were not outcomes associated with the teaching of the concepts in Burarra and this lead to some important curriculum work in mapping the knowledge the students completed in their first language, often outside of school.

I was introduced to 'both ways' learning, where the students were learning language and culture from home and school in English and Burarra. Ideally the children were learning the best of both cultures, but in some ways the power did not shift, even when some Aboriginal education workers became teachers after many years of interrupted study. I learned from the students the importance of respecting their voice and knowing their interests. Unless I could make something meaningful, practical and useful, the students wouldn't gain a deep understanding about anything. I became aware of the importance of explicit teaching in literacy to embed the understandings so they could transform the learning for use in other situations.

I am still learning about how much the students have taught me about effective teaching. I have a list of meta-cognitive learning strategies that we are continually adding to through informal unplanned conversations that reflect on the different ways students negotiate meaning in the classroom. I value the individual home backgrounds and provide students with choice in their learning. I know as a teacher I need to work with tensions constructed by the broader institution of schooling and the individual interests of the children. Teaching literacy is a complex process but then again children have taught me that they negotiate this complexity over many years before they begin school and they don't give up trying. If students do this without being paid, I have a professional responsibility to negotiate and mediate these tensions in my classroom so the students under my care develop effective strategies to deal with these tensions in their learning.

Reflection and discussion

Why did these people become literacy educators?

How do their circumstances and motivations compare with your own?

Conclusion

Throughout this chapter we have referred to policy initiatives such as the introduction of standardised literacy testing and professional standards. These reforms are generally referred to as standards-based reforms (Darling-Hammond, 2004) and they have been the subject of much debate. Their advocates claim that they are designed to improve the quality of teaching and learning in schools. Others argue that they have 'unintended consequences' which seriously undermine the capacity of schools and teachers to address the needs of children from culturally diverse communities. Your own entry into the profession has been shaped by these reforms, and for that reason it is likely to be very different from the way previous generations of teachers have been socialised into the profession.

As you navigate your own practice in these changed circumstances, ask yourself the following questions: Do you feel that standards-based reforms sustain or hinder your professional commitment as a literacy educator? Do you feel that your beliefs and values as a literacy educator are congruent with the beliefs and values that appear to be reflected in standards-based reforms? Do these reforms match your idea of what it means to be a professional?

The stories told by Robyn, Bella, John and Rachel should also prompt you to think about why you have decided to become a literacy educator. These stories have been told by teachers who belong to the Baby Boom Generation or Gen X, and so your story may differ simply by virtue of the fact that you belong to another generation.

Your own values and beliefs shape your professional practice in complex ways, and so it is worth periodically revisiting the question of who you are in an effort to be fully aware of how your approach to teaching might be influenced by your own education and life experiences. You might like to write an autobiographical account of why you want to become a teacher of literacy and think about the important influences in your life that shape the practices you bring to the classroom.

You could write this account in the first person (as 'I'), though you might also consider writing it in the third person (as 'he' or 'she'). Some writers feel that by recasting the events of their lives in the third person, they are able to develop a perspective on their experiences that might not otherwise be available to them. Now it's your turn.

References

Australian Institute for Teaching and School Leadership 2012, Australian Professional Standards for Teachers. <http://www.teacherstandards.aitsl.edu.au/OrganisationStandards/Organisation>

Authority, Australian Curriculum Assessment and Reporting Authority 2011, National Assessment Program. <http://www.nap.edu.au/naplan/naplan.html>

Bigum, C & Rowan, L 2012, 'When I grow up I want to be a cephalopod or the unbearable sameness of instrumentum cum docere', paper presented at the Critical Perspectives of Learning with New Media, The Learning with New Media Inaugural Conference, Glen Waverly, Victoria. <http://archive-com.com/page/776767/2012-11-28/http://chrisbigum.com/downloads/NLM.pdf>

Boomer, G 1992, 'Negotiating the curriculum' in G Boomer, N Lester, C Onore & J Cook (eds), *Negotiating the Curriculum: Educating for the 21st century*, Falmer Press, London, Washington DC, pp. 4–14.

Britton, JN 1975, *Language and Learning*, Penguin Books, Harmondsworth.

Comber, B 1997, 'Literacy, poverty and schooling: working against deficit equations', *English in Australia*, no. 119–20, October, pp. 22–34.

Comber, B & Kamler, B (eds) 2005, *Turn-around Pedagogies: Literacy Interventions for At-risk Students*, Primary English Teaching Association, Newtown, NSW.

Darling-Hammond, L 2004, 'Standards, accountability, and school reform, *Teachers College Record*, vol. 106, no. 6, pp. 1047–85.

Delpit, LD 1988, 'The silenced dialogue: power and pedagogy in educating other people's children', *Harvard Educational Review*, vol. 58, no. 3, p. 280.

Doecke, B & Gill, M 2004, 'Setting standards: confronting paradox', *English in Australia*, no. 129–130 , pp. 5–15.

Doecke, B Homer, D & Nixon, H (eds) 2003, *English Teachers at Work: Narratives, Counter Narratives and Arguments*, Wakefield Press in association with the AATE, Kent Town, South Australia.

Doecke, B, Kostogriz, A & Illesca, B 2010, 'Seeing "things" differently: recognition, ethics, praxis', *English Teaching: Practice & Critique*, vol. 9, no. 2, pp. 81–98.

Gannon, S 2012, 'Changing lives and standardising teachers: the possibilities and limits of professional standards', *English Teaching: Practice & Critique*, vol. 11, no. 3, pp. 59–77.

Heath, SB 1983, *Ways with Words: Language, Life, and Work in Communities and Classrooms*, Cambridge [Cambridgeshire]; Cambridge University Press, Cambridge, New York.

Moll, LC, Amanti, C, Neff, D & Gonzalez, N 1992, 'Funds of knowledge for teaching: using a qualitative approach to connect homes and classrooms, *Theory Into Practice*, vol. 31, no. 2, pp. 132.

Thomson, P 2002, *Schooling the Rustbelt Kids: Making the Difference in Changing Times*, Allen & Unwin, Crows Nest, NSW.

Chapter 3

Teachers researching their teaching

learning through practitioner inquiry

Anne Cloonan, Louise Paatsch and Muriel Wells

If being an educator in the 21st century centrally involves the capacity to inquire into professional practice, then the notion of inquiry is not a project or the latest fad. *It is a way of professional being.*

Alan Reid (2004, p. 3)

This chapter focuses on how you can reflect on your practice and engage in ongoing professional learning as a language and literacy teacher. We are working on the assumption that you think of yourself as an intellectual (Giroux 1988) who is critically engaged in your work, even though it can be incredibly difficult to maintain such a stance at the current moment, when teachers are being put under enormous pressure to improve educational outcomes. The emphasis placed by standards-based reforms, as proposed by Linda Darling-Hammond (2004), on improving performance on the part of both teachers and their students can sometimes undermine teachers' capacity to critically reflect on their teaching, especially when they feel pressured to 'teach to the test' in order to improve their students' results in standardised tests such as NAPLAN.

Yet a moment's reflection is enough to recognise the importance of teachers affirming their status as intellectuals and engaging in inquiry that might provide a perspective on such reforms.

People often use the term 'professional development' (PD) when referring to the learning that teachers need to do. Other people prefer to use the term 'professional learning'.

For a discussion of the currency of the terms 'professional development' and 'professional learning', see the opening sections of Brenton Doecke, Graham Parr, Sue North with Trevor Gale, Michael Long, Jane Mitchell, Jennifer Rennie and Judy Williams (2008).

'Professional development' brings to mind one-off PD sessions delivered by so-called 'experts'. Teachers who attend such sessions may find them stimulating, but when they return to their schools they often encounter difficulties in implementing this new knowledge, especially when it comes to persuading colleagues who have not shared their learning about the need for change. Such 'one-offs' often fail to acknowledge the context-specific nature of the issues with which literacy educators grapple in their school communities. 'Professional learning', on the other hand, signifies on-going collaborative reflection (Schon 1983) that is grounded in those communities, that emerges out of teachers' day-to-day professional practice and shapes it in significant ways, as teachers continually endeavour to extend their students' language and literacy.

Many people argue that for rich forms of professional learning to happen, schools and education systems need to adopt a view of teaching and learning that supports practitioner inquiry or school-based research conducted by teachers into their own practice (Cochran-Smith & Lytle 2009; Doecke, Parr, North et al. 2008; Parr 2010). This would mean thinking of yourself as belonging to a 'community of practice' and committing yourself to exploring the complexities of teaching with your colleagues, by talking, listening to and collaborating with one another, and reflecting on your work together.

The phrase ('communities of practice') is associated with the name of Etienne Wenger. See Etienne Wenger (1999).

In this chapter you will find three stories of practitioner inquiry arising out of three different school contexts. The schools involved use different words to name their approach to practitioner inquiry, including 'action research', 'participatory action research' and a 'whole-school approach'. We will honour their descriptions in the stories that follow.

Action research has a long history, dating back at least to the early twentieth century. According to Stephen Kemmis, Robbin McTaggart and Rhonda Nixon (2014):

> Different kinds of action research have emerged across different fields for many reasons, often because of the nature of the problems they confront … Because of the diversity, action research sometimes occurs under different names … [which] share some common key features. Each … rejects conventional research approaches where an external expert enters a setting to record and represent what is happening. (2014, p. 4)

Etienne Wenger also wrote *Communities of Practice: A Brief Introduction*, which provides a useful outline of this concept, making explicit links with educational settings. See <http://wenger-trayner.com/theory/>.

Action research recognises the capacity of people working in specific settings to actively participate in research in order to improve their practices (Kemmis, McTaggart & Nixon 2014). It is systematic, integrating 'action' with 'research' in an effort to bring about positive educational change. It acknowledges the power of teams of teachers collaborating together in order to identify and address issues in their professional practice. Teachers generate research questions relating to their practice in order to guide their inquiry into a shared area of concern. The cycle of action research involves teachers planning, taking action, observing and collecting evidence and reflecting on the effects (intended and unintended) of their initiatives, then modifying their practice in light of this new knowledge and planning what to do next (see Figure 3.1).

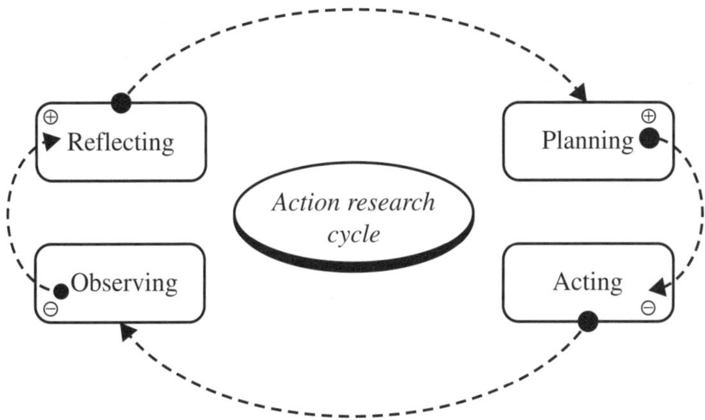

Fig. 3.1: *Action research cycle*

All three stories presented in this chapter mobilise elements of action research. However, the schools concerned adapt those elements according to the context of their school communities.

> The cycle of planning, acting, observing, collecting evidence and reflection followed by a new cycle of planning etc. is a common feature of action research projects, but action research has evolved over the years and has been adapted in many ways. See Wilfred Carr and Stephen Kemmis (1986), for an early and very influential set of arguments about the value of action research in school settings. Stephen Kemmis (2005) has revisited the question of action research and the importance of practitioner inquiry. For an argument about the application of Stephen Kemmis's idea of 'knowing practice' to the work of literacy educators, see Brenton Doecke, Bill Green, Alex Kostogriz, Jo-Anne Reid and Wayne Sawyer (2007).

Rosa is beginning her third year of teaching and is commencing at a new school that has just begun promoting practitioner inquiry as form of professional learning. Adam is a new graduate who has recently taken up his first teaching position at a school that has adopted a whole-school approach to classroom-based research. The final story presents Julie and Sophie, who have been teaching for five years in a school that has adopted action research as a school-wide initiative. We will explore how these teachers engage in professional learning within the different contexts of their work, learning about their efforts to investigate issues of importance to them and their students, the innovations they take and what they learn from them.

The language of practitioner inquiry will be evident in all three stories. A whole-school approach to professional learning, participatory action research, the action research cycle, collaborative learning, community of learners, observation, planning, taking action, inquiry based learning, feedback, reflection – all these terms illustrate how teachers are thinking about the different ways that they can research their own practices.

Reflection and discussion

What forms of professional learning have you experienced?

Do you feel that this learning has shaped your professional practice in significant ways?

What do you make of the difference between 'professional development' and 'professional learning'? How might teachers be best supported to engage in ongoing learning?

What kinds of professional learning have had most impact on your work as a language and literacy teacher? Think about the nature of that learning and the kinds of insight it generated into your professional practice.

Rosa joins a community of inquirers at a new school

It's late January and Rosa has just joined the Year 5/6 teaching team at Eastern Primary School (pseudonym), in a middle-class suburb in Melbourne. She is beginning her third year of teaching. Four of the five teachers in the team are also at the start of their third year of teaching, but she is the only one who is new to this school. The fifth member of the team, Heather, is an experienced teacher of twenty-five years who holds the position of the school's literacy coordinator. Rosa is surprised to learn that Sienna, with whom she will be team-teaching, has taken on school coordination of Information and Communication Technologies (ICT), even though she also has only two years of teaching behind her. That would never have happened at Rosa's previous school, where the lead teachers were given coordination roles, and most of them were about the same age as her parents.

She raised this with Sienna, whose reply made her think again about the nature of professional learning:

> The school's policy is to empower everyone to make his or her job more efficient, meaningful and rewarding. There's a belief in the value of tapping into the expertise, ideas and effort of everyone – we're actually obliged to step up and contribute to one another's learning – teachers, students, all the community. So I've felt pretty good that my ICT expertise has been recognised.

Rosa found Sienna's confidence inspiring, if a little intimidating. Over the holidays Rosa had read through the induction information manual for new staff, when she had been intrigued to read that the school adopted a model of 'Participatory Action Research', drawing on the ideas of Stephen Kemmis and Robin McTaggart (2005).

While Rosa recalled learning about participatory action research in some of her university units, she had found that such an approach was far from the norm at her last school. There the teachers had done PD sessions on areas of interest, sometimes together and sometimes individually. On their return to school, they had been obliged to present to the rest of the staff about the PD they had undertaken. But while Rosa sometimes found these presentations interesting, she wondered whether these new ideas really had any impact on the professional practice of teachers at the school.

Her new school's induction manual informed her that practitioner inquiry involved teachers 'wondering' about how to improve aspects of their work with students, and then working to deepen their understanding. The students' learning was meant to be matched by teachers' learning. One was a condition for the other. Just as teachers were seeking to develop their students' capacity to be reflective and imaginative, so they were working to develop their own capacity to engage critically and imaginatively in their work. Working collaboratively with colleagues, they would be able to move beyond 'taken for granted' ways of doing things. 'Yes', Rosa, thought, 'it was because so many things were "taken for granted" that I was often so frustrated at my last school.'

Rosa learnt that her team was to begin developing their 'combined research question' at their next meeting. She had maintained the habit of keeping a journal from her university days, and so in preparation for this meeting she began writing down her reflections about what a good question might be. Heather dropped by Rosa's classroom and gave her files containing samples of her students' work and their assessment results. The students had been asked to write a letter to their new teacher, indicating their strengths, interests and learning goals, as well as their hopes for the new school year. These were also included in the files. Before she left, Heather drew Rosa's attention to some assessment results that showed that many of the incoming Years 5/6 students could be further supported in making meaning from texts. The assessment showed that their capacity to infer meaning from texts could be strengthened. She remarked:

> Think about how important the capacity to infer is for children. They are bombarded with texts that they read, watch and listen to. Texts trying to sell them something or persuade them of something – on TV, on the internet – everywhere. They will start to turn 13 this year and then they'll also be on Facebook (if they aren't already). I will be arguing for this to be our research question at our next team meeting.

In preparation for meeting her new class, Rosa eagerly opened the files and sought out the letters from her new students. The first one read:

> **To my new teacher**
>
> We got new iPads last year but we didn't really do that much with them at school; just used apps for spelling and maths and stuff. I think that we should use the iPads more for reading books that you like and discussing them and reflecting on them with other people like in a book club – even with people not at our school. We could make our own books and films – not just using stuff that's already on the iPads.

As she leafed through the other letters, Rosa saw that many of the students mentioned the under-utilisation of the technology that they had been given. The range of interests was far-reaching, and their learning goals included many relating to social skills as well as subject-specific goals. The students were also preoccupied with the challenge of dealing with a range of different subjects and the associated reading and writing that they would be required to do at secondary school next year.

Rosa wanted to let the students know that she had read their letters. She was also keen to prepare for the meeting of the Year 5/6 teaching team, where they would start working towards identifying a research question. She made an entry in her reflective journal, when she was amused to find that she was asking more questions than making plans.

> Things on my mind. Staff are saying that the school could improve on incorporating ICT in meaningful ways – especially in literacy. I wonder what this means exactly. Heather thinks that the kids need more work on inferring. Why? I'd like to know more. The kids have a huge range of interests and I don't even know about their capacities yet. They are frustrated at the way they are using technologies. How can I find out more? I am really interested in this overlap between the technologies and literacy; and it seems the kids might be too.

You can see that her reflective journal is a crucial way in which Rosa sustains a conversation with herself about the complexities of her professional practice from day to day. Professional learning doesn't only occur in semi-formal settings when teachers meet together to discuss their practice, but it can be prompted by your day-to-day work, as you attend to the interactions that occur in your classroom.

Reflection and discussion

Have you experienced different approaches to professional learning at the schools where you have worked? What approaches have appeared to be effective? What approaches have been less effective? Can you say why? How important do you think it is for a school to adopt a whole school approach to professional learning?

You can see that Rosa has already learnt a lot about her students by reading the letters they have written to her. This has prompted her to think about a topic that she might research. Can you name a moment when you have begun to think differently about your work as a language and literacy teacher because of the writing your students have produced for you? You might also like to reflect on what you have learnt by observing students and listening to their conversations.

At the team meeting, team members tabled and discussed a range of evidence as a way of informing their decision-making, including test results, examples of student work, the students' NAPLAN (National Assessment of Program – Literacy and Numeracy) results, the letters from the students and notes from parent–teacher interviews held at the end of the previous year. Heather showed them student text responses that highlighted the need for deeper work on making inferences and reading more critically. Rosa looked at the range of evidence and saw that there was indeed a need to develop strategies to enhance their students' capacities to make meaning from texts. However, she also felt at a disadvantage, as the other teachers all knew their students, whereas she was a newcomer to the school. While she had looked through the students' files, their reports and test results, as well as reading their letters about their interests and frustration with the way ICT was being used in the school, she wanted a clearer picture of them – particularly as readers. She felt a little diffident about contributing to the discussion, but she nonetheless wanted to say something.

> I was thinking of giving them a homework task where they had to tell me on film how they see themselves as readers. That would help me get to know, and learn more about them as learners. And maybe how I can help them and further support their learning. It would also give them a reason to use the technology – in a meaningful way.

The team responded enthusiastically to Rosa's idea, deciding that they would all give students this homework task of creating a short movie. To scaffold the activity they decided to ask the students a set of questions: How do you see yourself as a reader? What are your strengths? What would you like to improve? How can your teachers support you to improve your reading?

As a way of analysing the students' movies the teachers decided to initially focus on three students from each class. They planned to present these students' responses to the questions at their next team meeting. Teachers were each to choose a student whom they considered to be 'struggling', a student 'working at a reasonable level', and a student who was 'sophisticated' in terms of his or her reading comprehension strategies. They were hoping that this would give them rich insights into how literacy learning was being experienced by students in their particular school community.

The following week the team viewed student responses to the task together. The student movie responses highlighted the varying levels of engagement with reading amongst the students. The teachers noted that many students whom they felt were 'struggling' gave signs of being utterly disengaged from print literacy practices. They simply failed to see them as meaningful. The teachers began to wonder whether they could explore the use of digital tools as a means of addressing these students' negative attitudes towards reading, with a view to ultimately improving their reading capacities. Rosa was enthusiastic about this new direction, as it matched perfectly her interest in the way new technologies could support literacy learning.

The team developed plans for teacher and student learning that they hoped would lead to student engagement with reading through digital tools. This included goals for student learning and actions for teachers to take in order to develop their understandings of the rationale for using a range of digital tools, as well as in an effort to build their confidence in employing them to enhance literacy learning. The teachers refined these plans continually, showing a growing understanding of the issues with which they were grappling.

Within this reflective phase of the participatory action research cycle the teachers engaged in collecting and analysing evidence about the students' progress in literacy. During fortnightly literacy team meetings teachers worked collaboratively as they discussed and developed understandings and engaged in professional reading in the areas of multimodality and comprehension.

> The literature on multimodality is vast. A good starting point would be the essays in David Cole and Darren Pullen (2010).

Team members undertook to become expert in the use of various technologies and took responsibility for sharing their learning with other team members. All team members kept reflective learning journals, as did the students. Teachers tracked and monitored students and brought evidence of their progression to each meeting in order to consider strategies for further intervention. The team developed the following research question as a focus for their professional learning:

> How can the integration of digital technology further develop students' capacities to make meaning from texts?

The team's focus was now on improving students' reading comprehension through using digital tools while engaging in an inquiry. The team designed an inquiry topic for their students that would provide a vehicle for them to answer their research question but also excite the students' interest:

> Imagining the future: How will contemporary technology change our world?

The Year 5/6 teaching team put their inquiry into action through the introduction of literacy contracts. Teachers developed a number of activities, including comprehension-based tasks related to the inquiry topic. These comprised 'must do' and 'can do' tasks, offering students a choice about how they went about conducting their inquiry. They developed intranet sites for each class, which linked to information such as contracts and home-based work.

Students read about, responded to and analysed texts about various technologies, such as smart phones. They listened to and analysed texts on iPods and iPads, read, played and critiqued internet games, and over time became engaged in analysing and writing weblogs (blogs), and creating glogs (interactive online posters) and wikis (that allow users to add or edit content), producing a range of texts in various forms.

> Chapter 4 provides another example of how teachers use new technologies to communicate with both their students and their families.

Rosa and the other Year 5/6 teaching team employed observation through the use of cameras to record students and teachers working. The recordings were then replayed as a prompt for both teacher and student reflection. The recordings and observations became yet another type of evidence of student learning. As Rosa explains:

> Teachers make a video recording of a group of students discussing literature including the sharing of thoughts, ideas and analysis of a text. The class watches the recording and gives feedback on the quality of discussion. We're seeing the complexity of understandings grow … and their capacities to articulate them.

Through watching the films and the discussion they stimulated, Rosa and the Year 5/6 teaching team observed that the initial impact of these changes was a deepened engagement for all students, regardless of the level of their capacity to handle print literacy. Students who had been disengaged from reading were willing, even eager, to undertake the technology-based reading tasks which were part of their literacy contracts. However Rosa reflected that while the students were engaged, they continued to need explicit teaching and support in developing more complex reading capacities such as inferring. As she wrote in her journal:

> There's been a big change in student engagement. They are all very excited and desperate to be able to use the technology … The students who aren't quite able to do inferential reading need more support and assistance. Even though the technology is helping to engage them, they still need support in looking for inferences. They are happier to try though.

When Rosa's students were given the task of reflecting on the technological tools introduced and how they supported their vocabulary development and capacity to infer meaning from text, a student whom she had previously considered to be 'struggling' wrote:

> I now know how to infer because I like the articles and like I know not all the answers are in the text, sometimes you've just got to think about the words and they may tell you a little clue but you've got to use your brain skills and work it out yourself … think about what you know about the world and other stuff you've read.

Heather oversaw periodic testing and recording of student comprehension against a standardised test. In comparing the results collected over time, the team observed a marked increase in aspects of their capacity to comprehend print texts. However in discussing the test results, teachers recognised that students had learnt things that the test instrument failed to explore. Rosa and her team expanded their own understandings of literacy in moving from a focus on print literacy to a focus on digital literacies. They wanted to give proper attention to the modes present in the multimodal texts (New London Group 1996; Cope and Kalantzis 2000) such as the way visual and audio dimensions contributed to the overall meaning of a text.

> For a theoretical rationale for teaching 'multiliteracies' see the New London Group (1996) and also the edited volume on 'multiliteracies' by Bill Cope and Mary Kalantzis (2000).
>
> Proponents of 'multiliteracies' argue that becoming 'multiliterate' requires students to develop proficiency in meaning-making in linguistic, visual, audio, gestural, spatial and multimodal designs; with multimodal being a combination of the other modes.

As Rosa explained:

> We're looking at digital literacies but we're not assessing the new skills that come with digital literacies, such as interpreting pictures and inferring or reading between the lines of what music in a text is implying. The writing on its own doesn't always give you the full story but when that picture is added or when that sound effect is added, or when that music is added, it creates a whole new meaning.

Rosa and her team's learning went beyond addressing their research question. In the process of undertaking their investigation, they developed expanded notions of comprehension and literacy. They reconsidered what constitutes comprehension in contemporary times when 'readers' (or would it be more accurate to say 'viewers'?) are making meanings from texts that involve an interplay between spoken and written language, visual images and audio. They had begun to consider the additional literacies required when students work in a digital environment.

You have seen from Rosa's story that the inquiry in which she was engaged involved strong collaboration between teachers. This was a feature of the culture of the school at which she was working. The cultures of schools are unique. The next story provides another example of inquiry-based professional learning as embedded in a whole school culture. In this school the principal and assistant principal are committed to developing a culture where people talk openly about their teaching, promoting the idea that they all belong to a 'community of learners'.

Adam moves from being a graduate to part of a community of learners

At the end of November Adam was ecstatic about being the successful applicant for a graduate teaching position in a Year 3/4 class in a rural school in Victoria. There were 16 teachers on staff, including ten classroom teachers, the principal, Shane, and his assistant principal, Sally, as well as Lisa, a part-time literacy coach, and three specialist teachers. Throughout January, Adam spent several days preparing for his new class and familiarising himself with the school's policies, including their Annual Implementation Plan. He learnt from discussions with Shane and Sally that the school was currently embarking on a whole-school approach to inquiry-based teacher professional learning. At the same time, the school was working on a whole-school approach to school improvement. This involved a cluster of schools within the regional network, with each participating school being required to select a whole-school focus for improvement.

During the first weeks of school, Adam came to realise that inquiry-based professional learning was new to all staff in the school, not only to him as someone who had just arrived. Previously, the school had sent individual teachers to professional development sessions (PDs) that were specific to particular content areas. Some teachers went to PDs around literacy, while others attended PDs on numeracy and ICTs. However, during the past six months, prior to Adam's appointment at the school, the leadership team, in collaboration with all members of staff, had agreed to undertake a 'whole-school approach' to professional learning. Shane and Sally both emphasised to Adam that he was a member of an active 'community of learners'. This meant that they were all learning: the principal, the assistant principal, everyone.

The concept of a 'community of learners' was not new to Adam. He had read and discussed the theories around community of learners in his initial teacher education course, and he had observed how some schools applied this concept during his professional experience placements.

> If you are interested in the 'community of learners' concept, you might like to read Barabara Rogoff, Eugene Mastusov and Cynthia White (1996). Etienne Wenger's (1999) concept of 'community of practice' is also relevant here, as is Jean Lave and Etienne Wenger (1991).

However, this had largely been with respect to how you can establish a sense of a 'community of learners' in classroom settings, involving teachers and their students, not with respect to the possibility of generating collaborative learning among a whole staff.

You will find a similar account of such a reorientation or refocusing on substantive issues relating to literacy teaching in staff meetings in Chapter 8.

During terms one and two staff meetings no longer took the form only of addressing administrative issues, but were dedicated to whole-school professional learning and collaboration around the teaching of literacy.

Prior to the first staff meeting, Sally asked the teachers: 'What do you want to know about, what do you want to learn?' Adam also noted that:

Such questions prompted self-reflection and rich collaborative discussions. It was such a change not to be talking only about administrative matters. 'Why are we doing what we are doing?' was the question that drove discussion at the meeting. After staff responses were collated, it was agreed that the focus for whole-school improvement and professional learning would be on literacy, and that initially special emphasis would be given to developing individual literacy goals incorporating the use of ICT. This focus was discussed with the year level unit leaders, then further planning occurred at year level unit meetings. Staff shared ideas as to how best to implement the focus at each specific year level. Adam contributed to the discussions with his colleagues during the Year 3/4 meetings. He drew on his personal knowledge and experiences gained throughout his university course and from his professional experience placements.

The first few staff meetings in term one were dedicated to looking at the data from the children's literacy assessments alongside teacher judgments about their students' literacy as they emerged from their day-to-day classroom observations. They were using data gathered from a number of different sources, and reflecting on how to interpret it in order to set goals for student. Adam recalls that:

We did a lot of talking in the after-school meetings about how to use the data and about grouping students … we looked at previous scores, anecdotal notes, and previous NAPLAN data for grade fours. We sort of brainstormed different ways and looked at different things to challenge our thinking and also how to improve our literacy teaching practices.

As part of this whole-school approach, Shane and Sally informed the staff that, in their role as school leaders, they were going to observe teachers in their classrooms at least twice a week. They would also meet with them individually once a fortnight to discuss the literacy data relating to their students and the rationale for selecting specific goals for literacy. Not surprisingly, Adam felt extremely anxious about the idea of these 'data meetings'. The thought of meeting with the principal and the assistant principal 'kind of freaked me out'. But he told himself that he wasn't the only one being observed. Shane and Sally were also going to be observing the classrooms of the most experienced teachers, saying that this was an opportunity for everyone to reflect and to learn.

Prior to his first meeting with Shane, Adam prepared all his literacy data on the children in his class. He used anecdotal records, NAPLAN results, PROBE test results and student work samples in order to develop an account of each child's progress. Adam recounts that during the meeting:

> Shane wanted to know … specifically who might be the ones who are struggling, who are our extension students? Who are those that can get lost … you know the ones in between … so basically we were looking at the students who were capable but weren't moving much … not much growth. Shane wanted to know why and pinpoint why and what we could do to move them along.

So far, so good. Although the meeting had been a little daunting, Adam felt that it had been productive, helping him to look at data in order to focus on 'specific students that you might overlook'.

Reflection and discussion

In this particular whole-school approach to inquiry-based teacher professional learning, student data were used as a basis for improving student literacy outcomes. What do such data really say about your students' literacy development? Why is it important to collect a range of data?

What is your experience of engaging with standardised test data, such as NAPLAN or that generated by other tests? How do you think such data compare with the insights you gain from your day-to-day classroom observations?

After the first term, Adam reflected further on the value of his meetings with Shane and Sally, and he came to feel that they had provided a good opportunity to build a relationship with them.

But Sally then informed Adam that she would be observing his literacy session during week four of the term, and again Adam felt a bit anxious. The whole thing began to remind him of his pre-service days at university, when he felt that he was being watched all the time. Once more he drew comfort from the fact that this was a 'whole-school practice', where even the most experienced teachers were to be observed. Adam had planned a session that incorporated individualised literacy learning goals for each child. He reflected on all the information presented at staff meetings regarding grouping students, incorporating the insights he has gained in his meeting with Shane. He was hoping that things would go well.

During the lesson Adam noticed that Sally was taking copious notes and that she was taking photos using her iPhone. He guessed that these notes and photos would be used as prompts for discussion in his next data meeting with Shane. But he still felt a bit uncomfortable, and he felt that he should make his discomfort known to Sally:

Adam: I can see you're writing. What are you writing?

Sally: I'm just, you know.

Adam: Can you please tell me now? I don't want to go for the next 45 minutes doing something that you think I should have changed.

Sally: Well I can see those boys are not really focused on what they're doing in literacy and I would probably now go and target some literacy learning goals for those kids first.

It was good that Adam spoke up, because after this session, Sally herself thought again about the protocols that she should follow when observing teachers. She acknowledged the need for teachers to be able to 'discuss the observations promptly and not to wait a week, they want immediate feedback'. Sally also realised that these observations were a time for building relationships and targeting specific professional learning needs of every teacher in the school. Staff were at 'different levels of their [learning] journey', and any feedback she gave to them should recognise that.

Reflection and discussion

These days, teachers are observed many times, not only in their teacher education programs but throughout their careers. Do you feel that such observations are valuable? What is required for effective classroom observation? What protocols do you think ought to be in place when observations occur? Have you observed many other teachers teaching? What have you learnt?

Adam also enjoyed his conversations with Lisa, the school's literacy coach. As part of his four hours of allocated planning time per week, he attended weekly meetings with her. During these meetings, she provided professional readings and suggested useful strategies to trial in the classroom. Lisa also took videos of Adam's teaching and made observational notes. They discussed these notes during the meetings, when further planning took place. In one particular meeting, Lisa asked Adam whether there was anything specific that he wanted to know about a particular student and possible ways that the student's literacy learning goals could be addressed. This led to a very rich discussion of the individual needs of students. Adam was also aware that the students in his class needed to be more aware of their own literacy learning goals and the need for the Year 3/4 students to take more responsibility for their own literacy learning.

During the next few weeks, Adam set up a class blog outlining the process for selecting specific literacy goals. He invited students to list the specific area of literacy

Chapter 4 and Chapter 8 also give accounts of teachers' efforts to make learning goals accessible to students.

that they felt they needed to work on, asking them to provide a reason for choosing this goal. He then set up a template asking students to write down their goal/s, stating when they achieved the goal/s and providing evidence for how they had accomplished them. He then set up a timetable schedule inviting students to nominate a ten-minute timeslot to meet with him to discuss their literacy learning goals. He would then meet with the students to ask them to reflect on the way they had achieved the goal and whether they had found the process useful to their literacy learning. Adam also provided each student with feedback during this meeting. One student commented:

If you have a goal then you keep setting your goal it's just yeah you try harder to achieve your goal.

Another student remarked:

If a few people are working on the same goal you can work in groups … so people are doing different things … so instead of doing stuff you already know how to do, each person's doing something challenging and working on their goal.

When asked how they achieved and provided evidence regarding their specific literacy goals, one student reported that:

So my first goal was to write more complex procedures and so then I typed in my action … I recorded how I achieved that by using our iPads and there's an app called 'show me' and I did it on that so you record it and you can draw on it it's like a white board on the screen that you can draw on it. And you can record what you're drawing and what you're saying.

Adam was 'gladly learning and gladly teaching', and he was pleased to share his students reflections on their literacy learning, as well as his personal reflections on his own learning with other members of the Year 3/4 unit team.

The unit team meetings provided opportunities for learning for everyone. It was exciting for Adam to know that some of the more experienced teachers had adopted some of his ideas and comforting to know that learning was happening for everyone. During one particular unit team meeting, one of Adam's experienced colleagues shared with him that:

You are always questioning yourself to make sure that you know that you're doing the right thing … and I think we're now a lot more open with the kids about what we're doing and why we're doing it.

Another colleague made this comment:

There is so much I have learnt now being a teacher, things that we didn't get when we were children sitting in classrooms … and now we say 'ahh that's why we learnt that', but the children in my classroom are actually having those discussions now. They get the point.

As the year progressed, the whole staff continued to share their learning experiences during whole-school staff meetings. Adam observed that these sessions were not only about learning from other teachers but also provided an opportunity for the leadership team to reflect on and share their own professional learning. For example, Shane had recently been to a 'celebration day meeting' with other principals in the region. This day was an opportunity for principals to share and celebrate the work that their schools had been doing to improve student literacy outcomes. Shane shared what he had learnt and discussed ways in which this new learning could be applied within the context of the current learners in the school. Sally also shared her experiences of a professional learning session she had attended at another school. Specifically, this session was about the curriculum standards for language and literacy levels. As a result of this session, she shared with the staff her interest in linking the whole-school focus of developing individual literacy goals with the curriculum standards levels. Sally talked about the importance of the whole school community understanding the language of these levels. As a result, the staff worked through adapting the literacy levels outlined in the curriculum standards documents into 'Kidspeak', under Sally's leadership and support.

> Chapter 8 provides another compelling example of how a teacher translated formal learning outcomes into language accessible to his students.

'Kidspeak' was one way that students could understand the language of the expected literacy outcomes of a particular year level and how these could be applied to their own literacy learning. It wasn't long before 'Kidspeak' was adopted throughout the school. Adam worked with his students around their individual literacy goals and supported them to align these with some of the literacy levels, where appropriate. He also set up his class blog so that parents had access to it, thus enabling them to know about the literacy goals their children had selected.

Reflection and discussion

Have you experienced professional learning as a 'whole-school approach'. What are the benefits and challenges to a 'whole-school approach' to professional learning? Do you feel that you should justify all your professional learning goals with reference to your school's priorities?

You can sense that all the professional learning at Adam's school was directed towards improving students' literacy outcomes, often as demonstrated by standardised test data. Do you feel that professional learning should always be justified in this way? Is there a direct link between professional learning and improved student outcomes?

The next story looks at the way teachers can pursue their professional learning by implementing an 'action research' cycle. Teachers are not the only ones who have adopted this well-known approach to situated learning. Professionals working in other institutional settings, such as health care, have also implemented action research in order to understand the complexities of their work. 'Action research' can be implemented with one or two colleagues, or it may be adopted by a whole school in order to bring about change.

Julie and Sophie combine action and research

Julie and Sophie teach in a regional primary school in Victoria. They have both been teaching for five years. Julie and Sophie's school joined a three-year long professional learning program that took on an action research approach to teacher professional learning. The approach at Julie and Sophie's school reflected many of the same features as the approach used at Rosa's school, including the phases of planning, acting, observing, collecting evidence and reflecting (see Fig. 3.1). You will also notice that aspects of their experiences are similar to Adam's professional learning. Julie and Sophie's school had similarly embarked on a 'whole-school approach' to practitioner inquiry as a key dimension of professional learning.

Julie and Sophie's school knew that one-off PD activities rarely lead to sustained change in teaching practices, whereas practitioner inquiry approaches to professional learning that is ongoing had been shown to lead to sustained change in practice (Blackley & Wells 2009; Comber & Kamler 2005; Darling-Hammond et al. 2009; Villegas-Reimers 2003). The school leadership team saw this ongoing action research approach to professional learning as an opportunity to trial what was, for them, a new way of creating sustainable change in pedagogy at their school.

The teacher professional learning program at Sophie and Julie's school involved three 'knowledge creation' days that focused on developing skills with learning technologies that could be used to enrich the teaching and learning in classrooms. This was followed by one day devoted to designing the research questions for their school. The school's action research project was conducted throughout the school year. They had decided to investigate the question: 'How can we use communication web spaces in the form of edublogs and wikis to build partnerships to personalise learning for our students?'

Julie and Sophie were both teaching in the junior unit, which consisted of two classes with 24 students in each. They became actively involved in the action research cycle of planning, acting, reflecting, observing and moving on to the next cycle of planning in the process of working with their students. They looked at their practice and identified an aspect of practice that they felt they needed to improve and then implemented the cycle. In Julie and Sophie's case, their area for investigation was a whole-school decision. Julie and Sophie's experience of participating in action research told them that, even though there is an expected sequence of steps, it is often a messy process. That is the nature of things when investigating the complexities of teaching and learning.

Let's hear what Julie and Sophie have to say about what they did in their own words:

> Our junior unit decided to look at ways to better integrate literacy with our inquiry unit which we called, 'Lights, Camera Action!' We also wanted to build stronger links with our parents. We decided to get our students to create movies to get our parents to use online blogging to give them feedback.

By integrating the teaching of literacy into their classes' inquiry unit, Julie and Sophie sought to provide a real purpose for the students' writing and the creation of multi-modal texts. This also provided an authentic context in which to help the parents take a more active role in their children's learning by developing their skills in providing constructive feedback to their children's writing and the creation of multimodal texts in the form of movies.

How to begin? Julie and Sophie knew that effective teachers 'start where the students are' so they decided to collect data directly from their students.

> We asked the students to use their journals to reflect on their attitudes towards writing. We asked them to reflect on the following questions:
>
> How do you feel about writing?
>
> What are you good at in writing?
>
> Is there anything that you don't like about writing?
>
> We then surveyed the students to find out what they knew about feedback. In the survey we asked a series of questions:
>
> What is feedback?
>
> What does it look like?
>
> What kind of feedback is most useful to you? Why?
>
> What kind of feedback is least useful to you? Why?

With this information, Julie and Sophie were in a position to plan to more fully engage their students through the creation of their movies. They were also committed to combining this activity with the use of online communication technologies to assist parents to provide their children with constructive feedback about the movies that they created.

We thought that one way to incorporate our inquiry unit called 'Lights, Camera Action!' with literacy and to provide the context for feedback was to ask the students to create movies. To do this we used an online movie creation site, which allowed our students to design and create their own movies. It provided students with the choice of background settings, characters, sound effects, movements, voices and themes. Students typed out their scripts in the online movie site and then used the tools available on the site to transform their scripts into movies.

Creating movies places a wide range of demands on students' literacy capabilities. They have to decide on the topic, the setting for the movie, the characters and the storyline. How should the characters be introduced? How might the conversation between characters be developed? What will happen in the movie to make it interesting and maintain the audience's interest? What sort of complication will happen? How will this be resolved? All these aspects need to be portrayed through the characters' gestures, movement and the words they 'speak'. The children have to plan in details the structure of their movie and also make decisions about camera angles and camera movement. When will they take the camera in close up? When in the script will they pan the camera out? Making movies is not 'easy'. Creating multimodal texts is complicated and challenging work. As Julie remarked:

During the movie-making process we expected our students to use feedback from their audience to continually improve their movies. To facilitate this, the movies were uploaded to the class edublog site where we encouraged parents to provide feedback to their children about their movies.

The decision to use a blogging site that allowed interactive communication was a powerful way to set up educational conversations within the school community.

At the start of the project the principal at Julie and Sophie's school ensured that all the staff understood the school's priorities. He stated that:

I want our school to develop strong partnerships between teachers, students, families and the wider community through the use of blogs and wikis. These web spaces can support us to become a learning community. All our classes will be able to share their work with an interested audience, therefore offering a diverse landscape in which to showcase our students' learning. Families love to hear about what their children are doing at school and this offers us a new way to do this, a way that can be accessed easily in and outside of school.

Julie and Sophie used edublogs to encourage their parents to be part of a collaborative learning community to support the students.

> We used edublogs as our web space provider for the online site. It allowed teachers and students to upload a variety of media such as images, movies and sound recordings. Feedback comments were posted on the class edublogs site and monitored by the teachers. It was like a class webpage with the bonus of interaction between parents, students and teachers through posting comments.

Because Julie and Sophie's inquiry-based professional learning was part of the bigger school project, they took the opportunity to set up sharing and learning experiences for other teachers across the school.

> We set up our edublogs site and then provided in-service sessions for other teachers on how to use edublogs effectively within their classrooms. An in-service day and several Professional Learning Team meetings were devoted to supporting the implementation of edublogs right across the school. Once edublogs was established as our site for communication, students were introduced to it and encouraged to access their class pages from home with their family. Parents were told about the site at parent–teacher interviews, in the mornings before school and through a letter.

Parents were encouraged to use edublogs as a tool to provide their children with constructive feedback about the movies they were creating. The teachers introduced the online movie site as a means to engage children in the inquiry unit and to enhance their writing and ICT skills. Through the use of the interactive white boards, teachers were able to demonstrate and model how to use the movie site and how to develop a conversation between characters in the movies. The students then had the opportunity to explore and experiment with the program before being asked to write their first script. Extra support was given to a small group of students who found the process challenging.

Throughout the writing process, students gave each other feedback about their storylines. Once the students' movies were completed and embedded into the edublog, parents and friends were able to post comments on each student's page. The students also presented their movies to the class on the interactive white board. The students used the 'Three Stars' and a 'Wish' method of feedback to respond to each other's movies. The 'Three Stars' represented three positive comments about the movie and the 'Wish' was expected to be a more critically analytical response that gave constructive feedback. Throughout the feedback process the students were encouraged to reflect on their experiences in their learning journals.

The teachers used reflective journals throughout the duration of their inquiry to reflect on any changes in their literacy pedagogies that they were experiencing. The writing of reflections in their personal journals combined with regular reflective conversations gave Julie and Sophie the means to think through the changes they were making and to modify their practice in light of those reflections. They regularly discussed what was working, what wasn't working so well, and possible changes that might improve the literacy teaching and learning in their classrooms.

One entry in Sophie's journal read:

> Now that everyone has received feedback on their first attempt at a movie, we are going to get them all to set a personal goal before writing their second script. The goal might be about any aspect of the movie. It could be how long their movie is, or getting them to make sure it makes more sense to the audience, or how engaging it is for the audience, or any other things that have come up in the feedback.

They repeated the process of writing and producing a movie, when once again they encouraged parents and family to give feedback. Julie and Sophie were aware that writers rarely write one perfect copy. They understood that writing is a process in which you plan, write rough drafts, edit and polish – all in an effort to create a final product for publication. Creators of digital texts are no different to any other writers. They need opportunities to work on and improve their creation over time.

To conclude the inquiry unit on 'Lights, Camera Action!', Sophie and Julie organised a movie premiere for the students to celebrate their achievements with family members. This movie premiere also provided opportunities for Julie and Sophie to reflect further, observing the children's achievements and planning for the future. You can learn an immense amount from the writing and other artefacts that students produce.

Both Julie and Sophie observed that student engagement in their own writing was improved by embedding writing into the inquiry unit of 'Lights, Camera, Action'. Crucial to this was the creation of multimodal texts and the feedback from parents as the audience. In doing this they incorporated an important, but sometimes forgotten, aspect of literacy work in which students share their work with a wider audience in mind (Buckingham 2007).

Reflection and discussion

You might now like to devise your own action research project. What aspects of language and literacy learning do you feel you would like to investigate? You might like to nominate one or two of your 'blind spots' for inquiry as areas where you feel that you would like to improve your understanding of language and literacy. It is obvious that Julie and Sophie were taking some risks in what they were doing, but that is in the nature of inquiry. There would be no point in an inquiry if you knew all the answers in advance.

You can see that, in addition to their interest in the potential of digital technologies, Julie and Sophie were concerned with questions that have traditionally preoccupied teachers of writing, namely how to inject into students a sense of purpose that might motivate them to write, as well as how they might benefit from feedback as they engage in the writing process. Perhaps you might focus on one of these topics for your inquiry. Do you feel that your students are always engaging in authentic, meaning-making activities when they produce school writing? Does this matter? Do you feel that digital or multimodal technology might be used creatively to enable them to engage in authentic communication with a larger audience?

Conclusion

Teachers who see inquiry as part of their 'professional being', as Alan Reid (2004) puts it, have much to contribute to an understanding of the complexities of language and literacy in school settings. Over the years both the Australian Literacy Educators' Association (ALEA) and the Australian Association for the Teaching of English (AATE) have done a great deal to promote the value of practitioner inquiry, publishing stories and other accounts of classroom-based research in their journals. Sometimes this has taken the form of reports about action research that has been implemented as part of a whole-school policy, as with the stories contained in this chapter. It should also be noted, however, that much of the material published by classroom teachers has not necessarily been generated through implementing an action research cycle, but is written from the standpoint of reflective practitioners who are thinking critically about their day-to-day work. They haven't made significant interventions or changes to their teaching in the way that Rosa, Adam, Sophie and Julie have done.

The history of practitioner inquiry is larger than that of action research. If you are interested in thinking further about the kinds of knowledge teachers are able to produce by reflecting on their practice, you might find it interesting to read Joe Kincheloe's (2003) book about teachers as researchers. A famous early example of advocacy for the centrality of classroom inquiry is the chapter on 'The teacher as researcher' in Lawrence Stenhouse's (1975) book. For studies with a focus on language and literacy, which also emphasise the importance of writing as a form of inquiry, see Graham Parr (2010) and Brenton Doecke and Douglas McClenaghan (2011). The STELLA project, mentioned in previous chapters, also provides valuable of examples of English literacy teachers writing about their work.

The teachers may have been prompted to write about an insight that became available to them as they were observing their students engaging in classroom talk. Or perhaps they are writing about something they have learnt from the stories their students have produced that has made them re-examine their assumptions about the best way to teach writing.

Another important element, after all, that the preceding stories have in common, in addition to being examples of 'action research', is that all the teachers involved kept journals about what they were experiencing. You may or may not find yourself working in a school that supports the kinds of collaborative inquiry into language and literacy in which Rosa, Adam, Sophie and Julie participated. But wherever you are, it is important to engage in reflective practice. Keeping a journal, as well as other forms of writing, is an important way of sustaining a reflective stance vis-à-vis the challenges you face as a language and literacy teacher.

References

Blackley, J & Wells, M 2009, *Supporting Teachers as Researchers (STAR): A Model for Sustainable Professional Learning*, paper presented at the Australian Teacher Education Conference (ATEA) Albury, Australia.

Buckingham, D 2007, 'Digital media literacies: rethinking media education in the age of the Internet', *Research in Comparative and International Education*, vol. 2, no. 1, pp. 43–5.

Carr, W & Kemmis, S 1986, *Becoming Critical: Education, Knowledge and Action Research*, Falmer, London.

Cochran-Smith, M & Lytle, S 2009, *Inquiry as Stance: Practitioner Research for the Next Generation*, Teachers College Press, New York; London.

Cole, DR & Pullen, DL (eds) 2010, *Multiliteracies in Motion: Current Theory and Practice*, Routledge, New York.

Comber, B & Kamler, B 2005, 'Designing turn-around pedagogies and contesting deficit assumptions' in B Comber & B Kamler (eds), *Turn-around Pedagogies: Literacy Interventions for At-risk Students*, PETA, Newtown, Australia.

Cope, B & Kalantzis, M (eds) 2000, *Multiliteracies: Literacy Learning and Designs of Social Futures*, Routledge, London.

Darling-Hammond, L 2004, 'Standards, accountability, and school reform', *Teachers College Record*, vol. 106, no. 6, pp. 1047–85.

Darling-Hammond, L, Wei, RC, Andree, Alethea, Richardson, N & Orphanos, S 2009, 'State of the profession: study measures status of professional development', *Journal of Staff Development*, vol. 30, no. 2, pp. 42–50.

Doecke, B, Green, B, Kostogriz, A, Reed, JA & Sawyer, W 2007, 'Knowing practice in English teaching? Research challenges in representing the professional practice of English teachers', *English Teaching: Practice & Critique*, vol. 6, no. 3, pp. 4–21.

Doecke, B & McClenaghan, D 2011, *Confronting Practice: Classroom Investigations into Language and Learning*, Phoenix Education, Putney, Australia.

Doecke, B, Parr, G, North, S, Gale, T, Long, M, Mitchell, J, Williams, J 2008, 'National mapping of teacher professional learning project: final report, DEEWR (trans).

Giroux, HA 1988, *Teachers as Intellectuals: Toward a Critical Pedagogy of Learning*, Bergin & Garvey, Granby, MA.

Hargreaves, A & Michael, F 2000, 'Mentoring in the new millennium', *Theory into Practice*, vol. 39, no. 1, p. 50.

Kemmis, S 2005, 'Knowing practice: searching for saliences', *Pedagogy, Culture & Society*, vol. 13, no. 3, pp. 391–426. doi: 10.1080/14681360500200235

Kemmis, S & McTaggart, R 2005, 'Participatory action research: communicative action and the public sphere' in NK Denzin & YS Lincoln (eds), *The Sage Handbook of Qualitative Research*, Sage Publications, Thousand Oaks, pp. 559–603.

Kemmis, S, McTaggart, R, & Nixon, R 2014, 'Participatory action research: communicative action and the public sphere' in NK Denzin & YS Lincoln (eds), *The Sage Handbook of Qualitative Research*, Sage Publications, Thousand Oaks, pp. 559–603.

Kincheloe, JL 2003, *Teachers as Researchers: Qualitative Inquiry as a Path to Empowerment* (2nd edn), Routledge Falmer, London New York.

Lave, J & Wenger, E 1991, *Situated Learning: Legitimate Peripheral Participation*, Cambridge University Press, Cambridge, New York.

New London Group 1996, 'A pedagogy of multiliteracies: designing social futures', *Harvard Educational Review*, vol. 66, no. 1, pp. 60–92.

Parr, G 2010, *Inquiry-based Professional Learning: Speaking Back to Standards-based Reforms*, Post Pressed, Mt Gravatt, Qld.

Reid, A 2004, 'Towards a culture of inquiry in DECS', occasional paper no.1, Department of Education and Children's Services: Government of South Australia. <http://www.decd.sa.gov.au/learnerwellbeing/files/links/link_72576.pdf>

Rogoff, B, Mastusov, E & White, C 1996, 'Models of teaching and learning: participation in a community of learners' in D Olson & N Torrance (eds), *The Handbook of Education and Human Development: New Models of Learning, Teaching and Schooling*, Blackwell Publishers, Oxford, pp. 388–414.

Schon, DA 1983, *The Reflective Practitioner: How Professionals Think in Action*, Temple Smith, London.

Stenhouse, L 1975, *An Introduction to Curriculum Research and Development*, Heinemann, London.

Villegas-Reimers, E 2003, *Teacher Professional Development: An International Review of the Literature*, UNESCO: International Institute for Educational Planning, Paris.

Wenger, E 1999, *Communities of Practice*, Cambridge University Press, Cambridge.

Wenger, E (nd), 'Communities of practice: a brief introduction', <http://wenger-trayner.com/theory/>

Chapter 4

Literacy teaching and learning in digital times

tales of classroom interactions

Muriel Wells and Glenn Auld

With the ubiquitous presence of technology, generating meaning in contemporary times harnesses influential technological capacities which have not only created a changed textual landscape . . . but . . . shifted the nature of interactions between people in their interpersonal, virtual, digital and textual spaces.

Christine Edwards-Groves (2012, p. 110)

Can you recall the technologies that were available to you when you were growing up? What kind of technologies do you remember your own school teachers using? Do you recall feeling excited when your teachers brought new technologies into the class? Did it make any difference to your learning or make you feel differently about school? How do those technologies compare with the technologies that are currently available to educators? How confident are you about using digital technologies in your teaching? Do you think it is important to use new technologies? How do you learn about the ways in which new technologies might enhance your classroom practice?

Over the past two or three decades increasing attention has been given to new technologies in education generally and in literacy education in particular. This attention has focused on multimodal technologies and social media that children and young people use in their everyday lives outside of school. James Gee argues that the practices of digital gaming reflect powerful learning, showing the complex cognitive operations in which teenagers engage when they play computer games (Gee 2003, 2007). Given the role that digital technologies play in young people's lives, some educators have questioned whether schools provide sufficient opportunities for them to use and learn from such activities (Lankshear, Green & Snyder 2000; Lankshear & Knobel 2003).

Catherine Beavis, Joanne O'Mara and Lisa McNiece (2013) have drawn on Gee's work to explore the complexity of digital gaming in Australian settings. Julian Sefton-Green (2000) and Andrew Burn (2000) have also developed useful arguments relating to the division between school literacy practices and the literacy practices (including digital literacy practices) in which children and teenagers engage outside school.

While some students are highly engaged in social media in out of school contexts, they are not necessarily able to use such media in schools and classroom settings and to reflect upon that use. How can schools possibly claim to be educating young people for the 21st century if they systematically exclude from the curriculum the digital literacy practices that are part of the modern world?

Digital technologies can also play an important role in making school relevant to young people. When teachers give them the opportunity to do so, children and teenagers typically show themselves to be very adept at using digital technologies to create texts, drawing on the meaning-making resources of popular culture. They are able to use such technologies to engage in authentic communication with one another, creating texts that they find personally meaningful.

For arguments in support of these claims, see Anne Haas Dyson (2009), Jackie Marsh (2009) and Brenton Doecke and Douglas McClenaghan (2009).

This is to envisage classrooms as social spaces in which teachers and students come together to share their experiences and to learn from one another, as distinct from traditional images of classrooms as places for drilling and skilling and learning the so-called 'basics'.

This chapter highlights some of the ways teachers can use new technologies to support teaching and learning in their classrooms. The vignettes that follow are designed to prompt you to reflect on your approach to teaching with technology. The first story captures the digitally mediated interactions that occur in Shannon's Grade 3/4 classroom, in the course of a series of lessons in which his students create a choose-your-own adventure in the form of a wiki. The second story introduces you to Shona, a Grade 3/4 teacher who uses tablet technology to provide individual learning experiences to her students. Taken together, these stories show the importance of understanding how digital technologies mediate the experiences of people in contemporary societies (Simpson & Walsh 2013), as well as the role those technologies play in educational settings. They invite you to reflect on how teaching and learning have been transformed by new technologies. This embraces both the literacy learning in which students engage in classrooms, when they use digital technologies to create and respond to texts of a variety of kinds, as well as the organisational work that teachers need to do in planning for literacy learning and teaching.

Shannon: creating digital texts

Imagine you are in a Grade 3/4 classroom in a large regional primary school. The children have just arrived at school, ready to commence their daily literacy block. Shannon, their teacher, has them sitting in a large group at the front of the classroom. He is using the interactive white board to lead the whole group teaching session.

> Okay, today we are going to start planning our next piece of writing. We are going to create a 'choose your own adventure' narrative. When it is finished we will publish it online in a wiki. I have registered our class on Wikispaces (you can find that site by going to <http://www.wikispaces.com>) which will allow us to publish all the pages we create for our 'choose your own adventure' narrative. We can publish all our pages and link them together to create an interactive multimodal text. We will have one shared page that will contain the introduction to our multimodal text and have links to all the other pages that you create for your sections of our adventure story.

Shannon believes it is important for the children to experience writing as a process, rather than simply focus on the outcome, the completed text. After all, published authors plan, draft, revise and edit their writing before it becomes a finished product.

A multimodal 'choose-your-own adventure' text promises to be the perfect vehicle to enable his students to see writing as happening over an extended period of time, as something involving planning, revising and publishing with careful decision-making happening along the way. Integral to the writing process is the way the students collaborate with each other through the drafting and editing of the text to come up with coherent text with an agreed clear purpose.

Reflection and discussion

It may be worth pausing before we go any further for you to begin to think about the literacy tasks embedded in this unit. As you read this vignette, try to identify the language and literacy skills that the students need to employ in order to complete this task. A 'choose-your-own adventure' is a type of narrative, and so the students will need to make decisions about the chronology of events, and the continuity of plot across the various pathways within the story. They will also need to think about the characters who are caught up in this adventure. This is a whole-class activity, which means that it will be important for them to work collaboratively, both in teams and as a class. A lot of talk will be necessary in order to get things done. Shannon has deliberately planned to integrate reading, writing, speaking and listening in this unit, in much the same way that language and literacy teachers have always done. But he is also passionate about new technologies, and so you might want to consider how these language modes are transformed through being facilitated by technology. What extra planning do you think this would necessitate?

We shall now pick up Shannon's story again at the start of the next lesson in this unit. Here is how he starts the lesson the next day.

Shannon: As I said we are all going to be working on parts of the same 'choose your own adventure style' multimodal text. Do you remember the one the Grade 3/4 kids at Bellaire Primary School made? It was called 'Terry the tennis ball'.

Students: *Nodding in agreement.*

Ethan: Yeah, it was cool.

Kaitlin: I'd like to have a go at doing that!

Aiden: I read 'choose your own adventures' all the time! I can't get enough of them!

Shannon: Remember how they had an introduction and then other pages so the readers could select their own pathway through the adventures of 'Terry the tennis ball'? No . . . everyone? Okay then let's take a quick look at Bellaire's to refresh our memories.

To view 'Terry the tennis ball' go to <http://terrythetennisball.wikispaces.com>.

Shannon: So, now we all have a clear picture in our minds of how our 'choose your own adventure' multimodal text might look.

The children indicate their agreement.

Shannon: We have discussed multimodal texts before. Can you remember what some of the modes that can be used in a wiki might be? Yes?

==

Phut, the lid came off the container. Terry was free at last. For so long he had been crammed up tight next to his two brothers in a can on the shelf in the sports store. Now he could see the sky and feel the air on his fluffy skin and he felt happy to be out. Straight away though he felt himself falling, down, down, down.

Soon Terry was bouncing, bouncing, bouncing before he

- **rolled down into ...**
- **was picked up ...**
- **down a hill ...**
- **got hit in a golf hole ...**
- **rolled down the road ...**
- **bumped into ...**
- **hit by a ...**
- **rolled by ...**
- **flow in the air and hit ...**
- **stopped at a ...**
- **sat their on a ...**
- **bounced to a ...**
- **popped in ...**

Fig. 4.1: *Adventures of 'Terry the tennis ball'*

Ben: Well, you've got to think about the writing, what the words say.

Zoe: And then you've got to think about pictures and even video that shows things moving around.

Aiden: I like it too when you hear sounds and music.

Shannon: Great, so you can add images, sound and video. They are some of the modes you can use in your scenarios. You might think of more as we work on our text.

The children engage in excited talk about multimodal texts they've enjoyed, not all of it connected with what Shannon now wants them to do, but he soon brings them back to focus on the task in hand.

Shannon: Okay … Okay … So, we are going to create our own 'choose your own adventure'. We are going to publish ours online in a wiki just like Bellaire did. We'll work together as a whole class to create the introduction page and then you will work in pairs to write, design and publish a scenario on your own pages that will be linked to the introduction. Now let's get started by brainstorming ideas or topics as well as the location for the introduction of our 'choose-our-own adventure' narrative.

All the students suggest possible ideas for the text. Shannon records their suggestions on the interactive white board. The students contribute ideas about the location and events that might happen in their 'choose-your-own adventure' story. Their suggestions include:

An adventure on Mars
A story about monsters
A time-travel adventure that goes back to the dinosaurs
An adventure that takes place in a zoo.

Shannon congratulates the students on having so many good ideas, and then remarks:

> Shannon: While they can't all be the setting or introduction for our whole class choose-your-own adventure, you might still want to use some of these ideas for your own stories.

The students eventually decide to write an adventure narrative that begins in the zoo.

> Shannon: Okay, do you want to change any of the ideas we decided on or are they all okay? James, what is your suggestion?
>
> James: Well, I'm wondering whether the location has to be a zoo. I thought it might be better if we set it in the Australian bush because the Australian bush is more interesting than the zoo.
>
> Shannon: Does everyone agree? Let's take a vote. (*Shannon counts the votes.*)
>
> Okay, the majority of the class prefers the zoo as the starting location. Sorry James. You might be able to use your idea in another piece of work. Now let's think about the types of multimedia we might use to make our text look and feel really interesting for our audience.

As you can see, the whole class has had the opportunity to contribute to the plan for the text. And although James wasn't able to change where the story is set, he seems happy to accept the majority decision and soon settles down to composing a zoo adventure.

The students then move into pairs to write the events that will be the optional pathways for readers following the introduction. Links to the various complications prepared by the students will be set up to take readers to their personal choice within the adventure. The students know from previous work on narrative that narratives usually follow a pattern of setting the scene, with complications to the plot that maintain the readers' interest. In the case of their multimodal 'choose-your-own adventure', readers will each be taken to one of the student's pages depending on their response to a question that concludes the introduction.

> Susie and Hayley are working together to create their scenario.
>
> Susie: Let's use your tablet to get started.
>
> Hayley: We have to make at least five slides on our storyboard don't we?

Susie: Yep, and we have to use at least three images too.

Susie and Hayley settle down to work on these tasks.

(*Later.*)

Hayley: Okay, I think our plan is ready. Let's send it to Mr B and see if he says it is ready for us to move on to the next step.

Susie: While we're waiting to get his okay, let's go and put the title of our scenario on the introduction page. Then we can go to our own page in the wiki and put our title in the there too.

It is worth noting here that Hayley and Susie are demonstrating their ability to use some task-specific vocabulary that Shannon, as their teacher, has modelled during whole class teaching sessions. They have also learnt some of this vocabulary through engaging with the 'choose your own adventure' from Bellaire Primary School.

At the end of the session Shannon brings the whole class together to share the learning and to suggest some tasks that they might complete as 'out-of-school' tasks.

Shannon has planned these lessons in order to bring together the knowledge that his students have about 'choose-your-own adventures' texts with the meaning-making capacity of digital technologies. During the early stages of their work together, the students have been preoccupied with details like setting and characters, i.e. the traditional features associated with storytelling, although this was also mediated by digital technology, with the students posting their pages on the class wiki. Now it is time to focus more squarely on the dimensions opened up by digital communication, and in the next lesson Shannon steers the class in this direction:

Shannon: Most of you have now completed your complications and have published them on the wiki. Now you need to consider the other modes of digital communication that you could use on your pages. Remember we discussed the various modes the other day?

Some students decide to add sound and some decide to add short movies to their complications. As Shannon monitors the students' progress he asks them how they will use multimodal elements to enhance their scenarios. So the unit unfolds.

What can we learn from Shannon's teaching?

We shall now leave Shannon's class in order to tease out some fundamental concepts of literacy that underpin his teaching.

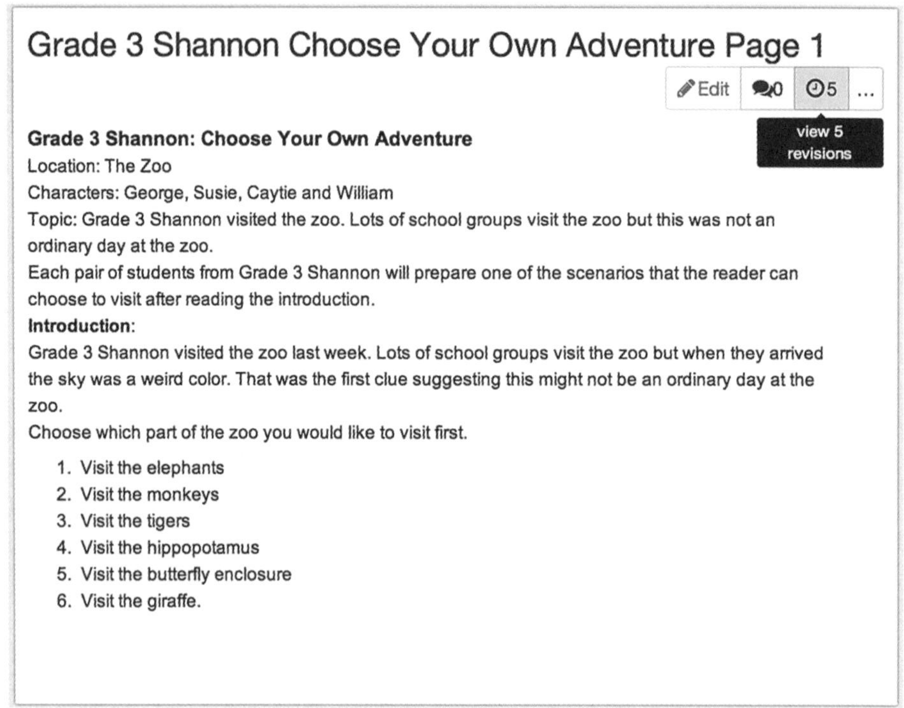

Fig. 4.2: *Shannon's grade's 'Choose-your-own adventure'*

In planning for these lessons, Shannon combined understandings about narrative texts as set out in the curriculum with his knowledge of the social networks that many students experience from their use of technology in out of school contexts. The fact that students might use social media does not necessarily mean that they are fully aware of the conventions that underpin the various genres and modes of communication that comprise it. There are multiple dimensions to digital texts, and Shannon tries to sensitise his students to this in these lessons.

In addition to wanting his students to learn how a conventional written text, such as a 'choose your own adventure', might be transformed by the use of multimedia, Shannon is also mindful of the value of the social nature of learning that can be facilitated by using digital texts. Colin Lankshear and Michele Knobel (2011) suggest that social media provide people with a more participatory experience in literacy. Whether or not you agree with this premise, this is clearly an aspect of the way that Shannon uses the wiki to give each student responsibility for the creation of different parts of the text, enhancing their sense of their obligations to other students, as co-creators of this text.

Your understanding of literacy for the 21st century does not mean abandoning your understanding of traditional print-based literacy. The fact is that both education departments and the wider community are insistent on the need to teach students traditional literacy skills, but it is also important for educators to be aware of the way new literacy practices often use different modalities to create different types of meaning. Lee Crockett, Ian Jukes and Andrew Churches argue that:

> The skills we learn to read, write and communicate have changed. In the age of multimedia, hypertext, blogs and wikis, reading is no longer just a passive, linear activity that deals only with text. Today, it's essential that all of our students have a wide range of skills beyond those that were needed in the 20th century, a range that includes the skills needed to function within a rapidly digital society. (2011, p. 17)

The word 'literacy' traditionally refers to reading, writing, speaking and listening effectively in a range of contexts. In the 21st century, 'literacy' has expanded to refer to a flexible, sustainable and ever-growing repertoire of capabilities in using and producing traditional texts as well as employing new communications technologies. Digital literacy has changed the way students create meaning by allowing them to convey meaning through sound, image, video and text to a wide audience. As David Buckingham has observed:

> The Internet, computer games, digital video, mobile phones and other contemporary technologies provide new ways of mediating and representing the world and of communicating. (Buckingham 2008, p. 74)

Digital literacy is changing not only the way children engage with their world, but also the way they learn about and understand their world. As technology becomes more and more accessible in the 21st century, many educators have been prompted to re-consider the diverse literacy skills and practices required to be literate, and their pedagogical repertoire has accordingly expanded in order to effectively engage young people in literacy learning.

Reflection and discussion

Shannon uses digital technology to scaffold a joint construction of text that integrates knowledge about digital and print-based literacies. He provides his students with opportunities to learn about digital texts, such as wiki, and print-based texts, such as a popular narrative genre, as integral parts of a shared learning experience. Crucially, he taps into his students' knowledge and interests, enabling them to engage in an authentic meaning-making activity.

These days the internet is full of texts that were originally print based. Recipes, advice on how to grow tomatoes, information about endangered species, newspapers, weather reports, comic books – you will find all these things and more on the internet. You might like to choose one of these text types and devise a series of lessons that would scaffold students into producing their own texts, taking care to ensure that you attend to both the conventions traditionally associated with these texts (as print texts) and the dimensions opened up by digital technologies, such as incorporating juxtaposition and hyperlinks, not to mention audio and visual effects.

Another way of exploring the meaning-making potential of multimodal texts would be to inquire into the multimodal texts that your students enjoy, such as computer games or video clips, and invite them to consider how they might produce such texts with the technology available to them.

How well does your current literacy teaching support students to construct such texts as part of their authentic meaning-making practices? How can you further develop your repertoire of literacy teaching pedagogies in order to facilitate these practices?

This vignette has focused on the way Shannon has enabled his students to use multimodal technologies to create their own 'choose-your-own adventure'. The following vignette, which tells the story of Shona's efforts to introduce into her school technologically mediated practices for monitoring students' learning, is somewhat different in character. Shona is still motivated, however, by a desire to empower students, enabling them to take ownership of their own learning. The vignette begins with an account of her presentation to staff about the initiatives she has taken to use technology to facilitate better assessment practices

Shona: using technology to monitor literacy learning

Shona begins her presentation to staff during their weekly staff meeting somewhat nervously, but then warms to the task. She has been asked by Greg, the principal, to explain the differentiated literacy teaching approach she has developed with her younger male colleague in their Grade 3/4 classroom. Shona wants to show the other teachers at the school how the children have been able to build on their capacity to set their own learning goals for reading and writing by using the technological platform that she has provided them. She shows how the children have gone about collecting evidence and recording it in online documents in order to demonstrate that they have achieved their goals. By doing this, she feels that they are taking further responsibility for their learning.

> Another example of how a teacher attempts to enable students to identify with the learning goals spelt out in mandated curriculum can be found in Chapter 8.

Shona: Hi Everyone, thanks for coming. I hope you don't find this too boring. I am sure you are all doing great things but Greg asked me to tell you about how we have changed our teaching of reading in the Grade 3/4. So the way we're teaching reading now is a lot more student-driven than the way that we've taught in the past when it was more teacher-controlled.

We've set up an Excel spreadsheet in Googledocs for reading. We call it a 'tracker'. In it we've recorded every English content descriptor for Levels 3 and 4 from our curriculum documents. We record them as learning goals for the students.

So I guess what we call a goal is actually a content descriptor adapted from the curriculum documents. Here's one example to show you what I mean.

Table 4.1: *The student tracker with the goals and activities from Level 3 reading and viewing*

Level 3 reading and viewing: Goal 1
My goal is to understand how different types of texts use different language choices, depending on their purpose.
Activity 1: Exploring text types.
Activity 2: Exploring narratives and informational texts.
Activity 3: Exploring tense in narratives and informational texts.

We pre-test the students. In the pre-test, every goal that we have in the tracker has a test question related to it.

If the student gets the question right, they write their name in bold for that goal. The first one they get wrong, they write their name in italics and that becomes their first goal.

The students click on a link under the goal that takes them to the relevant activities selected for that goal.

Table 4.2: *The tracker with the goals and activities for four students from Level 3 reading and viewing*

LEVEL 3 READING AND VIEWING: GOAL 1	LEVEL 3 READING AND VIEWING: GOAL 2
My goal is to understand how different types of texts use different language choices, depending on their purpose.	My goal is to understand that paragraphs are used to organise texts.
Robert Johnson	Robert Johnson
Yin Ma	Yin Ma
Mary Lee	Mary Lee
Gretal Smith	Gretal Smith
Activity 1: Complete the 'Explore text types' activity.	Activity 1: Complete the Ziptales.com activity about knowing when to start and end a paragraph.
Activity 2: Complete the 'Exploring narratives and informational texts' activity.	Activity 2: Complete the BBC website Skillswise topic about building up paragraphs.
Activity 3: Complete the 'Exploring tense in narratives and informational texts' activity.	

Students participate in the activity and once they complete it successfully they highlight their name in green under that goal. The key thing is that they track their own progress and record their achievements in the Excel spreadsheet in Googledocs.

We've tried to make it so that the students are totally independent when they're working on their goals but they're working on exactly what they need. So it's real point of need for them. I think that's the main difference that we've made this year: that the students themselves are able to use this means to identify where they're at and to take steps to improve.

The work of Shona and her colleagues shows how they are adapting their planning and teaching to address the requirements of the policy environment in which they are working and the possibilities opened up by contemporary technologies. This involves the use of both hardware, such the use of tablets, and software, such as online technologies like Googledocs and other online activities.

Their key aim is to personalise the learning of their students, giving them more autonomy with respect to identifying and then achieving their learning goals. Shona describes the relationship between teachers and students within this set-up, which she feels differs from the relationship that has traditionally existed:

> The way we, as teachers, have set it up we've got the curriculum goal, the students' names and underneath we have four to six links to different sites to goal-related activities that the students work through independently. So the first one could be a video explaining the concept that they're learning and they do two or three activities and then a test or an assessment task.
>
> So let's pretend I am a student. I have logged my results from my pre-testing, then I use my tablet to go to the Googledoc and I click on my goal tracker. My tracker comes up and I find my name in the class list. I can see my name in italics which tells me which goal I need to work on. Below my goal is a list of links to activities for that goal. I click on the link to my first activity.

Shona's teaching practice is anchored in the curriculum, as well as being focused on the individual needs of students. To map the students onto the curriculum, she uses pre-test data and student work samples. This information is used to map each student directly onto the learning tracker. The students then manage their own learning as they engage in their activities based on the goal in the learning tracker. The learning goal each student needs to work on is made clearly visible to them and the activities are matched to their individual needs. Shona has supported the students to work independently while she works with small groups or individual students to support their identified learning needs. An example of this is found in Figure 4.3. Robert, who from the pre-test results needs to work on paragraph structure, has been working on the BBC Skillswise activities about ordering sentences in a paragraph.

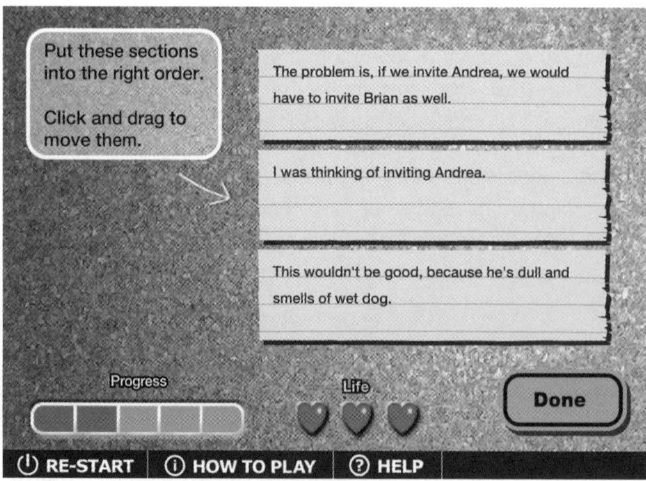

Fig. 4.3: *The BBC Skillswise website about paragraph structure presents this information as a simple game (reproduced with permission BBC Skillswise, <http://www.bbc.co.uk/skillswise>).*

Shona uses technology to give students access to learning activities in a way that develops her practice of differentiated scaffolded literacy. The individual work completed by the students is often modelled to the rest of the class in order for them to develop an understanding of the strategies and practices used by students to work independently. So the work in the classroom is a mix of individual, independent work around literacy learning activities and whole-class discussions about what and how students learn. As a result Shona is planning to meet the needs of all students in her class while using technology to provide a more individualised and targeted learning experience for her students.

The next section explores how the teacher makes judgments about the degree to which the students have completed their learning goals satisfactorily through completing the activities.

Students reflecting on their learning

A key dimension of this strategy is to enable students to take ownership of their own learning. To achieve this goal Shona uses Kidblog (<http://kidblog.org/home/>), an online blogging site that enables students to reflect on the learning they feel they have accomplished. This is what Shona said to staff in the weekly staff meeting where she gave a presentation about her initiative:

We also use Kidblog which is an online blogging site. Once students complete the activities and feel they have evidence to show they have achieved a goal they go to their page on Kidblog and they write in a reflection and post evidence to show they have achieved their goal.

After the students have posted their reflection and evidence on Kidblog they go back to the Googledoc tracker and highlight the next goal that they know they need to work on. It will be the next one that they got wrong in the pre-test. As a teacher at any stage, whether I'm at home or at school, I can look through the Kidblog to see how well the students reflected and what kind of evidence they posted.

Figure 4.4 shows how Shona can follow Robert's work using Kidblog. Shona has reiterated the learning on the blog and Robert has posted his response to what he learned from the activities relating to the construction of paragraphs.

But teaching and learning programs such as this one don't just work automatically when teachers set them up. Students have to be scaffolding into working in such autonomous and personalised ways. They have to learn how new processes work. Shona continues.

It's been a real process to teach the students that they must have evidence to show they have successfully completed an activity and that they must explain what they learned; so once I've looked at it I can see if they've got any misconceptions.

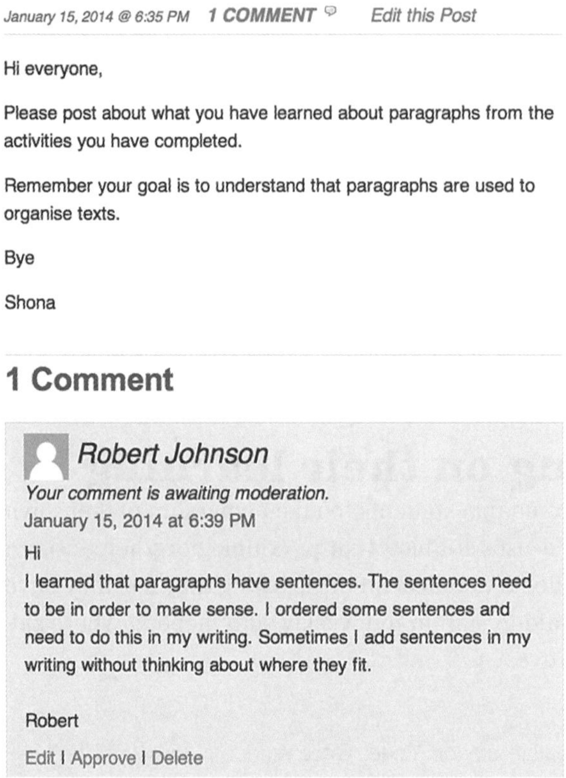

January 15, 2014 @ 6:35 PM   **1 COMMENT**   *Edit this Post*

Hi everyone,

Please post about what you have learned about paragraphs from the activities you have completed.

Remember your goal is to understand that paragraphs are used to organise texts.

Bye

Shona

1 Comment

Robert Johnson
Your comment is awaiting moderation.
January 15, 2014 at 6:39 PM
Hi
I learned that paragraphs have sentences. The sentences need to be in order to make sense. I ordered some sentences and need to do this in my writing. Sometimes I add sentences in my writing without thinking about where they fit.

Robert

Edit I Approve I Delete

Fig. 4.4: *A student's post on Kidblog reflecting on his learning about paragraphs*

Shona emphasises that even though students take greater responsibility for their learning, the role of the teacher is not reduced. It is, however, changed in noticeable ways. Teachers arguably have greater responsibility to monitor the learning of their students. Shona explains how she deals with possible misunderstandings and/ or learning problems.

> If I have any concerns about whether they have achieved a goal, I call them aside for a one-to-one conference or if there is a group of students who seem to have similar misunderstandings I bring them together for a small group conference. I always discuss their reflections with them and make sure they don't have any misunderstandings and that they are ready to move on to their next learning goal.

Shona insists that, while her methods might sound technologically driven, the teacher is still critical to the process of planning the testing procedures, identifying student needs, selecting activities to match each student goal, monitoring the student progress through the reflection, and providing small group and one-to-one teaching with students when required.

Reflection and discussion

What value do you see in the methods Shona uses in her teaching? Do you feel that they actually 'personalise' learning? Do you feel that students would be able to act with the degree of autonomy that she describes? How do you feel about the amount of work that the teacher is required to do?

How do you compare Shona's methods of assessment with the ones you currently use?

A community of learners

Sharing teachers' work as a form of teacher professional learning has become an accepted part of their school community in Shona's school. In staff meetings teachers regularly share the new ideas and innovative practices that they are trialling in their teaching. Shona points out that this kind of reflective practice can resonate beyond the confines of one classroom or year level and be taken up by teachers working at other year levels:

> Recently we had some of the Grade 1/2 teachers come and talk to us and ask how they could use this way of teaching, and we've been able to just instantaneously share our documents such as the goal tracker on Google Drive with those teachers so that then they can try using the goals with the students.

Setting up the goal tracker, putting in all the goals and selecting and making links to purposeful activities proved to be a massive task for the teachers.

> It was a really big task setting up the learning tracker in the beginning. We had to spend quite some time in dialogue so that we have a shared understanding about what each goal or curriculum descriptor means, so that we could put it into the student tracker. We've also spent a lot of time selecting appropriate activities for the students to engage in related to each learning goal. But now we have it set up and the children understand how to work this way it is fantastic because it is real differentiated learning.

How should we view the relationship between literacy and technology?

Let's now try to tease out some of the implications of Shona's professional practice in response to this big question.

Teachers have always been looking for technological aids to make their work easier. Depending on your age, you might have experience with teaching with different types of technology, such as tablets, interactive whiteboards, computers, laptops, videos, televisions, data projectors and DVD players. All these things have had a big impact on classroom life at various times. Video cassette recorders and overhead projectors were once prized artefacts purchased through the efforts of many parents' hard work at fetes and other fundraising activities. There was a time when parents put a lot of effort into collecting supermarket dockets in order to purchase a Mac computer for their school as part of a promotion campaign by a major supermarket chain. And a decade or so earlier, a teacher who had a projector's licence was once considered to be at the forefront of technological innovation. A lot has come and gone, as various technologies have become outmoded. If the past is anything to go by, your current use of technology as a teacher will probably be seen as obsolete by many of your peers in years to come.

But it is easy to make a fetish of technology, as though we're achieving something educationally valuable by keeping up with the latest. It is the larger purposes that are being served by the technology that are important, not the technology itself. If we look at Shona's work as a teacher, she is approaching technology as a medium through which to support her negotiation of the curriculum and learning goals with her students. Ursula Franklin suggests 'new means of technological linkage need to be explored, which would facilitate cooperation without centralization or oppression by scale' (1992, p. 128). Shona is also using technology to engage in professional conversations with her peers around the networked resources they can source to support their teaching practice. She is committed to catering for the range of abilities in her classroom and to putting her students in a position where they can take responsibility for their own learning. These are practices that she will continue to develop throughout her professional life as a teacher, drawing on whatever technologies are available.

Reflection and discussion

What approaches to technology do you bring to your teaching? How do you feel your professional practice has been enhanced by new technologies? Are you always comfortable with the way technologies are used in educational settings? Do you always feel that they are serving valuable educational purposes?

Do you see value in Shona's approach to supporting an individualised or targeted learning experience for students?

To what extent can students have an individualised learning experience when the goal they are following is pre-determined by a centralised national curriculum?

The other important practice that Shona has developed using technology is self-directed student learning, using social networking sites such as Kidblog and

Googledocs. While it would be possible to encourage students to think of themselves as belonging to a learning community without these social networking sites, Shona feels that her work has become more effective by her use of this technology. She believes that the new literacies embedded in these sites are more participatory, collaborative, and distributed in nature than conventional literacies.

> Colin Lankshear and Michele Knobel (2011) argue that social practices around the use of technology are increasingly a part of every teachers' business.

She is not, in short, simply promoting technology for technology's sake, but emphasising the value of technology for achieving these larger goals. Her focus is on the relationships in which the use of technology is embedded. She does not imagine that a classroom of the kind she aspires to create can simply come about by applying new technologies. She sees value in Kidblog for providing a record of students' work that can be accessed by the teacher to make comments and also for the parents and caregivers to see the child's progress. Kidblog is a vehicle for bringing teachers, parents and caregivers together around the interests of the child.

> There are other social networking sites that support these types of activity, such as Edmodo, Ning, edublogs and Wikispaces.

Reflection and discussion

Any innovative practice that you adopt has a ripple effect that you might not be able to predict. Should Shona, for example, allow the parents or caregivers of her students to have access to the blogs and comments on what they have achieved? Should she be more active in involving parents and caregivers in the negotiations about learning goals that she is attempting to facilitate with her students? Would this be a good idea?

The potential use of social media in your teaching can raise concerns among parents. Some parents, for example, might see this as being at odds with a focus on more traditional literacy practices, such as those associated with standardised testing. Then there are the concerns that parents have about the content of such social media, not to mention the phenomenon of cyber bullying. What rationale would you be able to give to parents who challenge you about this emphasis on social media?

Conclusion

The wider community has embraced multimodal texts in a variety of forms. Newspapers, books and other texts are now available in digital form, and so it follows that school-based literacy learning should reflect this cultural shift. Print-based texts ('conventional texts' as they are called in the Australian Curriculum) still play an integral role in teaching reading and writing but classroom literacy learning needs to thoughtfully integrate a variety of texts to support students in their efforts to engage in authentic meaning-making activities. Shannon has shown you one possible way in which to draw on and extend students' use of multimodal texts for literacy learning. You have no doubt experienced other ways in which to exploit such resources that go beyond simply an emphasis on reading, writing, speaking and listening. Shannon's story highlights how the multimodal nature of such texts challenges us to rethink what we mean when we refer to these language modes. It might be more meaningful to use words like 'viewing' or 'creating' or 'composing' when thinking about the production and reception of such texts.

Taken together, the stories of Shannon and Shona indicate the range of uses to which new technologies might be put in educational settings. You might like to think about whether those uses are always compatible. Shannon, for example has a belief in the imaginative potential of his students to use new technologies in innovative ways that conceivably exceed what he had in mind when he designed his unit of work on choose-your-own adventures. Often when teachers enable their students to use new technologies in their classrooms, they are surprised by the creativity their students reveal. Shona on the other hand, is promoting the use of technologies to monitor students' achievement of mandated learning outcomes – a goal which, on the face of it, seems more conventional in nature, despite the fact that she is using the most up-to-date technology to achieve it, as well as emphasising student autonomy by enabling them to make the learning outcomes their own.

Anne Turvey, John Yandell and Leila Ali (2012) show how learning outcomes can become a straitjacket, limiting students' sense of their potential. See Brenton Doecke and Douglan McClenaghan (2009) and Wayne Sawyer (2005) for similar arguments.

It is up to you to judge the worthiness of the goals to which new technologies are applied. What we want to say, finally, is that there is no denying, as Christine Edwards-Groves puts it, the way technology has decisively changed the nature of 'the interactions between people in their interpersonal, virtual, digital and textual spaces' (Edwards-Groves 2012, p. 110). As committed language and literacy teachers we should obviously be committed to exploring this new communication landscape.

References

Beavis, C, O'Mara, J & McNiece, L 2013, 'Literacy learning and computer games: a curriculum challenge for our times' in C Beavis, J O'Mara & L Niece (eds), *Digital Games: Literacy in Action*, Wakefield Press, South Australia, pp. 3–11.

Buckingham, D 2008, 'Defining digital literacies' in C Lankshear & M Knobel (eds), *Digital Literacies*, Peter Lang, Oxford.

Burn, A 2000, 'Repackaging the Slasher Movie: digital unwriting of film in the classroom', *English in Australia*, vol. 127–128 May, pp. 24–34.

Crockett, L, Jukes, I & Churches, A 2011, *Literacy is Not Enough*, Corwin, California.

Doecke, B & McClenaghan, D 2009, 'The content of students' writing' in R Beard, D Myhill & J Riley (eds), *The SAGE Handbook of Writing Development*, 1st edn, Sage, Los Angeles and London, pp. 374–86.

Dyson, AH 2009, 'Writing in childhood worlds' in R Beard, D Myhill & J Riley (eds), *The SAGE Handbook of Writing Development*, 1st edn, Sage, Los Angeles and London, pp. 232–45.

Edwards-Groves, C 2012, 'Interactive creative technologies: changing learning practices and pedagogies in the writing classroom', *Australian Journal of Language and Literacy*, vol. 35, p. 99.

Franklin, UM 1992, *The Real World of Technology*, Anansi, Concord, Ontario.

Gee, JP 2003, *What Video Games Have to Teach Us About Learning and Literacy*, Palgrave Macmillan, New York.

Gee, JP 2007, *Good Video Games + Good Learning: Collected Essays on Video Games, Learning, and Literacy*, Peter Lang, New York.

Lankshear, C, Green, B & Snyder, I 2000, *Teachers and Technoliteracy: Managing Literacy, Technology and Learning in Schools*, Allen & Unwin, St Leonards NSW.

Lankshear, C & Knobel, M 2003, *New Literacies: Changing Knowledge and Classroom Learning*, Open University Press, Buckingham.

Lankshear, C & Knobel, M 2011, *New Literacies: Everyday Practices and Classroom Learning*, 3rd edn, Open University Press, Maidenhead.

Marsh, J 2009, 'Writing and popular culture' in R Beard, D Myhill, RJ & M Nystrand (eds), *The Sage Handbook of Writing Development*, SAGE, London, pp. 313–24.

Sawyer, W 2005, 'Writing = learning' in B Doecke & G Parr (eds), '*AATE interface series'*,Wakefield Press in association with the Australian Association for the Teaching of English, Kent Town, South Australia, pp. 129–45.

Sefton-Green, J 2000, 'Beyond school: futures for English and media education', *English in Australia*, vol. 127–8, May, pp. 14–23.

Simpson, A & Walsh, M 2013, 'Teaching reading in a digital age: towards an understanding of pedagogic practice' in A Goodwyn, L Reid & C Durrant (eds), *International Perspectives on Teaching English in a Globalised World*, Routledge, London.

Turvey, A, Yandell, J & Ali, L 2012, 'English as a site of cultural negotiation and contestation', *English Teaching: Practice & Critique*, vol. 11, no. 3, pp. 26–44.

Supporting intercultural engagement in literacy education

Anne Cloonan, Joanne O'Mara
and Sarah Ohi

Education is the most powerful weapon which you can use to change the world.

Nelson Mandela

Australia has, for several decades, espoused multiculturalism, although this rhetoric has now been shaken by the controversies that surround refugees. Even so it remains the case that educational policy and practice in Australia have variously acknowledged the diverse cultures and languages of students in schools.

Recently there has been a pronounced shift away from deficit constructions of students from language backgrounds other than English to teachers recognising and drawing on the rich cultural and linguistic resources, often called 'funds of knowledge', attributed to the work of Luis Moll, Cathy Amanti, Deborah Neff and Norma Gonzalez (Moll & Amanti et al. 1992). As a literacy educator, you will typically find yourself in classrooms that reflect a diversity of cultures and languages. Within such settings, issues associated with multiculturalism and the flow of people around the world are not simply topics for debate, but matters that you and your students negotiate each day. This is often a richly rewarding experience, but it can involve challenges that cause you to interrogate your own values and beliefs, in much the same way that teachers like Rachel and Bella (see Chapter 2) were prompted to think about the way their lives have shaped their work as literacy educators.

In this chapter we introduce you to three teachers in very different school contexts, who share an agenda for incorporating intercultural understanding into their literacy teaching. The teachers' school settings are quite different and so their starting points and actions also differ.

This chapter arises out of a research project in which we had conversations with a range of teachers who were investigating the importance of intercultural understanding in Australian schools. In the Australian Curriculum, the general capability of intercultural understanding is described as follows:

Students develop intercultural understanding as they learn to value their own cultures, languages and beliefs, and those of others. They come to understand how personal, group and national identities are shaped, and the variable and changing nature of culture. The capability involves students in learning about and engaging with diverse cultures in ways that recognise commonalities and differences, create connections with others and cultivate mutual respect.

Gunilla Holm and Harriet Zilliacus (2009) suggest intercultural understanding has an emphasis on 'interaction and dialogue's between individuals from culturally and linguistically diverse cultures. Learning about other cultures is not seen as sufficient; rather intercultural understanding is nurtured through experience, communication and engagement across cultures (Liddicoat et al. 2003).

Claudia is a Year 3/4 teacher in her second year of teaching at an inner-city school with students from diverse backgrounds. Angelina is a graduate Year 5 teacher at an independent school with a diverse student cohort in an affluent suburb of a large city. Patrick is a Grade 6 teacher at a middle-class suburban school with a narrow mix of students from a few distinct groups. Each of them has engaged in significant professional learning in their efforts to develop practices that are more sensitive to cultural diversity. This has had both an intensely personal character for them, sending them back to think about their own values and beliefs, as well as an inter-personal character, in that it is learning that they have shared with others at their schools in an effort to bring about whole school change.

We have organised this chapter around their stories, which we have written on the basis of conversations with each of them. The chapter connects intercultural understanding with teaching and learning in literacy classrooms.

Reflection and discussion

As you read the narratives you might like to think about the examples they provide of teachers working with linguistic and cultural diversity and reflect on your own context and experiences. Are the decisions and actions they take ones that you would take if you were in their situations? How feasible would it be to follow their examples in other school settings?

Claudia moves beyond 'Harmony Day' using cultural resources and texts

After spending time travelling through Asia and Europe, Claudia began working at a co-educational government school that has a population of about 400 students with 40 per cent coming from language backgrounds other than English. Two per cent of students are Indigenous and there are many students whose grandparents migrated from Greece and Italy after the Second World War. Saudi and Indian full-fee-paying students are represented, as are students from Chilean, Ethiopian, Eritrean, Somalian, Sudanese and Vietnamese backgrounds. The staff includes a Somalian multicultural teacher aide who speaks multiple African languages and acts as a bridge to the community. As Claudia describes it:

> We've got everyone here: some families living in the flats are refugees, or children of refugees, mostly from Africa; others are here from overseas to work in high flying corporate jobs; others are inner-city gentry, Queen's Counsels and so on.

Now in her second year of teaching, Claudia teaches a Year 3/4 class. She knew from her previous experience that incidents sometimes occurred, particularly in the playground, which permeated her students' intercultural relationships. The Year 3/4 boys play soccer with great passion, both in and out of school. Sometimes during their play, students have engaged in behaviour that has had racist overtones. Or at least this is what some of them have reported, because the details of the incidents have been hard to confirm, beyond someone relating that 'he looked at me bad'. Similarly, boys and girls occasionally seek teacher intervention when others have made comments about their diet, or their activities during play time, or their clothing; all things that reflect cultural and religious differences. When asked how she responded to such incidents, Claudia responded, 'I reinforce the school values that it's not respectful to comment on others' behaviours, appearance and beliefs … or to touch someone else or their belongings'.

In addition to teaching her Year 3/4 class, Claudia has joined a newly formed curriculum team, which has representatives from each teaching team, including the specialist teachers. Her recent extensive travel has heightened her awareness of the challenges and rewards in communicating across cultures. Growing up in Australia as the child of immigrant non-English-speaking parents, she is aware of how the children of immigrants often need to negotiate a pathway between the dominant culture and their own beliefs and values. As part of the intercultural understanding team she has the responsibility for students to make connections between their own worlds and the world of others and to negotiate difference in a respectful way across the whole school. Claudia had hoped that by joining this team, she would be able to develop her confidence in teaching in a more culturally sensitive way. At their first meeting the school coordinator led a discussion differentiating between intercultural understanding and multicultural education.

A key point of discussion at the initial meeting of this team was the difference between 'multiculturalism', a word that everyone knew, and 'interculturalism'.

> For further reading about interculturalism see Greg Noble and Scott Poynting's (2000) work 'Multicultural education and intercultural understanding: ethnicity, culture and schooling'.

An intercultural perspective puts emphasis on interaction and dialogue between individuals from culturally and linguistically diverse cultures, rather than simply tolerance of diversity (UNESCO 2006). It is not enough just to learn about other cultures (as in multiculturalism), but attention should be given to nurturing cultural sensitivity and understanding through engaging with each other and negotiating the similarities and differences between us. This resonated with Claudia, both at a personal level and with respect to the kind of social relationships that she wanted to encourage in her classroom.

> Knowing what people I associate with and my family say – it's a problem. And my family comes from overseas as well, but still see other cultures … well they don't understand them because they don't have the same beliefs or cultural values and they don't talk to people from other cultures. You assume these kids have a lot more understanding because they are growing up together and its just part of who they know, who their classmates are. But I wonder how deep the understandings are … it can be scary to talk about as you don't know where the discussion is going to go.

The school traditionally celebrates Harmony Day in March each year, usually through an across the school theme. The curriculum team decided to make Harmony Day one of its first responsibilities. The previous year the school had invited the school community in to work with teachers to conduct a series of one-off workshops highlighting aspects of culture. Claudia reflected that the focus was on difference between students and their families (for example wearing different clothing, eating different food) and overlooked the opportunity to explore similarities. In Claudia's words:

> That was a real 'ah-ha' moment for me. Unless we are careful, this approach can actually reinforce the dominant group as the norm and other students as different and perhaps exotic, for example 'Aussies' wearing footy jumpers as opposed to our African students in colourful national costumes. We have to be careful not to promote stereotypes or we can be giving false impressions and failing to get to real engagement. It has to be about communication.

Rather than a 'one-off' experience, the committee decided that they wanted the work that students engaged in around Harmony Day to be ongoing, and a way for the children in each class to get to know one another at this early stage in the year. They settled on the theme of 'Many people, one Australia' and each year level undertook an integrated literacy/art project that was themed around the students' unique identities. It was a broad approach allowing teachers of each year level to interpret and implement it in their own way. Claudia actively supported this initiative.

> We really need to start thinking of ways that intercultural understanding can be embedded into all that we do rather than confined to a special day. At the moment we are all about 'the big event' – the five Fs of 'food, festivals, flags, folktales and fashion'. Literacy seems a natural place to start embedding intercultural understanding because we're all teachers of literacy, and literacy permeates all learning.

It might be valuable to pause here to reflect on what Claudia has told us about her school.

Reflection and discussion

Think about Claudia's 'ah-ha' moment. What are your thoughts about her ideas about 'difference'? What approaches have you observed in schools towards promoting cultural sensitivity and respect for difference? How would you describe the difference, if any, between multiculturalism and interculturalism? What role do you think you should play as a literacy educator in school change directed towards enhancing intercultural understanding?

Claudia and her Year 3/4 colleagues actively looked for opportunities to develop intercultural understanding in their current curriculum offerings. In Art lessons, their students had been working with an artist-in-residence developing memory boxes. These involve students selecting images and artefacts that represent aspects of their cultural memories and placing them within a box or tin to present a narrative. Rather than develop a separate activity they decided to enrich and expand the development of memory boxes to include oral and written reflections on memories through the use of memory journals and filmed oral presentations on their tablet devices.

To begin the memory journal students wrote and drew about themselves, responding to the prompt, 'Who am I?'. Three of the students' responses are reproduced below.

Table 5.1: *Student responses to the prompt 'Who am I?'*

EXTRACT FROM IDA'S MEMORY JOURNAL	EXTRACT FROM YIN'S MEMORY JOURNAL	EXTRACT FROM OMAR'S MEMORY JOURNAL
My Nonna and Nonno came from Italy. My dad was born in Australia. My grandpa, great grandpa and grandma came from England. My mum is Aboriginal and I am Aboriginal and I have Aboriginal grandparents and Aboriginal cousins. I go to Mt Martha with my Italian cousins. On the holidays I am going to Echuca with my Aboriginal cousins. I go to meetings with my Aboriginal cousins. At these meetings we talk about the history of Aboriginals in Australia.	I am here from Vietnam because my father is working for Vietnam Airlines. I love Carlton [Football Club] and sausages and mash. When I lived in Japan I did origami and Sudoku. In Vietnam we have a dragon festival.	My mum is Egyptian. My dad is Lebanese. I am all of these and Aussie too.

Such texts prompted Claudia to think about students' unique backgrounds and experiences in their out-of-school lives and the depth of knowledge that students bring to their curriculum experiences. She became aware that many of her students had multiple backgrounds that were far more complex than she had assumed.

The texts were really powerful. I realised the students had disclosed a lot about themselves in these narratives: things about their families, their lives. There were also things students spoke to me about that didn't make it into the written texts because of their sensitivity, like students who had family living overseas – deep, close, personal things. In an ongoing way I wanted to honour their work through sharing it but I felt a responsibility to create a safe environment to do this, one that would support them to continue to disclose things about themselves. Respect and boundaries are important.

Claudia remembered her own experience of speaking a version of English at home that was very different from the English she was taught at school. She remembered learning to adjust her language for classroom learning. Sometimes she would adjust not only her speech, but the way she presented her thoughts and experiences in order to make them more like those she associated with the 'dominant culture'.

See Michael Clyne (2005) and Alex Kostogriz (2005) for discussion about the ways in which teaching and learning are mediated by socio-cultural understandings.

She was now determined that in her own teaching practice she would provide her students with opportunities to engage in genuine exchanges about their cultures and experiences. This was what she was trying to do with the memory boxes.

Claudia and her colleagues worked to address both the creation of an environment for respectful intercultural engagement and for the honouring of student work. They asked students to adopt and extend on the sentence stem: In our class we think that everyone should have the right to...Following discussion, students wrote their suggested 'right' in 'speech bubbles', and photographs were taken of each individual. A display of the sentence stem and student responses in speech bubbles with photographs of students was prepared and hung in a prominent position visible to students and classroom visitors. Students' examples of completion of the sentence stem included:

In our class we think that everyone should have the right to

...be treated fairly

...laugh, to love and to be free

...stand up for yourself

...have a family and friends

...have a culture

...be healthy and safe.

Claudia then read the text *We Are All Born Free: The Universal Declaration of Human Rights in Pictures* (Amnesty International 2008). The students compared their responses to the rights agreed on by the United Nations after the Second World War. Following the comparison, additional rights were suggested by students and added to the display. This display then served as a constant reference point for Claudia and her class, framing conversations and providing a point of appeal when rights were seen to be violated.

Claudia thought about the potential of the students' texts to stimulate intercultural understanding to the wider school community. Many of students' completed texts remained in their portfolios, seen by an audience limited to herself, and perhaps a few other students and parents. To honour their work, and to encourage student pride in the development of authentic texts that would promote intercultural engagement, Claudia and her colleagues decided to display the memory boxes, journals and oral narratives as an art exhibition and to invite the school community to an evening launch of the display. Claudia invited her students to write and make audiovisual representations of their oral narratives on their tablet devices. They rehearsed this work with a peer for review, gaining and giving critical feedback. This prepared them for discussing their texts with the broader community audience.

The launch of the exhibit was a real event, with students' discussing their texts with their peers, teachers and parents. The Art room was transformed into a gallery with presentations on tablet devices displayed with each student's memory box and journal.

Reflection and discussion

What experiences have you had in engaging with other languages and cultures – in and out of schools? What initiatives have you experienced that draw on students' languages and cultures as resources for learning? What might you do as a literacy educator to provide opportunities for creation and critique of texts that might enhance a sense of the value of diversity and difference? What challenges do you envisage to implementing an intercultural policy of the kind that Claudia's school implemented?

While Claudia draws on family background, personal experiences of travel and school-based experiences to inform her work around literacy education and intercultural understanding, Patrick brings very different experiences to his teaching and understanding of interculturalism.

Patrick develops intercultural understanding and skills

Patrick is a Year 6 teacher at a middle-class suburban school. The school has a mixed population, with large groups of recently migrated Asian students from Taiwan and Hong Kong and large groups of Caucasian students whose ancestry is from post-Second World War Europe and earlier English and Irish migrations. There are small numbers of students from other backgrounds.

Patrick has worked at the school for five years and is an enthusiastic participant in the school's intercultural understanding focus. Before working at the school, he had not really grappled with issues of race or difference in his life and had little knowledge of other countries, beyond the basic geography he had learned in school.

> When I first came to the school, I didn't really even know anyone who wasn't white or, you know, from a different background. I didn't have any friends who weren't white. I know that sounds bad, but really it was just that I hadn't met anyone. Everyone was really, well, basically the same as me when I grew up, and even at uni, in my teaching course … I think most of the people were white…

Although he grew up in a large city, Patrick lived mainly in a largely English-speaking, white, middle-class suburb. He had never been out of Australia, and did not think about issues such as how people from diverse nationalities and cultural backgrounds fit into Australian society and how Australia was positioned in the world. When he first came to the school, he did not really think that the school would need to do any kind of work on race or intercultural understanding, as he did not think that there were any problems of this kind in his city. He had a kind of colour blindness; for him such tensions simply did not exist. As a young person, Australian English was so normalised to him that he did not even consider that he had an 'accent'. He acknowledges that if someone had asked him previously what intercultural understanding in primary schools meant, he would have said that it was the festivities like Multicultural Day and 'raising money for other countries when they faced natural disasters'. Now he realises that intercultural understanding is much more than that, and he has since developed strong intercultural understanding through the experiences and opportunities given to him at the school.

When Patrick joined the school teaching team he did not realise that he was also joining them on a journey of intercultural understanding. But the work that Patrick has subsequently done on the school's intercultural understanding focus has proved to be the area of professional learning where he feels the most satisfaction and growth. The staff and leadership team at the school are very enthusiastic and committed to the development of intercultural understanding. When Patrick started at the school, it was already embarking on a program of studies of Asia and had Mandarin as its study of languages other than English. The principal was committed to furthering the studies of Asia, in line with the changing population at the school. She saw this as central to both enabling the school to reach its population, and embracing the changing nature of Australia and Australia's physical location and place in the world. The school curriculum is now embedded with studies of other cultures. It has a strong Mandarin language program, a sister school in mainland China, studies of other cultures through the texts studied in language and literacy, the artworks produced in Art classes. The teaching team at the school has invested considerable energy in embedding both the values and content of intercultural understanding into the school curriculum.

After five years of working at the school during this time of change, Patrick is now at a point where he feels very confident with intercultural understanding.

> I feel really confident with the intercultural understanding part of the curriculum. It is pretty amazing really, especially seeing that I had no experience in this area. We have such a great team here at the school though, and every one has really supported me to get on board with the program. I think the trip to China was really important. I made some great friendships with teachers from the other schools, and we stay in contact. It is great. We come from the other side of the world, but at the end of the day, we're teachers, and have similar issues and problems. It's just all about the kids really.

Patrick recognises his personal growth through his encounter with this aspect of the curriculum. He has been on a school trip to the sister school in China, has had professional conversations with teachers at the sister school and has worked on programs with them. This travel and getting to know teachers from another culture has made him feel like he belongs to an international network of teachers, all of whom are working in their students' best interests. He is enthusiastic about this work, and keen to really make a difference to the way that students in his school work together. He finds that the students generally are very inclusive and accepting of each other, but every now and then he faces a race-based issue, and he always tries to successfully resolve it. He is used to discussing different cultural issues with his students, and he feels confident when working with students from different cultures. Patrick recognises now how race and culture play out for many of his students. They encounter small sneers of racism everyday as a regular part of their lives.

Patrick has noticed that some of the issues at the school are around using language to exclude others. This can be tricky to deal with because the school does not want to make a rule where students may never use their mother tongue or home language. Patrick describes how a group of girls came to see him because they felt that they were being excluded by other girls because they spoke Mandarin. When he delved into the issue, he found that the bilingual girls always spoke Mandarin on the playground and that non-Mandarin-speaking girls felt as though they were being excluded from their play. It got to a point where the non-Mandarin-speaking girls were retaliating by not including anyone who spoke Mandarin in their games. Patrick organised an open forum with the girls and they all talked through the issues about how the use of language can be a way of excluding others. The girls decided that it was up to all of them to work together on this, that it was very important for everyone to use their home language to communicate with their friends, but that everyone needed to be aware of how language had the potential to include some and exclude others. Patrick felt that this was quite a tricky issue to deal with, but through handling this incident successfully, he was more determined than ever to develop a more structured and critical approach to teaching multicultural values in his literacy classroom.

Patrick has experienced a shift from thinking about intercultural understanding as being the content of the curriculum to thinking about it as signifying a deeper set of inclusive values and empathy for others. This has also occurred as he has become more aware of his own views, of his own position as it has shifted in relation to intercultural issues. While he would never have thought of himself as being 'racist', with his growth in professional knowledge, he realises that he once held stereotypical beliefs and attitudes that were racist and narrowly monocultural in nature.

It is weird really. When I first came here, I would have said that there is no racism in Australia, but really I just meant there was no racism on my street. Now I can see it everywhere, and I am kind of super vigilant. I almost over-react, like someone who has given up smoking does when other people smoke. You know, and they can't stand the smell of smoke at all. I just want to solve every situation that has even a sniff of racism.

Patrick examines his own actions and thoughts, as well as trying to develop intercultural understanding where he can. He is always looking for examples from the media, because issues presented in the media are at a remove from schoolyard incidents as children experience them, when a lot of heated emotion comes into play. From not even thinking about race as an issue, Patrick now sees racism around him everywhere. He sometimes witnesses racism in small everyday moments that he would not have thought remarkable previously, like noticing a shopkeeper raising his or her voice to a customer who does not speak fluent English. Now he notes it and tries to act to help the situation.

Reflection and discussion

What place should mother tongue or home language have in school? Do you feel that Patrick handled the situation of the Mandarin-speaking girls appropriately?

How confident are you in dealing with issues like this? How can racism be tackled in schools? What might you do as a teacher of language and literacy?

You have seen that Patrick became quite experienced in identifying and addressing issues in relation to cultural difference and building understanding within the school context. We will now turn to Angelina, and her experience of introducing a literature focus and laying emphasis upon the value of personal stories to sensitise people to cultural difference and the need for cross-cultural dialogue. This was once again in line with a whole school commitment to promoting intercultural understanding. As you read the following narrative, you might like to consider the value of using 'stories' to encourage the building of intercultural understanding in her classroom.

Angelina taps into students' 'funds of knowledge'

Angelina was born in Australia, as were her parents, but her mother's family originally migrated from Macedonia. English is the only language in which Angelina is fluent and she considers herself to have been brought up in what she calls 'the Australian way of life', with lots of sport, social gatherings and a love of the beach and bush. Angelina is a graduate teacher whose first appointment is as a classroom teacher for children in Year 5. She works in a large school of nearly 600 students in an affluent south-eastern suburb. The students come from a diverse range of cultural backgrounds from more than twenty different countries, but the most common backgrounds are Indian, Sri Lankan and Sudanese. The school community is quite transient, as people tend to rent in this well-established suburb for a while, prior to purchasing a home in one of the surrounding new housing developments.

Angelina's school decided that intercultural understanding needed to permeate all areas of the curriculum. Staff spent time discussing the meaning of 'culture' and then reflecting upon their own cultural identities. This was because they believed that you firstly need to understand your own cultural identity before you can truly understand the identities of others and engage in meaningful intercultural exchanges.

Angelina commented that a key realisation for her was the fact that everyone has a distinct cultural background, regardless of whether they have lived in Australia for a long time or they've just arrived:

> We all came from somewhere and its important to recognise and value that and then try to understand one another's backgrounds and how we can work together from there. I never thought I was very Macedonian, but reflecting upon the values that I uphold and understanding how they differ to the views of others has led me to question this. My gran would be thrilled.

The school has a growing number of students who were born overseas and migrated to Australia with their families. Some have arrived as refugees and many others have come to Australia for their parents to engage in further study and upgrade their qualifications. Prior to working in this school Angelina assumed that low socio-economic status in families was directly associated with low levels of parental education, but a recent experience changed her views on this. While preparing for a class excursion to visit Scienceworks, Angelina approached a family who had not yet returned the permission slip and payment for the excursion and found out that the family couldn't afford it. After engaging in discussion with the child's mother, Angelina learned that she was highly proficient in English and that she was a medical doctor from Sri Lanka, here to upgrade her qualifications to an international standard. Her husband was working in a factory and studying a Masters degree in engineering part time. Angelina shared this story with staff and together they discussed the importance of genuinely getting to know their students and their families at a deeper level in order to better understand their needs and open up avenues for communication. For Angelina, this story showed that teachers need to be constantly sensitive to their own preconceptions and embrace opportunities to think and see differently.

Angelina belongs to a teaching team comprised of four Year 5/6 teachers, all of whom have many more years teaching experience than her. The team decided to use literature as a focus to develop students' literacy and intercultural understanding. They felt that doing so would provide a seamless introduction to discussing valuable issues that could firstly be explored in the meaningful context of shared stories and then branch out into talk about the children's own lived experiences.

Angelina's school committed to creating classroom blogs. Each teacher shared interesting teaching activities, reported about events and celebrated students' achievements in their online space for the entire school community to access. Angelina's classroom blog was well designed, and other staff approached her for assistance. In addition, her team leader asked her to develop an intercultural understanding literacy blog in which the team and later the entire school staff could share their teaching ideas and experiences and the rich array of literature that they had used and found valuable. She compiled a list of the teams' resources and had staff add critical reflections about the activities. Angelina worked collaboratively with the school librarian who alerted her to related websites, newly released titles and books purchased. Here is an entry that a Year 4 teacher at Angelina's school contributed to her Intercultural Understanding blog about his plan to use a book called *The Little Refugee* (Do & Do 2011) with his class.

A blog entry by Andrew T.

Grade 4 teacher

The Little Refugee *is an award winning picture storybook written by Anh and Suzanne Do. It's an inspiring story describing Anh's story of arrival in Australia. Fleeing a life of poverty in war-torn Vietnam, his family and friends boarded a fishing vessel and set sail. The many challenges that they faced on their treacherous journey are introduced, including hunger, thirst, fear and pirates. The story then describes the challenge of settling into a new way of life in a new country. This story is characterised by a sense of hope and is a testament to the power of love and resilience.*

If you go to this website you'll find a pdf with teaching suggestions

<http://www.allenandunwin.com/default.aspx?page=94&book=9781742378329>

I've selected some activities from here and I'll let you know how they go in next week's update.

As well as the dissemination of information about resources, the Intercultural Understanding blog was also used to share thoughts about how the children were responding to the curriculum. Below is a blog entry written by Angelina for other staff to read about a recent classroom episode and how a focus on literacy and intercultural understanding was embedded into classroom activities.

Teaching suggestions for *The Little Refugee*
<http://www. allenandunwin. com/default.asp x&page=94&book =9781742378329.pdf>

Building intercultural understanding: Year 5P's ongoing journey

By Angelina P, 20th June

Last week one of the children reported on a news item in which someone of an Indian background in Sydney had been robbed by a group of teenagers from the Pacific Islands. They described a version of the incident in detail and the children were clearly intrigued, 'oohing' and 'aahing' in response as the story was told. Observing the children's responses, I decided that the issue was worthy of discussion as I wanted to ensure that the children were not left feeling distraught about what they had heard. I also wanted them to think about the text being discussed. We searched the internet and found a brief article about the incident and discussed the following points:

- *Whose perspective was being portrayed and for what purpose? (authorship, audience/readership)*
- *What difference would it make if the reporter had not provided information about the people's cultural backgrounds?*
- *What could have been the motivation behind the incident?*
- *What kind of solutions could be considered?*
- *How would changing the headline title of the article change the impact of the story?*

I was very proud to find that, on the whole, the students engaged in responsible discussion about the story. They started to realise the importance of critically analysing a text considering its source, purpose and the effect of the words used.

But following this discussion I noticed that Afa, a Samoan student, became unusually quiet and withdrawn, and I was concerned that this may have been because Pacific Islanders were portrayed in a negative manner. I tried to speak with him about his feelings but he reassured me that he was fine. There are only a few Pacific Islander children at our school and Afa, in my class, is one of them. As a child, I remember that I never met anyone else at school who was Australian and part Macedonian and so I would state that I was Australian, a full Australian. I had felt disconnected from Macedonian culture and wanted to build a sense of belonging among my peers. It was easier to be Australian, as the other children had no idea where Macedonia was. I decided to make a conscious attempt to introduce the class to an opportunity to learn more about Pacific Island cultures through literature. I wanted Afa to have the opportunity that I missed out on: the opportunity to feel that your cultural background is truly valued.

Over the past month my class has spent Tuesday afternoons reading short traditional stories that originate from a range of cultures. We began with stories from Australia and have also worked on stories from China and India. Following the reading, we engaged in rich discussion about the meaning of the story and the values and beliefs that are advocated. I also provided time for the children to reflect upon their own beliefs and they had to create a response of some sort i.e. a written piece, a visual response (digital poster, slideshow), a podcast. This week I selected a Samoan story called 'Sina and the Eel' (Goodchild & Potter 2005). I was hoping that focusing on this story might help Afa bounce back and be his happy self again. You can read the two following diary entries (one by Ryan and one by Afa) and decide for yourself if you think I achieved this.

Two diary entries from Year 5P 'Sina and the eel: a Samoan story'

1   Our class read this book and learned about the Samoan legend of how coconut trees came about. After we talked and answered questions about it we did an art activity, which was about the eel. We had to create symmetrical patterns and match them to make a design. My friend Afa comes from Samoa and he did these really nice tribal patterns and it looked excellent! By Ryan

2 I was so surprised that we read a Samoan story in my classroom. That's never happened before! When our teacher started reading I was excited and nervous at the same time because I wasn't sure what the other kids would think.

Everyone ended up being really interested. They liked how it had a scary twist and then a happy ending. After the story they asked me all about Samoa and my family's lifestyle and beliefs. It was like I was the expert and they all wanted to know more. We all talked about our lives and found out that the way I live in Australia has lots of things in common with the other kids…and some big differences. There aren't many other Islanders at my school and I felt really proud when the class loved my artwork. It was an awesome day! By Afa

Angelina stated that she was determined to ensure that Afa's renewed engagement in class would last beyond that one 'awesome day'.

When Angelina's class read the Samoan literature it became the stimulus for interesting conversations among the students. Initially focusing upon Samoa and Afa's life, it then became the springboard for each student to share and reflect upon their lives as well. Angelina realised that tapping into her students' existing funds of knowledge and genuinely valuing them in the classroom was empowering and served to engage them in their learning. She also found that through purposeful planning teachers could use stories and literature from a range of genres in the classroom as the basis for children to further explore their own cultural identities and to better understand and relate to those around them. Angelina's school found the use of literature to be instrumental in supporting staff in introducing the concept of intercultural understanding to their students and to nurture their ongoing knowledge and skill development in this area. The use of well-selected literature was powerful in enabling children to learn through vicarious experiences by putting themselves into someone else's shoes. They seemed to be developing empathy and respect for cultural difference and were beginning to understand their own biographies as important and ongoing.

Reflection and discussion

What lessons can you draw from Angelina's story with respect to your professional practice as a literacy educator? How do you feel about the way she handled the situation with Afa? Can you think of moments when what you have learnt about the languages and cultural backgrounds of your students has caused you to critically revisit some of your assumptions as a literacy educator?

Conclusion

The stories in this chapter have all been about teachers who have reflected critically on the different cultural experiences they bring to their teaching of literacy and intercultural understanding. This includes Patrick, who recognises that while his culture might be dominant, it is still only one culture among many, shaping his view of the world. Through their engagement with particular students and their backgrounds and needs, these teachers have all developed a deeper awareness of the cultural re-sources of students and their worlds of experience. This has enabled them to draw on those worlds of experience as a resource for learning.

The school communities in which each of the teachers work are fostering their understanding about difference and about how to work together more effectively. The school contexts differ, but each can be thought of as a site for teacher inquiry into cultural diversity. Collaboration with colleagues, engagement with the broader school community and a preparedness to tackle difficult issues are leading to deeper understandings of literacy and difference on the part of both teachers and students.

References

Amnesty International 2008, *We Are All Born Free: The Universal Declaration of Human Rights in Pictures*, Frances Lincoln Children's Books, London.

Australian Curriculum Assessment and Reporting Authority (ACARA) 2013, The Australian Curriculum v 5.0. Retrieved 24 March 2014 from <http://www.australiancurriculum.edu.au/GeneralCapabilities/intercultural-understanding/introduction/introduction>.

Clyne, M 2005, 'Writing, testing and culture' in B Doecke & G Parr (eds), *Writing = Learning*, Wakefield Press in association with the Australian Association for the Teaching of English, Kent Town, South Australia, pp. 120–9.

Do, A & Do, S 2011, *The Little Refugee*, Allen & Unwin, Crows Nest, NSW.

Goodchild, R & Potter, L 2005, *Legendary Art: Using Stories to Teach and Learn about Art*, User Friendly Resource Enterprises, Christchurch, New Zealand.

Holm, G & Zilliacus, H 2009, 'Multicultural education and intercultural education: is there a difference' in MT Talib, J Loima, H Paavola & S Patrikainen (eds), *Dialogs on Diversity and Global Education,* Peter Lang, Frankfurt am Main and New York, pp. 11–28.

Kostogriz, A 2005, '(Trans)cultural spaces of writing' in B Doecke & G Parr (eds), *Writing = Learning*, Wakefield Press in association with the Australian Association for the Teaching of English, Kent Town, South Australia, pp. 104–19.

Liddicoat, A, Papademetre, L, Scarino, A & Kohler, M 2003, 'Report on intercultural language learning', Department of Education, Science and Training, Commonwealth of Australia, Canberra.

Moll, LC, Amanti, C, Neff, D & Gonzalez, N 1992, 'Funds of knowledge for teaching: using a qualitative approach to connect homes and classrooms', *Theory into Practice*, vol. 31, no. 2, p. 132.

Noble, G & Poynting, S 2000, 'Multicultural education and intercultural understanding: ethnicity, culture and schooling' in C Scott & S Dinham (eds), *Teaching in Context*, Australian Council for Educational Research, Camberwell, Victoria, pp. 56–81.

United Nations Educational, Scientific and Cultural Organization (UNESCO) 2006, *UNESCO Guidelines on Intercultural Education*, UNESCO, Paris.

Chapter 6

Inclusive literacy education

Joanne O'Mara and Louise Paatsch

If we want to progress education reform and change, then the importance of value positions that are grounded by social and cultural beliefs about education, learning and difference need to be acknowledged

Suzanne Carrington, Joanne Deppeler and Julianne Moss (2012, p. 1)

The literacy classroom: working to each child's potential

In Australia, all young people have a right to attend their local school and to receive a good education. These rights are strongly protected in law.

The *Melbourne Declaration on Educational Goals for Young Australians*, ratified by the State, Territory and Commonwealth Ministers of Education meeting at the Ministerial Council on Education, Employment, Training and Youth Affairs (MCEETYA) in 2008, has two goals. First, that Australian schooling should promote equity and excellence.

> You would find it useful to read the whole of *The Melbourne Declaration on Education Goals for Young Australians.* This document emerged out of negotiations between the Federal Government and the Australian states and territories, and provides a blueprint for educational reform in all sectors.

Second, that all young Australians should become successful learners, confident and creative individuals, and active and informed citizens (Commonwealth of Australia 2005, p. 7). This includes young Australians who have a disability.

For young people with a disability, these rights are explicitly affirmed and protected under the Australian Institute for Teaching and School Leadership (AITSL). The standards developed by AITSL make specific reference to teaching students with disabilities. Standard 1.6, for example, states that proficient teachers should 'design and implement teaching activities that support the participation and learning of students with disability and address relevant policy and legislative requirements' (AITSL, 2014).

Such requirements are directed at eliminating discrimination in the area of education and training against people on the grounds of disability. They are designed to ensure that people with disabilities have the same rights to equality of education and training as the rest of the community, promoting recognition and acceptance within the community of the principle that persons with disabilities have the same fundamental rights as the rest of the community.

It is important that everyone develops literacy skills, both for pragmatic purposes and for the pleasures to be gained from reading stories and other imaginative texts. The level of speaking, listening, reading and writing that each individual develops radically impacts on their ability to live their life in an independent and fulfilling way. This is particularly true of young people with disabilities, for whom the difference between living independently or not may depend on incremental gains in their literacy skills (Driedger & Hansen 2011).

> You can read the standards developed by the Australian Institute for Teaching and School Leadership (AITSL):
> <http://www.teacherstandards.aitsl.edu.au/DomainOfTeaching/Professional Knowledge/Standards/1>.

Children who have additional needs are sometimes given extra funding to support their progress in schooling. This is generally when the child has a disability, such as Down Syndrome, autism, physical disabilities or sensory impairments, such as significant hearing or sight loss. For children who receive additional funding in Australia, usually the school has a choice about what to do with the funding in terms of how they support the child. Funding approaches vary across states and countries and frequently change with government policy. Usually the greater proportion of the money pays for a teacher's aide, who works alongside the student and teacher, often offering support across the rest of the class as well.

You can read Ben Whitburn's (2013) work for an extended discussion of positive and negative aspects of teacher aides in the classroom.

Schools often have many students who are not funded but require significant amounts of additional help. To allocate their resources to meet the needs of all students is one of the greatest challenges for schools. Sometimes students can fall through the cracks, with their needs unmet from year to year. Some may have learning disabilities that are difficult to assess. Often these students lose interest in school, can become positioned as 'a problem', and spoken of as if they are deficit in some way, implying that nothing of significance can be done to help them to develop. As teachers, it is our role and responsibility to work with all of our students to help them to achieve their best. When teachers work in partnership with coordinators and leadership teams, they have a better chance of successfully meeting the literacy needs of all students in their class.

This chapter prompts you to think about both the challenges and the rewards of including all students effectively in the literacy classroom in order to enable them to reach their full potential. We present two case studies drawn from our own work and experiences, and ask you to think about how the teachers, students and other key players worked with each other, and what you might do in the same situation. The first case concerns Brooke, a second year graduate teacher, who is working with Emily, a Year 1 student who has Down Syndrome. The second case is about Eloise, an experienced teacher working with Nicola, who has a profound hearing loss and is fitted with bilateral cochlear implants. Both cases document how a general classroom teacher works in a team with other specialist support staff to include students with disabilities. In Brooke and Emily's case we focus on reading and writing, and in Eloise and Nicola's case we look at speaking and listening. You will be invited to reflect on the advantages of an inclusive education for students with and without disabilities and the professional rewards obtained by teachers when they work with students with disabilities, as well as some specific approaches and strategies to work towards success.

To read more about inclusive education see Julie Allan (1999, 2010) and the work of Michele Moore and Roger Slee (2012).

Reflection and discussion

Think about how we all rely on literacy practices in our everyday life. How literate are the people you know who have disabilities? What strategies, supports, devices and tools do they use to develop, maintain and extend their literacy practices?

Brooke and Emily: gaining confidence and skills together

Brooke is twenty-four and has been teaching for two years. This year she is teaching Year 1 in a middle-class school in Melbourne. She has a child in her class, Emily, who receives extra funding support as she has Down Syndrome.

You might like to know more about Down Syndrome and how to support students with Down Syndrome in the classroom by visiting <http://www.downsyndrome.org.au>.

At the beginning of the year Brooke was really worried about what it would be like to teach someone with Down Syndrome. She worried about not having enough knowledge herself, not having the skills that might be needed, and whether there would be an impact upon the rest of the class. Brooke did not know anyone with Down Syndrome before she started teaching Emily, which really contributed to her fears. She simply did not know what to expect. She felt that she was not really prepared to work with children with additional needs. She was also worried about how she might work with the teacher's aide, who was much older and very experienced.

At the end of the year of teaching Emily, Brooke was extremely enthusiastic about her inclusion in the class. She reflected on what she had learnt from working with Emily: that children with Down Syndrome can learn to read well, they can achieve academically and make significant progress in their academic work from year to year. Brooke had been surprised with how much Emily was capable of achieving and how easily she fitted in with the class. Her reading was six months above the level expected for her year, and Brooke had a strong sense of achievement about what she and Emily, as well as the school-based team and Emily's parents, had achieved together. She was full of praise and admiration for Emily, particularly her high level of persistence and motivation. Rather than being the 'scary' challenge that she had imagined it might be, teaching Emily was extremely satisfying and something she had really enjoyed. Before she had Emily in her class, the only knowledge she had had of Down Syndrome were stereotypical perceptions. That is: an expectation of low academic achievement, with such children being consigned to a special school in order to learn basic 'life skills' because of their inability to keep up with the rest of the class. This year Brooke had developed her professional expertise in working across the range of needs that she found in her classroom every day, and she had become open-minded about teaching children with additional needs, realising that if she planned her literacy program by using the interests of the children as the starting point, she could effectively plan to meet the needs of each individual child.

Elaine, the teacher's aide, had already been working at the school for some time, and the amount of funding allocated to Emily meant that Elaine could be in the classroom for three hours a day. Brooke at first felt a little intimidated by having Elaine in the classroom, as it felt like surveillance of her teaching, well beyond how she was working with Emily. However, Elaine recognised this and was very proactive in talking through how they might work together productively. Elaine supported Brooke, but did not interfere in the classroom, and she was of great assistance not only to Emily, but to other children in the class. Elaine explained to Emily that she saw her relationship with Emily and Brooke as a partnership based on mutual respect. It took some time for Brooke to feel totally comfortable with Elaine, because Brooke was not comfortable about having this older, experienced aide in the room while she was still developing her own confidence and expertise as a teacher. However, after several months they had developed a very productive and supportive professional relationship, and Brooke could see how helpful Elaine's work had become to Emily's progress.

Enhancing literacy practices: the place of teachers' judgments

Early in the year, the Year 1 students were tested to ascertain their reading levels. Students whose reading tested below a certain point qualified to have additional reading support in the school Reading Recovery program (Clay 1994).

Reading Recovery, a very famous remedial program developed by Marie Clay (1994), targets students in Year 1. This is based on the assumption that students who are performing below the expected achievement level in literacy at this point of schooling can benefit significantly from a focused one-on-one program. Although there are disagreements between literacy teachers and scholars about the 'best approach' (Tunmer, Chapman et al. 2013), the program has been adopted widely in Australian schools and is successful for some students.

Emily qualified for the program and started to work with Leslie, the Reading Recovery teacher. This program provided intensive one-on-one sessions for half an hour per day. Leslie worked very closely with Emily, monitoring and assessing her progress constantly.

The Reading Recovery program has a continual cycle of teaching, assessment, reviewing, and then teaching, enabling the teacher to work very closely with the child and draw on the child's interests. The program is often criticised, both for being too holistic (it is not a phonics-based program) and for being too prescriptive (with respect to the series of strategies it embodies to expand the repertoire of literate practices).

Reading Recovery suited Emily extremely well. Many children with Down Syndrome have auditory processing, articulation and hearing issues. For these children, a phonics approach is not suitable, as they may not hear the words clearly, and so focusing on this dimension of literacy adds to their confusion. It is better to consider more visual strategies and to adopt a whole language approach, as in the Reading Recovery program. One of Leslie's primary concerns was getting to know Emily, and choosing content in which Emily was interested. The Reading Recovery program also has a writing component, and Leslie helped Emily to compose writing that was about Emily's life, her family, friends, hobbies and interests.

Emily was very engaged with the program and really enjoyed the sessions with Leslie. Most importantly, she had a very strong sense of achievement and was very aware of the progress she was making. Her parents worked with her on the additional activities at home, an important part of the program. Leslie worked with Brooke to give the children in the class who were working on the Reading Recovery program support, and Brooke kept Leslie up-to-date with the classroom program so that the children participating in the Reading Recovery program were still able to participate fully in the life of the classroom.

Classrooms are language intensive environments, saturated with both spoken and written language. For children with intellectual disabilities this can be very challenging, and making themselves understood clearly is a priority. Emily also worked with a speech therapist, Danielle, once a week at school. Children with Down Syndrome generally have difficulties clearly articulating their speech. This is partly physical, as they often have low muscle tone, a normal sized tongue and a smaller mouth cavity. It is also partly intellectual, as they may not have developed all the sounds and language constructions yet.

In class, Emily sometimes found it difficult to make herself understood. She was very motivated to become clearer in her speech, and really wanted the other children to understand her all the time. Emily's motivation and personal goals enabled her to work with the speech therapist in a very collaborative way, even though Emily was only seven. Elaine attended the speech therapy session with Emily, and having the aide attend meant that Danielle could give Elaine strategies and tips for assisting Emily to make herself understood in class, as well as some specific exercises that she could practice with Emily when time allowed. In this context, Elaine was able to fill Danielle in with information about Emily's progress in the classroom and highlight any specific issues she was having with her speech in the classroom context. Oral reports were found to be an area Emily struggled with, so Danielle focused on those for a few sessions, giving Emily, Elaine and Brooke some strategies about how to best organise these for success. Emily's parents were also in frequent contact with Danielle, and they paid for all of the sessions. Emily had some therapy sessions at home, which gave a chance for Danielle to update the parents, and she also sent them written reports of the school sessions. Because most of Emily's clarity issues were in the more public space of the classroom rather than in the home, her parents and Danielle agreed that school-based sessions were the most effective for Emily's progress.

All the students who received additional funding have a meeting each term with the parents, the inclusion co-ordinator, the classroom teacher and the teacher's aide. These meetings are to set goals for the student, review progress and to share experiences, tips and feedback. In Victoria, one of the conditions of schools receiving additional funding for students is that they hold these meetings. Brooke was very nervous for the first meeting, as she was not sure what would be expected of her. However, she found the meeting was very productive as it gave her a chance to report on Emily's progress and to seek advice about how to best support her in the classroom. It was very much a team approach, and the parents and school team swapped information about Emily's likes, dispositions and challenges. Brooke felt really young and inexperienced, especially meeting with these older educated parents, but Emily's mum saw her after school and told her how happy they were about the meeting, and that she had some great ideas about what to do. Brooke realised that this approach, which was very organised in Emily's case because of her funding, was a great way of thinking about the development of literacy for all the students in her class. Many of these middle-class parents were very demanding, and sometimes Brooke felt as though they were suspicious of her. She realised that all the students in her class relied on a team approach, with the work in the classroom and the work the parents did with reading to their children, hearing their children read and demonstrating everyday literacy practices in the home coming together to support each child in their literacy learning.

One thing that Brooke was worried about throughout the year was Emily's writing. At the beginning of the year she wrote completely backwards, in mirror writing. When Brooke held the writing up to a mirror she could read it clearly. Sometimes Emily would write things the right way around if Brooke or Elaine sat with her guiding her. Brooke was worried about this and felt that she might need some specialised help, as she did not know what to do. She consulted the junior school coordinator, who told her that she had seen this before with children who had a developmental delay or who were younger in the class and that the mirror writing generally corrected itself over time. The coordinator also told her that if children have a known developmental delay such as Down Syndrome, then teachers do not need to intervene as this will usually self-correct and the child will be accessing a range of additional support services. However, like any issue you may have with a child in your class, if you don't know what to do, it's best to seek further advice from senior school leaders and paraprofessionals working with the school. Even though Brooke knew that Emily's writing would reverse, she was surprised when Emily began to naturally correct her work towards the end of the year. By the beginning of Year 2 Emily mostly wrote correctly.

The family and school had agreed to report Emily's progress, using the standard progression points employed in general reporting. The family realised that Emily would not always be at the expected level, but the parents wanted Emily to be assessed using the same measures of progress for other students in the class, alongside the very valuable formative assessment that the teachers completed regularly. They explained to Brooke that they felt that if her academic work was 'off the books' that teachers might not think of her as advancing academically. They wanted her to be included as much as possible, and they felt that this was a part of that inclusion. Emily's parents also felt that these measures were ones understood by all teachers in the school and across the state, so that these results on her report card communicated her progress in ways that could be shared and reflected upon. Brooke realised that this was a very good method to use, because while the progression points are simple markers that do not reflect the fullness of any child's skills or learning, they did enable her to have a set of markers about where Emily was at different moments in time. Emily showed a huge amount of progress: six months ahead in reading, up to the mark in composition/writing and six months behind with her speaking and listening. She could look at the report from the year before, and because the shared language of the state's progression points had been used, she could see her development over time. This was also invaluable for communicating with other teachers, as everyone was working with the same set of standards, and so Emily's teachers could see from the report what Emily had already achieved and how to plan based on her needs.

Both Brooke and Emily's mother have noted how important Emily's literacy skills are to her. At school she is able to participate in all of the activities in English and other subjects quite independently because of these skills. While the instructions and some of the tasks may sometimes need to be modified for Emily, having very solid literacy skills makes her inclusion more complete, as Emily is able to read instructions and complete tasks on her own, as well as participate in group work. When the class is working in a multi-aged setting, Emily is able to use her reading skills to read to younger children in the class, and Brooke has noticed that this is valued by those students as well as giving Emily a sense of high esteem. Emily has a brother who is two years younger, and she often reads to him, and helps him out with his reading when he reads to her. The family all enjoy reading, and Emily can participate in this family practice by reading the books that she enjoys. Emily's mother reports that Emily uses her literacy skills effectively at home: she makes a shopping list, and on the weekend she goes with her mother and does the family supermarket shopping – they have two lists, and Emily gets a trolley and does half of it. She can write greeting cards and letters, sort the mail and add events to the family calendar. She can also read the calendar to know what is on at school. Her family are excited that the school is moving to a 1 : 1 iPad program, and they are hoping that Emily will keep an electronic diary that she can use to plan her week. All of these authentic literacy practices in the home further extend Emily's skills and interest in literacy, showing her that literacy has an important place in her life, that reading is both functional and pleasurable.

Reflection and discussion

Brooke has drawn on a wide range of resources and supports in her partnership with Emily. One of the features of Emily's case is the rich language and literacy environment she experiences at home and her parents' positive approach to developing her language and literacy skills. How might you work with parents across the range of abilities in your classroom to support their child's language and literacy? What have you learnt from Brooke's story that might be applied to your teaching of all children?

Eloise and Nicola: working together within a multidisciplinary partnership

Eloise is an experienced teacher who has been teaching early years students for the past eight years. This year she is teaching Year 3 for the first time. Throughout the past eight years, she has worked with many children with additional needs within her inclusive classroom, including students with physical and intellectual disabilities. However, this year she was informed that there was a new student to the school in her class who had a hearing loss. Nicola has a profound hearing loss and was implanted with bilateral cochlear implants at the age of eighteen months. Previous school reports indicated that her reading and writing were 'at grade level'. Teacher comments also showed that Nicola was shy and appeared to have some challenges with mixing with her peers. Reports from her speech language pathologist and her visiting teacher of the deaf showed that Nicola had age-appropriate language skills, although she had difficulties with using complex language structures in both spoken and written language. It was also recommended by her teacher of the deaf that Nicola would benefit from being exposed to a wider range of experiences that would assist with the development of her vocabulary.

You might like to know more about the cochlear implant and how it works by visiting <http://www.hearing.com.au>.

Eloise was feeling anxious about her own lack of knowledge in working with students with hearing loss. She did not know much about the cochlear implant, although she had read in the newspapers and heard on TV that it was also known as the bionic ear and that it could help people hear.

You may want to read further about the impact of hearing loss on spoken language development on students with cochlear implants and hearing aids by reading: Peter Blamey, Julia Sarant, Louise Paatsch, Johanna Barry, Catherine Bow, Roger Wales, Maree Wright, Colleen Psarros, Kylie Rattigan and Rebecca Tooher (2001).

For a further information on Australian sign language you may want to visit: <http://www.auslan.org.au/>.

Eloise had many unanswered questions and was certainly facing her 'blind spot', to pursue the metaphor introduced in Chapter 2 of this book. How did this device work? Did the cochlear implant restore Nicola's hearing? What did she have to do in order to support Nicola in the class? Did Nicola speak or did she use Australian sign language (Auslan)?

Did she need to learn sign language herself? How would Nicola communicate with the other children? Who would she need to work with in order to address Nicola's specific needs? What was the role of the visiting teacher of the deaf? Where would she go for professional learning?

Reflection and discussion

You can see that Eloise has identified a gap in her own professional learning, even though she is an experienced teacher. What are some of the challenges you have faced with your own learning when working with students with specific needs in inclusive environments?

Two weeks before the start of the school year, Eloise received an email from Nicola's mum requesting a time to meet to discuss Nicola's specific needs. Eloise spoke with her principal about arranging a meeting with all involved in Nicola's learning and development. Eloise was experienced with running parent support group meetings and had formed strong collaborative relationships in the past with many paraprofessionals who supported students with intellectual and physical disabilities. Once again, Eloise was a little anxious about working with a new group of parents and paraprofessionals. The meeting was attended by Nicola's parents, her visiting teacher of the deaf, and her case manager from the bionic ear institute who was a speech language pathologist who had been working with Nicola since her implantation. Also present at this meeting were the principal, the assistant principal and the inclusion coordinator. All talked about Nicola's specific needs in the areas of spoken language and literacy. Nicola's parents were particularly concerned with the need to continue to develop her spoken language in order to support the development of her social skills, and highlighted the potential challenge of making new friends. They had chosen spoken language, rather than signing, as the main mode of communication for Nicola because it was the language of the home and of her community and stated the need for her to be able to communicate effectively with others at home, at school and within the broader community.

Nicola's case manager, Liza, discussed how the cochlear implant worked and ways to optimise the listening environment. In particular, Liza talked about ways of reducing the background noise including placing rubber stoppers on the bottom of chairs, covering tables with materials that would absorb the noise, covering display boards with felt and placing rugs or mats on the linoleum floor of the classroom. She also introduced the team to the sound system that Nicola would use. This included showing the Soundfield system and the device that Nicola wears that is connected to her cochlear implant that directly link to the speaker's voice.

> You might be interested in reading further about how Soundsystems work in inclusive classrooms. You could read further at <http://www.mediaaccess.org.au/category/taxonomy/education-terms/soundfield-amplification-system>.

Liza also directed Eloise to a number of useful websites which described hearing loss, how the cochlear implant works, how to troubleshoot the equipment when it breaks down, and materials that could be used with teachers and students to help them to understand hearing loss.

Nicola's visiting teacher of the deaf, Melanie, talked about the purpose of her weekly visits to the school and the importance of ongoing communication between all involved with Nicola's learning. Melanie discussed that she would be withdrawing Nicola from the class for about 45 minutes each week to work specifically on Nicola's speech, listening and language skills. She also suggested that it would be useful to meet with Eloise after each visit to talk about goals for Nicola's ongoing learning and development. Further outcomes from this meeting included planning ways of ensuring a 'whole-school approach' to the inclusion of Nicola within her new school community. This included arranging dates for specific presentations to be given by Melanie and Liza to staff, students and parents regarding hearing loss and the implications for Nicola's speech and language development.

> For more information about hearing loss and cochlear implants see <http://www.hearing.com.au> and <http://www.cochlear.com/wps/wcm/connect/au/home/>.

At the conclusion of the meeting, Eloise's head was 'spinning' with all the new knowledge and the realisation that there was still so much to learn. She was on a continuous journey of acquiring new knowledge but she knew that she was not alone. Everyone was learning and she knew that she had enormous support. Drawing on her past experiences of working with students with specific learning needs, she knew that in order for inclusion to be successful, students needed to feel that they were 'members' of the community and not 'visitors' as identified by (Antia, Stinson & Gonter-Gaustad 2002). It was critical that everyone continued to work together to address the needs of all students in the class. Nicola was one of 24 members of the Year 3 class.

Reflection and discussion

You can see how important it is to bring all stakeholders together to talk about the specific needs of the student. What other factors does a school need to consider when developing a whole-school approach to inclusion?

Throughout the first three weeks of Term 1 both Eloise and Melanie conducted many assessments in order to gain a more comprehensive understanding of Nicola's specific language and literacy needs. Eloise carried out the Year 3 assessments for numeracy and literacy, including listening and speaking. Eloise mapped Nicola's progress against the curriculum standards. It was evident that Nicola understood that spoken, visual and written forms of language are different modes of communication. She also used simple vocabulary about familiar topics. However, it was apparent that Nicola was not able to use a wide range of vocabulary in new topics and was hesitant to experiment with vocabulary to suit the audience and purpose.

Melanie also conducted a number of assessments. These included more formal language assessments as well as collecting samples of Nicola's conversational skills, including one ten-minute conversation between Nicola and Melanie, and another between Nicola and one of her peers. After all data had been collected Eloise met with Melanie to collate results and develop Nicola's individual learning plan. Melanie reported that she had some concerns with the structure of the conversation between Nicola and her friend, but she felt that they would monitor her interactions more closely throughout Term 1 to enable her to settle into her new environment. Eloise felt that she needed to target Nicola's vocabulary, as it was evident in both her written and spoken language that she used very simple language and did not appear to use emotive language in her text responses and within her interactions with her peers. Once again, both Melanie and Eloise wanted to monitor Nicola's progress throughout the term as she began to get to know other children in the class. During this meeting Eloise suggested that these co-constructed goals should be discussed with Nicola, her parents, Nicola's case manager and others involved in Nicola's learning. As a result, a meeting was scheduled where goals were discussed. Nicola's own goal was to be understood by her peers, to make friends and to 'do well' at her school work.

Reflection and discussion

Other chapters in this book have highlighted the importance of children articulating their own learning goals. Think about the inclusion of Nicola in the development of her own learning goals. How have you included students with disabilities in understanding and developing their learning goals? In what ways do you ensure that the learning goals of students with disabilities are understood by all those involved in their learning?

At the end of first term a meeting with all those involved in Nicola's learning was held. It was clear from this meeting that everyone had an understanding of Nicola's learning needs. It was also evident that these speaking and listening goals were integrated into every aspect of her learning, not just in the individual sessions with the paraprofessionals. Everyone discussed Nicola's progress and made adjustments, where necessary, to her individual learning plan. Eloise reported that Nicola was making friends and had appeared to settle in well in her new class. Eloise had learnt to operate the Soundfield system in the classroom and children had become accustomed to using the microphone when speaking in class. Interestingly, other students had reported the benefit of the teacher using the microphone in the whole-group class activities, as it was easier to hear the teacher's voice and that the background noise was reduced.

Eloise had also worked hard on developing synonyms and antonyms for specific vocabulary. She had also worked with Nicola within a small group of students who had similar vocabulary goals. She worked on developing emotive language by connecting feelings with possible vocabulary used to express such feelings. These small group sessions not only supported vocabulary growth, but also provided opportunities for spontaneous talk around the teaching and learning. Such incidental talk promotes turn taking, listening, responding and taking the perspectives of others in the group. Eloise had recorded some of these interactions on her phone and presented them to everyone attending the parent support group meeting, including Nicola. Eloise used these recordings as a way of highlighting the positive interactions as well as those where further work was needed. In particular, it was noted that Nicola was able to initiate conversation, take turns and pause appropriately. However, it was also evident that she was not attending to some of the subtle cues used in talking with her peers. These included: establishing mutual eye gaze during talk, attending to feedback from the listener, sensitivity to the change of topic by her peers, and an ability to extend the topics. Eloise talked with Nicola and asked her about her own challenges when interacting with others in the group. Nicola reported that she found it difficult to know when someone had changed the topic and often she didn't know anything about the topics they talked about. Nicola also said that she was unaware of the subtle differences in meaning in some of the non-verbal cues such as head nods and change in listener's eye gaze. It was noted that these would form the basis for future goals for both individual and small group sessions.

Melanie and Liza also shared the strategies they used with Nicola in their individual sessions. Melanie had developed her sessions around the specific topics and themes that were being covered in the classroom. These included inquiry-based topics, the numeracy and literacy goals, and the arts and physical education topics. Specifically, Melanie worked on frontloading the possible vocabulary that may be used in these topics and themes. In particular, she worked on developing multiple meanings for words and set up activities that provided opportunities for Nicola to manipulate words to be used in different contexts and as different parts of language (e.g. the noun 'colour' can be manipulated to be an adjective 'colourful' or a verb 'coloured'). They also worked on how words could be used creatively in humour, sarcasm and colloquial language, all aspects that are critical for the development of literacy and social skills.

David Dickinson, Linda Cote and Miriam Smith (1993) as well as Megan McClelland, Claire Cameron, Carol Connor, Carrie Farris, Abigail Jewkes and Fredrick Morrison (2007) provide insights into these dimensions of language development.

Liza worked with Nicola on developing her pragmatic skills, that is, the social use of language. She set up scenarios around real life situations whereby Nicola would need to role play particular situations. For example, one scenario was around playground interactions. Nicola was to imagine that she went out to play and wanted to join in with a group of peers. The aim of this activity was to expand ways to initiate conversation and enter a group. This included developing appropriate and varied question types, non-verbal cues, statements and the appropriate use of objects to engage her peers. Liza also invited some of Nicola's friends into the sessions to take part in these scenarios. Liza also recorded some of these sessions and talked through these interactions with both Nicola and her friends.

Eloise took note of the many strategies that were discussed and thought about other students in her class who might benefit from this type of teaching and learning. She began to implement some of the strategies with the whole class, keeping in mind Nicola's specific goals. In particular, she began to explore with all the students, the subtle cues used in conversation to convey different meanings, including both verbal and non-verbal cues. She also linked these oral communication skills to other aspects of literacy learning, including supporting students to investigate how these face-to-face cues could be represented in multimodal texts. All students benefitted from this emphasis on spoken language and its explicit link to literacy learning.

Eloise also identified the need to read further on the impact of a hearing loss on the development of conversation, language and social skills, and the importance of talk for all students. Liza and Melanie directed her to a couple of key readings while Eloise located her own readings through the library and from within the Primary English Teaching Association Australia (PETAA) of which she is a member.

Some of the readings that Eloise accessed were Louise Paatsch and Dianne Toe (2014), Dianne Toe and Louise Paatsch (2013). She also drew on Janet Scull, Louise Paatsch and Bridie Raban (2013) and Christine Edwards-Groves, Michele Anstey and Geoff Bull (2014).

Reflecting on the year, Eloise had learnt many things about working with students with hearing loss. She had also learnt a great deal about the importance of talk and its impact on the development of literacy and social skills for all students. While it appeared that Nicola was a good communicator and appeared to understand, there were many subtle spoken language skills that still required attention. It seemed that Nicola, like many other students with communication difficulties, learnt to develop a number of 'coping strategies' that may seem, on the surface, to show attributes of a competent communicator. However, when you observe more closely and go beyond the limited speaking and listening progression points outlined for teachers in curriculum standards, there are signs that there may be many challenges for these students. Such challenges could be easily overlooked.

Reflection and discussion

Think about how the teachers in these two examples have used curriculum standards to monitor children's literacy development. What are the limitations you have identified in your own literacy teaching of only using progression points outlined within curriculum standards to capture the uniqueness of all students in your class? How do you develop a complete literacy profile of every child that recognises their individuality? Do you think teachers should use common systems to report upon all children?

Ensuring that all children are literacy learners

Brooke and Eloise's reflections on working respectively with Emily and Nicola, their families and others involved in their learning led to changes in their own practices. They broadened their assessments beyond simply mapping what Emily and Nicola did against the outcomes outlined in state-specific curriculum standards (though Brooke also respected the desire expressed by Emily's parents to maintain a record of her progress against those standards). Understanding the specific needs of one particular student prompted them to think further about the needs of all students in their classes. They were reminded how the language and literacy needs of students move beyond the physical space of the classroom. As language and literacy teachers, they were active participants in their own professional learning and were willing to take on the new challenges.

> You can explore more about teacher professional learning in Chapter 3.

Reflection and discussion

You have seen that both Brooke and Eloise held stereotypical notions about disabilities. As well as finding out more about specific disabilities, you might also consider ways to diversify your teaching in order to enable every child in your class access to the activities you have planned. How might you adapt your literacy program to accommodate all learners in your classroom? Here is a list of starting points for thinking about this:

- Get to know the child's interests and strengths: What are her/his preferences? How does she/he respond to different activities?
- Assess where the student is at: use both formative and summative assessment to plan your teaching and learning and record the student's progress.
- Modify activities to have multiple entry points.
- Expect all students to achieve their personal best.
- Develop collaborative relationships with the child, the parents and other staff who work with the child.
- Develop an inclusive environment where all children are members of a learning community.

You will teach many children who require extra supports and help but do not qualify for individual funding. When you have children who you identify as needing extra support you will need to take professional action.

- Research reliable sources of information, not hearsay or last night's TV program.
- Consult and collaborate with senior colleagues at your school, who will generally support you in meeting with the parents of the child, seeking additional support and external help.
- Check current policies, funding arrangements and protocols.
- Set up regular meetings with parents, paraprofessionals, support staff and students to ensure that all have an understanding of the specific learning goals. Discuss the adjustments and accommodations required for learning.
- Integrate learning goals across all aspects of the curriculum.
- Seek support for your own learning.

Conclusion

In this chapter you have witnessed two classroom teachers working with a number of paraprofessionals in different ways, with the common goal of understanding the learning needs of students with disabilities. You have also seen that many of the strategies used within intense individual sessions can be applied to different contexts and with all members of the learning community.

The developmental paradigm dominates many of the approaches to teaching children with disabilities. Such standards might have inbuilt blind spots, making it difficult for teachers to recognise the specific needs of children. This paradigm assumes that children develop and progress in a specific, sequential order when they are ready and ignores the impact of their environment on their learning. In reality, every child is different, and children are as much a product of their personal dispositions and their environment as they are of their abilities. As we have seen in the two cases discussed in this chapter, students who have disabilities can achieve great success at school, and teachers can work in partnership with other professionals, families, students and the wider school community to achieve very successful literacy outcomes.

References

Allan, J 1999, *Actively Seeking Inclusion: Pupils with Special Needs in Mainstream Schools*, Falmer Press, Philadelphia PA.

Allan, J 2010, 'The sociology of disability and the struggle for inclusive education', *British Journal of Sociology of Education*, vol. 31, no. 5, pp. 603–19. doi: 10.1080/01425692.2010.500093

Antia, SD, Stinson, MS & Gaustad, MG 2002, 'Developing membership in the education of deaf and hard-of-hearing students in inclusive settings. *Journal of Deaf Studies and Deaf Education*, vol. 7, no. 3, pp. 214–29. doi: 10.1093/deafed/7.3.214

Australian Institute for Teaching and School Leadership 2012, 'Australian professional standards for teachers'. <http://www.teacherstandards.aitsl.edu.au/OrganisationStandards/Organisation>

Blamey, PJ, Sarant, JZ, Paatsch, LE et al. 2001, 'Relationships among speech perception, production, language, hearing loss and age in children with impaired hearing', *Journal of Speech, Language & Hearing Research*, vol. 44, no. 2, pp. 264–85.

Carrington, S, Deppeler, J & Moss, J 2012, 'Cultivating teachers' beliefs, knowledge and skills for leading change in schools', *Australian Journal of Teacher Education*, vol. 35, no. 1, pp. 1–13.

Clay, MM 1994, *Reading Recovery: A Guidebook for Teachers in Training*, Heinemann, Portsmouth, NH.

Commonwealth of Australia 2005, 'Disability standards for education 2005', Commonwealth of Australia, Barton, ACT.

Dickinson, D, Cote, L & Smith, M 1993, 'Learning vocabulary in preschool: social and discourse contexts affecting vocabulary growth', *New Directions for Child Development*, vol. 61, pp. 67–78.

Driedger, D, Hansen, N 2011, 'Making a connection: literacy, disability and quality of life, participatory action research approach final report', Canada, Ottawa IL. <http://www.ilcanada.ca/article/literacy-405.asp>

Edwards-Groves, C, Anstey, M & Bull, G 2014, *Classroom Talk: Understanding Dialogue, Pedagogy and Practice*, Primary English Teaching Association Australia, Newtown NSW.

McClelland, MM, Cameron, CE, Connor, McDonald, C, Farris, CL, Jewkes, AM & Morrison, FJ 2007, 'Links between behavioral regulation and preschoolers' literacy, vocabulary, and math skills', *Developmental Psychology*, vol. 43, no. 4, pp. 947–59. doi: 10.1037/0012-1649.43.4.947

Ministerial Council on Employment, Education, Training and Youth Affairs (MCEETYA) 2008, *Melbourne Declaration on Educational Goals for Young Australians*.

Moore, M & Slee, R 2012, 'Disability studies, inclusive education and exclusion' in N Watson, A Roulstone & C Thomas (eds), *Routledge Handbook of Disability Studies*, Routledge, New York, pp. 225–39.

Paatsch, LE & Toe, DM 2014, 'A comparison of pragmatic abilities of children who are deaf or hard of hearing and their hearing peers', *Journal of Deaf Studies and Deaf Education*, vol. 19, no. 1, pp. 1–19. doi: 10.1093/deafed/ent030

Scull, J, Paatsch, L & Raban, B 2013, 'Young learners: teachers' questions and prompts as opportunities for children's language development', *Asia-Pacific Journal of Research in Early Childhood Education*, vol. 7, no. 1, pp. 69–91.

Toe, DM & Paatsch, LE 2013, 'The conversational skills of school-aged children with cochlear implants', Cochlear Implants International, vol. 14, no. 2, pp. 67–79.

Tunmer, WE, Chapman, JW, Greaney, KT, Prochnow, JE & Arrow, AW 2013, 'Why the New Zealand National Literacy Strategy has failed and what can be done about it: evidence from the Progress in International Reading Literacy Study (PIRLS) 2011 and Reading Recovery monitoring reports', *Australian Journal of Learning Difficulties*, vol. 18, no. 2, pp. 139–80.

Whitburn, B 2013, 'The dissection of paraprofessional support in inclusive education: "You're in mainstream with a chaperone"', *Australasian Journal of Special Education*, vol. 37, no. 2, pp. 147–61.

Chapter 7

Homework

a window into community literacies

Glenn Auld and Kirsten Hutchison

We need to examine what literacy activities our students are engaging with out of school and consider how we can form bridges to support students within school. This will give us the opportunity to think more clearly about what literacy is being supported where. In addition, we need to pay attention to the complex blend of new and old media, which are central to the experience of the everyday cultures of childhood and adolescence.

Pahl and Rowsell (2005, p. 70)

What do you remember about homework? Did you like homework? Did it always seem useful? Why do you think your teachers set homework? Did you ever need to ask anyone else for help when you did your homework? What resources did you use when completing homework tasks?

This chapter looks at the ways in which literacy practices circulate between home, school and social and community spaces. It invites you to think critically about the kinds of literacies students engage in under the guise of 'homework', why teachers might wish to ask their students to do homework and how they might employ homework more effectively as a means to building bridges between school and community. Homework is a word that conjures up memories and associations for just about everyone. In this chapter we are exploring 'homework' as it is enacted in a variety of social spaces, with a range of child and adult participants, from specific tasks set by teachers, through to informal learning between young people and their parents around technology. Yet while homework is a highly visible practice – we suspect that just about every teacher sets homework in one form or another – it also prompts reflection about things that may not be so visible to you as a teacher. Can you, for example, imagine how the children in your class actually go about doing their homework when they get home? Can you imagine how long it takes for them to complete the tasks you set them? Do you feel confident that they would have the resources and the support to do these tasks? And do you feel that homework really plays an important role in enhancing their language and literacy?

More to homework than meets the eye

We are using the practices associated with homework as a way of examining relationships between home and school. We firstly want to explore some ways in which parents interact with their children around homework and literacy learning. Like the other authors of this book, we are working on the assumption that literacy is complex, multiple and increasingly technologised. We also assume that learners are variously situated within diverse communities that vary according to their location and the socio-cultural practices of people within them. When they engage with school and community-based literacy practices, our students draw on what Luis Moll has characterised as 'funds of knowledge' (Pahl & Rowsell 2005, pp. 71–2), and one of our purposes in this chapter is to make visible some of the ways that homework might be used as a vehicle to tap into those funds. But we are also cognisant of the challenges of social, economic, linguistic and cultural diversity for teachers, and aware that dominant school-based literacy practices can reproduce social inequalities if we don't think carefully about how we teach them, and how they might connect with the literacy practices in which students engage at home. So we want to begin by considering this issue of inequality and pointing to some theoretical resources that might enable you to critically reflect on your professional practice as a literacy educator with this question in mind. These theoretical resources have been immensely valuable to us in our own attempts to understand the diverse social settings presented in the vignettes that comprise this chapter.

We are thinking especially of the work of Pierre Bourdieu, a social theorist who has been influential in explaining and theorising the relationships between inequality and education.

A useful introduction to Bourdieu's work is found in the edited collection by Michael Grenfell (2008). James Albright and Alan Luke (2008) provide some interesting ideas on how Bourdieu's work is used in literacy education. Michael Grenfell, David Bloome, Cheryl Hardy, Kate Pahl, Jennifer Rowsell and Brian Street (2012) have explored how Bourdieu's work forms the basis of several ethnographic studies of literacy education.

Bourdieu's three key concepts of 'habitus', 'capital' and 'field' have been taken up by educational researchers to make sense of how social inequality operates through educational systems and institutions, such as the family. He argues that groups in society experience the world differently according to their class location, using the word 'habitus' to name the ways of seeing and being in the world that characterise those groups. He shows how 'habitus' mediates an individual's life trajectory and the forms of capital to which he or she has access (Bourdieu & Passeron 1990). Habitus produces 'individual and collective practices', (Moll, Amanti, Neff & Gonzalez 1992) within schools and families, through the mobilisation of various kinds of 'capital', which we can think of as the cultural, social, economic and emotional resources available to people as they participate in social settings. In this chapter, we'll use some of Pierre Bourdieu's language as a way of refocusing on the familiar school literacy practice of homework. This will be a way of making the familiar strange (to borrow a saying that anthropologists commonly use), enabling us to think about such practices in new ways.

We'll begin by introducing two families, whose children attend Grevillia Primary School. Our description focuses on the unique conditions shaping the familiar school practice of homework. The following stories are constructed on the basis of research that Kirsten has done into the social practice of homework in diverse settings. As you read the following stories, you might like to notice the kinds of language, texts, technologies and networks these families have available to them.

To read more about the social practices of homework read some of Kirsten's research. In these texts Kirsten outlines the importance of gender and homework (Hutchison 2012) and how homework is seen through the eyes of children. (Hutchison 2011)

These distinctive family resources are what Bourdieu would call the 'capitals' that are present and activated within families and communities.

Two families

We know that homework often serves as a communication channel between parents, children and teachers, and as such it might be viewed as a fairly neutral or innocent mechanism, whereby schools encourage their students to develop dispositions that will lead to academic success. But what this fails to take into account is the social and cultural contexts within which homework is done that shape what children are able to accomplish, that is to say, the distinctive sets of behaviours or dispositions Bourdieu calls 'habitus' that serves to advantage some students and disadvantage others.

> Pat Thomson also talks about this idea of students possessing various skills, attitudes and knowledge which may or may not be visible or built on at school. In her book *Schooling the Rustbelt Kids* (2002) she argues that all children come to school with 'virtual school bags', which are full of various cultural and linguistic resources. However, only some children get to open their bags and make use of what is inside. Many children's knowledges, experiences and practices remain invisible and unused at school.

When you read the following stories, you might like to reflect on the dispositions they reveal and how as a literacy educator you might begin to address the issues they raise. These two vignettes provide usefully contrastive examples of the ways children from different families engage with homework. How would you characterise the 'habitus' of each family? How well does this 'habitus' match what happens in school?

Gina and Katya: 'It's your homework'

Gina is an active, athletic ten-year old, with a passion for dancing. Her mother Katya works night shifts as a nurse, and so she's available to pick up Gina and her younger sister Alice from school and take them to their after-school activities. She has a strong commitment to working with her daughters on homework and also volunteers as a parent helper in Alice's Grade 1 class on a weekly basis. Her husband Nat, is also an active participant in the girls' homework routines. Gina squeezes between thirty minutes to an hour's homework each week into her busy timetable of after-school activities, which include tennis, swimming, aerobics, dancing, singing and acting classes. Her mother encourages her in these activities, although they impose a demanding routine. Katya prepares dinner in between picking up the girls from school and supervising homework, before transporting them to their activities, bringing them home and putting them to bed, finally heading off to work night shift at the hospital.

Gina often struggles to complete homework, because of her many extra-curricular activities and because she finds the work difficult. Homework, in fact, is a major source of tension affecting her relationship with her mother. Katya has recently discussed this with Gina's teacher and they have agreed that Gina should work independently without relying on her mother's help, because of the conflict this creates between them. Yet Katya finds it impossible not to intervene because the homework tasks devised by the teachers at Gina's school are complex, often requiring research and writing skills that Gina cannot confidently apply at home. This week, for instance, her homework is to write a report on the effects of the gold rush on Victoria. She sits at the kitchen table, which is covered with papers, pencil cases, an iPad, a laptop and a couple of library books, while her mother prepares an early dinner for her and Alice, which they'll eat before they head off to dance class. Despite Katya's insistence that 'It's your homework', both Gina and her mother are working together on the report. Katya is frustrated at Gina's apparent inability to use the resources assembled on the table to complete the task. The effort required from both of them in order for Gina to write each sentence is intense. It is Katya who reads, identifies and paraphrases the relevant information, all the while peeling carrots and preparing other vegetables. She has neither the time nor expertise needed to scaffold Gina towards the development of these skills. She does not know the necessary strategies for summarising and 'putting it in your own words'.

By contrast, the following vignette provides a glimpse of quite a different set of attitudes and exchanges around the common practice of homework. This vignette focuses on Sam, a classmate of Gina's. Although they are given identical homework tasks, the conditions for doing it are very different for these two children. In reading this vignette, you might like to consider the 'capitals' that Sam's parents are able to draw on as they support him in his education.

Sam, Maya and James: 'Part of the game'

Sam also attends Grevillia Primary School. According to his parents, James and Maya, Sam's experience of school has always been positive: he is articulate, academically and socially able. Sam's attitude towards homework is a mix of resignation and resentment. He would 'rather not have it' and finds it 'a bit boring'. He does homework for 30 to 45 minutes, three nights a week, and despite being resentful, he usually gets involved, and even finds some enjoyment in it, at least according to his father. Sam encounters few problems and is consistently rewarded with positive feedback from his teacher. For this family, the practice of homework produces minimal stress and only occasional conflict. James is a tertiary-educated full-time father, who happily put aside his unsatisfying career in the public service to bring up his children. He draws on abundant supplies of cultural, social and emotional capital to support his children's education. In addition, he is also extensively involved as a volunteer helper at the school: supervising and organising sporting activities, transporting children on excursions, working at the canteen, fund raising, as well as maintaining his children's participation in a wide range of extra-curricular sporting, cultural and social activities.

Sam's parents are often anxious about whether he is sufficiently challenged by homework tasks and is extending himself intellectually. They believe that homework provides an opportunity for children to pursue excellence and develop skills, interests and understandings beyond what is possible within the classroom. They acknowledge homework as 'part of the game' of schooling, and expect that Sam will take homework seriously and may even find satisfaction in it. They want him to challenge himself, but do not wish to compromise their relationship with him by being too demanding. They would like to help him develop the habit of self-critique through dialogue with them. Maya is especially conscious of her role in developing Sam's literacy. She reads his drafts and makes suggestions as to how he can develop his writing. She also encourages him to read and discuss literature. As a homework task each term, Sam and his classmates are required to undertake a literature project, which involves reading a book of their choice and completing three tasks from a wide ranging list of activities. Maya guides Sam's choice of text and activity. She offers him literary books she has read that she predicts he will also enjoy, and helps him to structure his reading so that he completes the book in time. She encourages Sam to do at least one of the more challenging literary tasks, along with the craft, art or quiz-type activities that are usually set.

Reflection and discussion

What similarities and differences have you observed between the ways these families participate in the ritual of homework? It's obvious that Gina is struggling with homework, while for Sam it hardly poses any problems at all. Why might this be so? And what could you do as a literacy educator to help Gina? Should this be the focus for a whole-school literacy policy? If so, what measures do you think should be adopted? What problems do you anticipate might be encountered through implementing it? And how might they be overcome?

Homework can mean different things to different children

For Gina, the family resources that she has available to her for homework are not readily transformed into cultural and intellectual capital (as Pierre Bourdieu would put it) that is useful to her at school. The school emphasises the importance of developing independent learning skills, and sees such skills as being one of the main educational purposes of homework. But this does not get around the fact that Gina is locked into anxious dependence on her mother to provide her with answers. Her anxiety may be somewhat surprising, given the fact that she has ample material resources available to her, such as computers, internet access, relevant information texts, dictionaries and electronic spell checkers. Despite these resources, however, homework serves only to confirm Gina's lack of confidence in her abilities, and she requires intensive support to successfully negotiate the complex literacies involved in writing a research report. Although Katya is willing to help her daughter, the sets of specialist teaching skills required are not available within this family. Nevertheless, project-based work is the predominant form of homework, and this kind of homework is actually requested by the middle-class parents in this school. They view open-ended, independent research tasks as valuable learning opportunities for their children to extend their capacity to express themselves.

Katya does not share this view about the value either of homework or such open-ended tasks. Time is a scarce resource for both her and her daughter. Over-tiredness, interrupted sleep patterns, a demanding job and a commitment to her daughter's education conspire to overstretch Katya, as she struggles to meet the numerous daily deadlines punctuating her domestic and pedagogical work. Katya's philosophical opposition to homework means that she finds it difficult to summon any enthusiasm for it, and so the potential for building intellectual capital for her daughter through her participation is limited. Homework in this household argu-ably functions to reinforce failure, since Gina's poor performance only leads to more hours being spent in doing homework. Katya could be speaking about herself when she comments:

> At this point they have so many pressures and they don't need it. To me it's just one more pressure they don't need.

Despite a plentiful supply of resources, both parent and child experience homework as stressful, emotionally charged and ultimately unattainable.

Reflection and discussion

Imagine that you are Gina and Sam's teacher. How would you negotiate the issue of homework with both them and their parents? How might you be able to elicit the information from each family that we have just presented to you and act upon it? What do you feel the role of parents and other family and community members should be in shaping homework? To what degree do you think homework should be achievable by all students without parental involvement? What forums exist for teachers and parents to communicate and negotiate expectations around homework, not only as a whole school policy but as something that is tailored to the needs of each individual child?

Would it be possible to design homework in such a way that it was explicitly directed at both students and their parents? What might such an approach look like? What rationale could you give for implementing homework in this form?

By contrast, James and Maya, as tertiary-educated professionals, are confident in their knowledge and educational beliefs and even at times assert the superiority of their understandings over those of their teacher. In this family, you can see how homework is a site for 'value adding', where concepts introduced at school are built on through discussion and purposeful parental involvement. James's parents are aware of 'the game' of schooling and are able to effectively mobilise their cultural capital and authoritative knowledge base in order to give him support. They draw on a range of skills and practices from their own educational histories to bolster Sam's confidence and effectiveness as a learner. Within this family, Sam is directed towards cultural activities which signify middle-class status (Bourdieu 1986) and which are rewarded at school: the ability to read and interpret books, to write and perform with an awareness of audience, the confidence to think independently and strive for excellence. You can see how his parents are skilled in supporting the educational work of the school and are able to use their middle-class family 'habitus' to advantage their son in educationally significant ways.

Homework: a community project

Homework is often viewed as an individual responsibility. As we have just seen, Grevillia Primary School regards it as an important means through which to instil in students a sense of the importance of developing independent learning skills. Increasingly, however, schools are recognising their responsibility for scaffolding children into homework practices, providing after-school support for children to get their homework done. Community organisations sometimes set up homework centres to cater for the needs of students whose home life may not support them to successfully complete homework tasks.

The following story (which again derives from Kirsten's research) describes a community centre that addresses the needs of students from culturally diverse backgrounds, many of them refugees. When reading this story, you might like to weigh up the feasibility of such an initiative in other settings. What purposes, beyond enabling students to complete their homework, might be served by such community centres, from your standpoint as a literacy educator? We are presenting the following scene to you in its multi-levelled complexity, presenting detail that shows that the students involved were using the centre for their own purposes, as well as for doing homework. You might like to consider the multiple purposes that the centre serves. You might also speculate about the value of the homework they are required to do, and consider whether it is meaningful to them. Might it be possible for other types of teaching and learning to occur in this space instead of those that are associated with the traditional notion of 'homework'?

Beyond *home* work: community-based literacy spaces

The Brick Street Learning Space is located in an inner-city warehouse in Melbourne and serves as a community education hub for a multi-ethnic, socio-culturally diverse population, which includes refugees from Afghanistan and, most recently, the Sudan. The centre provides adult education, English language classes, vocational and computer classes and offers advocacy, support and information for newly arrived migrants. It also offers a free after-school program in which young people work with volunteer tutors and mentors on homework and creative arts projects, such as music recording and performances, visual arts, filmmaking and photography.

A group of regular Year 8 students, Tahir, Amir, Leo, Senai and Declan, sit around a table working on Maths and Studies of Society and Environment (SOSE) homework. Amir, a highly competent, focused student, confidently occupies the role of Maths tutor, moving around the table, answering questions, directing their endeavours and reassuring his friends as they check their understanding. First, he demonstrates to Tahir with a calculator how to move through a stage he's stuck on. He then explains to Leo, who's uncertain what the question is asking, that he has to find out the length of one side of the triangle. Amir then looks over Declan's shoulder and assures him that he has the correct answer. Senai also has questions about the Maths homework, which Declan offers to explain. She ignores this and instead asks Justin if he's done it and will do hers as well. Justin has his backpack on and is about to go home, but willingly and rapidly completes her sheet before he leaves.

According to Senai, students regularly do one another's homework and teachers never notice. She places two political newspaper articles on the table, which she has to analyse and works on them for about ten minutes, before announcing how boring the task is. She moves to a computer and begins to research an essay on the life of Andy Warhol. Using Google, she types in 'Where was Andy Warhol born?' then pastes the required information into her essay, editing until it becomes 'her own words'.

The co-ordinator, who has been moving between other students working on the computers, delivers two books about Warhol's art and they briefly discuss the images on the covers, although Senai doesn't open the books. While she is writing her essay, Senai takes part in a conversation with some friends from her class on Skype. After five minutes, she gets a blank CD from her bag, opens up a music download site and looks for the tracks she wants. She burns a selection of music and plays samples of the various tracks while she researches and writes her Warhol essay. Her other friends regularly drop in to remind her about dance practice or invite her somewhere, but she stays until she has finished homework due the following day. Unlike the boys, she does not play computer games and instead talks to her friends on Skype and via SMS and listens to music for relaxation while she works.

Amir joins Senai and the others on the computers just after 4 pm and begins playing online computer games while simultaneously listening to sound files for use in his radio show, an English assignment which requires that Year 8 students work in groups to plan and broadcast an hour of music and interviews on a community radio station. As the other boys finish their Maths, they join Amir at the computers, moving between game playing and developing their radio shows.

Reflection and discussion

All the students at the Brick Street Learning Space are 'doing homework', but their ways of completing the tasks are diverse, as are the meanings various students ascribe to homework. You might find it useful to re-read the vignette and to consider the various learning behaviours evinced by the students. Are these patterns of behaviour familiar to you? How do you feel about them? Do you feel that they reflect meaningful learning? Could schools do more to create such spaces for learning?

The opportunity for collaboration between students as they do their homework together is one of the attractions of the centre. Tahir, Amir, Leo and Declan draw on each other's knowledge and expertise to complete their homework. Amir, as a highly competent Maths student, scaffolds the learning of his peers, circulating around the group, answering questions, modelling and reassuring, just as a teacher, tutor or perhaps a parent would. By contrast, Senai takes a more pragmatic approach to the Maths task and simply wants to get it done. She does not seem to find any meaningful learning in the activity and, when a friend is willing to do the work for her, she quickly moves onto the next homework task. The homework tasks her teachers set appear to hold little interest for her and she is intent on moving through them as quickly and efficiently as possible. At the Learning Space, homework nonetheless becomes a collective, shared endeavour, rather than an individualised, solo effort. There is the possibility of enjoying the company of friends, intellectual and emotional support for learning and access to expert assistance and technological resources that may not be readily available in students' homes.

Each experience of doing homework, whether at home alone at a computer or at the kitchen table while dinner is being prepared, or at an after-school program with friends and other adults, reflects the affordances of placed, spatialised literacies.

See the text about place-based pedagogies and multimodal literacies by Barbara Comber, Helen Nixon and Jo-Anne Reid (2007).

In the Brick Street Learning Space, students are free to collaborate in learning, teaching and creating with their peers and with mentors. They move easily between school ordained literacy tasks and their own interests, accessing music and engaging with friends for their own pleasure. This is a 'passionate affinity space' (Gee & Hayes 2011) where everyone can create and everyone can mentor and teach and also be mentored and taught. The boundaries between 'work' and 'play' merge as students freely access the available technological and human resources and use them for their own, unique purposes.

All the vignettes that have been presented nonetheless raise thought-provoking questions about the differences between the activities at home and school and the consequences for literacy learning of students who move between these places. The literacy practices engaged in by the students in these different locations is something to be mindful of when teaching literacy.

Scott Bulfin and Dimitris Koutsogiannis (2012) suggest that teachers need to be wary of setting up home–school binaries, where home literacies are seen as innovative and creative while school literacies are constructed as dreary and dusty. Their research concerning young people's use of digital literacies highlights the ways that young people multi-source their literacies across home and school.

Thinking about how literacies are situated can be a productive way for teachers to work across the domains of home and school. How might homework be conceptualised to enable you as a literacy educator to transcend the divide between school and home literacy practices? What might we learn from the technologically mediated practices of young people (as shown, for example, by the way Senai engaged in a Skype conversation) that might help us to conceive of homework in more innovative ways?

Situated learning

The next story, which draws on research that Glenn has carried out and is narrated by him, tackles this question from another direction.

You might say that his focus is on the literacy practices in which young people engage at home or in their community and how these might suggest ways to rethink the teaching and learning of literacy that occur in school. The setting is an Indigenous community, where Glenn has been inquiring into the way young people can appropriate communication technologies (specifically iPhones) for their own purposes. As we move into this space well beyond any school walls, you might consider the kind of teaching and learning that is occurring, as Rachel Thomas, an Indigenous education worker, engages with Taris about how to use the apps on a mobile phone. What does this vignette suggest about the way we should conceptualise the relationship between school and community? What might we learn from it with respect to the practice of setting homework?

> You can read some of Glenn Auld's work about mediating Ndjébbana on touch screen computers (Auld 2002) and the use of mobile phones in a remote community (Auld 2012).

Learning around a mobile phone in an Indigenous community

I have known Rachel Thomas and her family for over twenty years. As a member of the Kunibídji community, in Arnhem Land in the Northern Territory, Rachel is one of the 250 people in the world who prefer to speak Ndjébbana as their first language. I lived in Rachel's community, learning about teaching for ten years, followed by visits for a period of over another ten years. Whenever I revisit her community I find that am still learning. As part of my research, I was invited by Rachel to observe how her son, Taris, was learning to download songs on a phone. Such visits to Rachel's house are very rewarding as they reveal to me what literacies and practices are valued by Taris in an everyday context.

The sound of the clapsticks becomes louder as I walk to Rachel's house where a funeral procession is happening at a house nearby. When I arrive at Rachel's house, I feel uneasy being the only non-Indigenous person in the vicinity of the funeral. From under the shelter next to

Rachel's house where I am invited to sit, we have a clear view of the funeral events. Rachel explains that it is another clan group and so it is okay to download the songs on the phone.

As an Indigenous education worker and a respected elder in the community, Rachel has a wealth of understanding about education in a remote community. Taris, on the other hand, is more focused on the $30 phone card that I have just given Rachel to recharge the mobile phone for him to download a song for the first time.

Rachel begins by giving the phone to Taris and provides him with instructions in his first language, Ndjébbana, about how to recharge the phone. The only English words that are being spoken represent numbers. Once the phone has been recharged, Rachel provides Taris with instructions in Ndjébbana about how to navigate on the Telstra BigPond site to download a song by Michael Jackson.

To the background of singing in Burarra from the funeral across the road, Taris negotiates instructions in Ndjébbana from his mother about a screen in his hand that displays English to him. I am not sure if Taris or Rachel understands how the buttons on the screen are linked to content sitting on a server somewhere in the world far away from their community.

Taris navigates through the buttons without much of a problem, following the concise instructions provided by Rachel. As he comes to each new screen, Taris shows Rachel the screen so he can navigate through the buttons to the next stage of downloading the song. He is able to search the songs on the Telstra BigPond internet site for Michael Jackson to be downloaded with help from Rachel. She scaffolds the spelling of the words and the graphics on the Telstra site with Taris. Once the search engine has listed all the songs by Michael Jackson, Rachel begins explaining how to scroll down the screen. Here is some of the dialogue in Ndjébbana with translations in English:

Rachel: *Barra-nána Djébba.* (Look that one.)

Rachel: *Number six Barrakanana.* (Look at the number six one.)

Taris: [Busy.]

Rachel: *Ma.* (Yes.)

Rachel: *Djawardaya, Djawardaya.* (Up, Up.)

Taris: *Djíya?* (This one?)

Rachel: *Djawardaya this side.* (Go up this side.)

Rachel: *Djawardaya, djé-yarra.* (Go up that way.)

Rachel: *Koma, djéyabba.* (No, not that way.)

Rachel: *Yaka-ngádja djawardaya.* (Close that one, go up.)

Rachel: One more *djawardaya.* (Go up one more time.)

Taris: *Djíya?* (This one?)

Rachel: *Yaka-ngádja* arrow. (Go where the arrow is pointing.)

Rachel: *Koma djéyabba.* (Not that way.)

Rachel: *Djíya djíya* arrow *dawardaya.* (That one, that one put the arrow up there.)

[Taris pressed another button.]

Rachel: Rub off *djanabera.* (Rub it off you made a mistake.)

Taris: *Agh ngawákka ngawákka ba-kkúndja.* (Agh I will go back, I will go back one more.)

Taris is still having trouble navigating the screen to download his preferred song, and so Rachel uses a number of metaphors to explain how he can move the icon down the screen. There is no word for 'scrolling' in Ndjébbana. Rachel is using the words 'hold' and 'down' in Ndjébbana. These metaphors complement Rachel's hand gesturing that she is using to explain the concept of scrolling on the phone to Taris. He is highly motivated to complete the activity in order to get the song in his phone.

Once Taris finds the song, he checks he has the right one by tapping a button on the screen that plays the first few seconds for free. He confers with Rachel before downloading the song to the phone. Once it is downloaded he touches the speaker button. We can all hear the beat of the Michael Jackson song, which forms a strange contrast to the radically different rhythms of the clapsticks in the background. As the song progresses, Taris begins singing. Meanwhile the women involved in the nearby funeral begin wailing to show their grief.

This story shows the complex teaching and learning that can occur between an adult and a child in a community setting, highlighting the social, cultural and technological contexts of literacy in a home environment. Taris's literacy learning was made possible because of the respect he had for Rachel, her knowledge of the literate activity that he wanted to learn, and her understanding that Taris needed to 'do' the downloading himself, even if he made some mistakes along the way. Besides this knowledge, the activity was also dependent on Taris getting something from being literate, in this case a Michael Jackson song on a mobile phone.

One way to explore these relationships is through the notion of giving a gift. Literacy learning could be seen as a gift to children and young people, as suggested by Alan Luke (2008). Rachel was giving Taris knowledge about how literacy works in the process of downloading a song. Each set of instructions was a new gift to Taris that enabled him to appropriate the skills required under her guidance.

You might like to think about the gifts of literacy you bestow on your students in a school context. Students are happy to receive these gifts when they are motivated by the knowledge that they are achieving something worthwhile through developing their literacy. Your students need to sense that the activity is meaningful, and that it serves a real purpose, just as Taris was motivated to learn because he wanted to download Michael Jackson.

The interactions between Rachel and Taris are complex, showing how literacy happens in everyday informal learning environments outside school. Rachel and Taris are talking in Ndjébbana, one of the three languages they could use to communicate with each other. The screen on a mobile phone, however, is displaying English. This means that both Rachel and Taris are participating in complex interpretive activities that involved switching from one language to the other, as Taris talks and listens to Rachel in Ndjébbana, in between reading and viewing English screen on the phone.

Taris is bombarded with meaning at particular moments in this story, but he persists because of the scaffolding he receives from Rachel, who encourages him to engage in risk-taking. The literacy learning might be said to be local as well as global. The communication on the phone is being mediated by an extensive network coordinated by a server somewhere in the world a long way from their community. Yet Rachel's instructions in Ndjébbana are highly specific to this area of Australia. Without these local and global literacies coming together, Taris would not get his song in this literacy event. He and Rachel are operating at the interface between Ndjébbana and English, and their interactions have a hybrid quality that is rich and complex.

The effectiveness of the scaffolding that Rachel provides derives from the opportunity for Taris to listen and speak in his preferred language, Ndjébbana. Skutnabb-Kangas (2008) suggests people have the right to be educated in their preferred language. The scaffolding upheld Taris's right to engage with others in his preferred language. Tensions are not only the norm for literacy educators, but also for the students they teach. An important dimension of this vignette is that Taris was choosing to pursue his purposes in both languages. As a literacy educator you need to consider the tensions that Taris and many other bilingual children face when they attend school, where these kinds of decisions are made for them in English, as part of the institutionalised practices of literacy education. It is crucial to imagine what it is like to be them, to try to see the world from their standpoint. Becoming a teacher of language and literacy is not just a matter of learning how to teach, but of imagining what it is like for your students to learn.

Reflection and discussion

What literacy purposes does homework serve in your teaching? Does homework help you to cater for the diversity of students within your classroom? Or does it actually disadvantage certain students? Does the homework you set take into account parents, siblings and community networks? How do you design homework in a way that it is not simply an individualistic student endeavour? How might you engage with community 'funds of knowledge' through devising homework tasks? How might you go about ascertaining the beyond-school literacy practices of your students? Might this in itself be posed as a homework task?

Conclusion

Obviously what you take from the stories that make up this chapter will depend on your own approach to teaching literacy and on the community in which you are teaching.

Yet it is worth pausing to think about the differences between home literacies and school literacy practices, and how homework might be used more effectively to bridge the gap between these domains. David Barton (2008) has suggested that different literacies are associated with different domains of life, and this holds true for the literacies of homework, whether it is a matter of family members negotiating around a kitchen table, downloading songs in an Indigenous community, or SMS-ing friends while doing a school assignment in a community centre. By knowing the domains of literacy that students go home to each day, teachers can provide stronger matches between home and school literacies in order to make their learning manageable.

The stories show how homework is completed in domains unique to each individual student. Although all the stories are about homework, you can see that homework signifies something very different in each setting. When designing homework you might consider how various people, places, activities, texts and time constraints mediate the work you receive from your students. You may be blinding yourself (remember the cephalopod metaphor in Chapter 2 of this book!), if you treat homework only as something generic, as though it is simply something that students do.

The stories in this chapter suggest that negotiating with students about their learning could extend beyond the walls of the classroom to take place outside of school. Literacy learning happens outside of school, in the form of a host of everyday events, and we have a professional responsibility as teachers to map this learning onto the curriculum. Sometimes, as happens in the story about Gina and Katya, the homework set by the teacher clashes with the literacy practices of home, suggesting that literacy educators need to develop a better understanding of this difference.

From a very young age, students from marginal backgrounds negotiate a pathway between home and school literacies (Barton 2013). The stories in this chapter have shown the social importance of literacy, and how meanings are socially constructed and negotiated. You might like to explore the out-of-school spaces where your students' literacy learning is taking place. Teachers who look for literacy learning in out-of-school spaces will not only find evidence of the rich diversity of ways in which students are making meaning, they will also gain an insight into what it is to 'be' a young person in changing social and technological times. Understanding how their out-of-school literacy practices might support the developing identities of young people is a strong foundation on which to learning experiences at school.

References

Albright, J & Luke, A (eds) 2008, *Pierre Bourdieu and Literacy Education*, Routledge, New York.

Auld, G 2002, 'What can we say about 112,000 taps on a touch screen computer?', *Australian Journal of Indigenous Education*, vol. 30, no. 1, pp. 1–7.

Auld, G, Snyder, I & Henderson, M 2012, 'Using mobile phones as a placed resource for literacy learning in remote Indigenous communities', *Language and Education*, vol. 24, no. 4, pp. 279–96.

Barton, D 2013, 'The threat of a good example: how ethnographic case studies challenge dominant discourses' in J Kalman & BV Street (eds), *Literacy and Numeracy in Latin America: Local Perspectives and Beyond,* Routledge, New York, pp. 214–19.

Bourdieu, P 1986, 'The forms of capital' in JG Richardson (ed), *Handbook of Theory and Research for the Sociology of Education*, Greenwood Press, Connecticut, pp. 241–57.

Bourdieu, P & Passeron, JP 1990, *Reproduction in Education, Society, and Culture*, Sage in association with Theory, Culture & Society, Department of Administrative and Social Studies, Teesside Polytechnic, London and Newbury Park California.

Bulfin, S & Koutsogiannis, D 2012, 'New literacies as multiply placed practices: expanding perspectives on young people's literacies across home and school', *Language and Education*, vol. 26, no. 4, 331–46. doi: 10.1080/09500782.2012.691515

Comber, B, Nixon, H, Reid, JA & Primary English Teaching Association (Australia) (eds) 2007, *Literacies in Place: Teaching Environmental Communications*, Primary English Teaching Association, Newtown, NSW.

Gee, JP & Hayes, E 2011, *Language and Learning in the Digital Age*, 1st edn, Routledge, Abingdon and New York.

Grenfell, M (ed) 2008, *Pierre Bourdieu: Key Concepts*, Acumen Stocksfield, Durham.

Grenfell, M, Bloome, D, Hardy, C, Pahl, K, Rowsell, J & Street, BV 2012, *Language, Ethnography and Education: Bridging New Literacy Studies and Bourdieu*, Routledge, New York.

Hutchison, K 2011, 'Homework through the eyes of children: what does visual ethnography invite us to see?', *European Educational Research Journal*, vol. 10, no. 4, pp. 545–58.

Hutchison, K 2012, 'A labour of love: mothers, emotional capital and homework', *Gender & Education*, vol. 24, no. 2, pp. 195–212. doi: 10.1080/09540253.2011.602329

Luke, A 2008, 'Using Bourdieu to make policy: mobilising community capital and literacy' in J Albright & A Luke (eds), *Pierre Bourdieu and Literacy Education,* Routledge, New York, pp. 347–62.

Moll, LC, Amanti, C, Neff, D & Gonzalez, N 1992, 'Funds of knowledge for teaching: using a qualitative approach to connect homes and classrooms', *Theory Into Practice*, vol. 31, no. 2, p. 132.

Pahl, K & Rowsell, J 2005, *Literacy and Education: Understanding the New Literacy Studies in the Classroom*, Paul Chapman, London.

Skutnabb-Kangas, T 2008, 'Language rights and bilingual education' in J Cummins & NH Hornberger (eds), *Encyclopedia of Language and Education*, 2nd edn, vol. 5, Springer Science + Business Media LLC, New York, pp. 117–31.

Thomson, P 2002, *Schooling the Rustbelt Kids: Making the Difference in Changing Times*, Allen & Unwin, Crows Nest, NSW.

Chapter 8

Planning for teaching / planning for learning

Gaelene Hope-Rowe and Maria Nicholas

... we must begin from where the children are: ... there can be no alternative ...

James Britton (1972, p. 134)

I can still vividly remember the door closing behind me. Highly respected members of the school community were deciding my fate around a table piled with documents and planners. They were searching for a graduate teacher, a piece of the puzzle, to fit in with their school's philosophy and direction. I nervously approached the panel with a tentative smile and a secret anxiety and sat down ready to hear the verdict that was to decide my immediate future. I studied the panel members' faces for any insight into the result, but clearly they had played poker before. 'Thomas', the Principal started, 'If I understand correctly, you are prepared to go into that classroom with all those students and instil in them a love for learning, so welcome to the school'. We shook hands and the door opened for me. Four years have passed and I am now a Year 6 teacher at a primary school (Preparatory Year to Year 6) along the coast of Southern Australia.

Thomas

In this chapter you will be hearing more from Thomas, and reflecting on the complex decisions he makes when planning for literacy learning and teaching. In addition, you will be presented with two other accounts of planning for learning and teaching: one by Gaelene that arises out of her work as a literacy teacher within a middle years context; the other by Maria about her experiences of whole-school planning within a primary school.

A common theme running through these accounts of planning is the need to focus on the students you are teaching. These days, teachers are expected to plan their lessons and develop curriculum with regard to the outcomes mandated in official curriculum documents. They also need to ensure that what they do accords with whole school policy. Even more pressures can be imposed by the need to ensure that their students are ready for system-wide literacy testing, such as the NAPLAN tests. The paper work required to show that what you are doing accords with official policy can be enormous. With all these demands being made on teachers to comply with policy mandates at a school, state and national level, there is a danger of slipping into box-ticking that loses sight of the students. The three examples of planning presented here reflect a common concern on the part of the teachers involved – Thomas, Gaelene and Maria – to meet whole-school and system-wide curriculum and assessment requirements while remaining responsive to the needs of their pupils.

The stories that comprise this chapter provide examples of planning for learning and teaching, not models. As with all the narratives presented in this book, you are invited to reflect critically on what is being done and to consider whether it is something you might wish to do or whether it would even be feasible to implement such an approach. Although the stories presented in this chapter are quite diverse, they have been chosen to reflect the multiple dimensions of planning, ranging from Thomas's focus on his own class to Maria's account of the dynamics of whole-school planning. Gaelene's story also prompts thought about links between primary school and secondary school and the responsibilities of both primary and secondary teachers for the welfare of pupils as they make the transition from one sector to the other. Taken together, these stories are intended to encourage you to think about all the things you need to consider in order to engage in effective planning, including a knowledge of policy at a school, state and national level, as well as theoretical resources relating to language and literacy development. But before all else, we are asking (echoing the epigraph we have taken from James Britton): how can you ensure that you begin where the children are?

Thomas's story: beginning with the child

Consider this: have there been times when you have felt challenged by the suspicion that the language we use to talk about literacy is inaccessible to students? Would it enable your students to take more ownership of the learning that you are expecting them to accomplish if the official curriculum could be worded in ways that they could understand?

Thomas is one who has faced such a challenge. In Thomas's Year 6 classroom, planning begins with careful assessment of students. The students are placed at the centre of the process as Thomas translates the language of the Australian Curriculum into 'Kidspeak', involving them in goal setting, planning and assessment.

Thomas aims to personalise the learning and to differentiate reading and writing tasks so that all students are working at their instructional level for optimum achievement. In his approach there are strong links between learning, assessment and curriculum planning that are maintained through continuing conversations between the students, parents and himself as the teacher.

Here is how Thomas explains his approach:

For an account of a similar initiative to translate the language of official curriculum into terms which students can use and understand, see Shona's story in Chapter 4.

To meet the fresh challenges that accompanied the introduction of the new national curriculum, I developed a planning and teaching framework that could be used to map the current Language and Literacy skills and understandings for each student from Preparatory right through to Year 10. It takes the teacher curriculum terminology from Level 1 (end of Preparatory), to Level 10 (end of Year 10), and translates it into learning intentions for the students. This way, students know exactly what they're learning, why they're learning it and how their learning can be applied to real life situations. To engage students in reading, they need to see purpose in the activities they complete. Additionally, because the curriculum is translated into simple student-friendly language, the framework can be used to inform my lessons, assessments and reports. I give each of my students a bookmark with the learning outcomes expressed in language that they understand. An example of a student-friendly translation of some of the national curriculum standards into 'Kidspeak' as printed on a bookmark is shown in Table 8.1.

Table 8.1: *Thomas's student bookmark*

LEVEL 4	STRATEGIES TO USE
Standards Statements (Australian Curriculum Assessment and Reporting Authority, n.d.) (not included on the bookmark but included here in bold to show the translation into 'Kidspeak')*	
Students understand how content can be organised using different text structures depending on the purpose of the text: Can I understand at least three pieces of information from a magazine, newspaper, novel, diagram, letter or song? *Analysing newspaper article – Concept map – Character cards – Advertisement – Recipe – Magazine cover – Letter – Art Attack*	Using what I already know Predicting Finding key words Questioning and thinking aloud Reading and retelling Re-reading to check meaning
Students read and view different types of texts, identifying how they vary depending in either complexity and technicality, depending on either the approach to the topic, the purpose and the intended audience: Can I explain why authors write different text types? E.g. Narratives, poems, song, persuasive, newspapers, letters, postcards, advertisements, signs and magazines. *Advertisement – Teacher conference – Letter to character – Narrative music – Interview author – Read and create poetry*	Using what I already know Asking why the author wrote it Asking who s/he is writing it for Looking at the text structure and layout Looking at the pictures and other visual effects Looking for key words (connectives) Predicting and confirming Inferring and drawing conclusions
Students build literal and inferred meaning to analyse and evaluate texts, for example making inferences about a person's motivations and intentions and consider how this impacts on the audience Can I predict and infer events in my novel? Can I explain how it will affect the characters and plot? *Little Bebop – Sticky notes – See, think, wonder – Re-write final chapter – Greatest performance*	Using what I already know Retelling events Finding key events Re-reading to check meaning Predicting Summarising characters and plot Inferring and drawing conclusions
Students recognise how authors and illustrators choose techniques to hold a reader's attention and elicit an emotional response. Can I relate the information in a novel to something that happens in real-life? *TV broadcast part 1/2 – Venn diagram – Interview character – Newspaper headline/picture – BTN – Life – Culture shift*	Retelling and re-reading Summarising Picturing events and characters Activating prior knowledge Linking to what I already know Inferring and drawing conclusions

Students identify and explain characteristic text structures and language features used in a range of imaginative, informative and persuasive texts to meet the purpose and audience of the text.

Can I understand that some texts are written for different audiences?

Advertisement – Teacher conference – Letter to character – Narrative music – Interview author

Asking why the author wrote it

Asking who s/he is writing it for

Predicting and confirming

Looking at the text structure and layout

Looking at the pictures and other visual effects

*Outcomes statements in official curriculum documents, such as the Australian Curriculum, can change. The key point that Thomas is making concerns the desirability of translating existing outcomes statements into language that is accessible to a wider audience, including students.

I felt that this framework would be a good way to combine the explicit reading strategies that were taught in many literacy programs operating in schools, with the expectations in the national curriculum. I was aware that the CAFE (Boushey & Moser 2009) and the Fountas and Pinnell (2010) 'Benchmark Assessment System' were popular literacy resources that were used by many teachers and schools. Our school was using both, so I incorporated elements of both to make the framework a flexible 'living' thing that I could own, as well as my students. Visiting teachers often asked me if the framework I was using was only suitable for one particular aspect of literacy teaching. My answer was no, and that was what made it so effective. The framework was designed with a need to focus on the explicit teaching of reading strategies, with room to add and change the strategies, whenever I hear of and learn of other strategies that might work with my students.

The student bookmark that Thomas designed to accompany his framework is one way he makes the curriculum accessible, involving them in a conversation about their learning by providing a shared language for understanding and communication.

Reflection and discussion

What steps do you take in your own planning to make the curriculum accessible to students? Do you think that Thomas's strategy would enhance their learning? How would you be able to gauge that you have successfully opened up the curriculum, enabling them to take ownership of their learning?

Thomas certainly feels that his initiative has been successful, though he needed to go further, as he explains:

My students were starting to take control of their learning and monitoring their progress. However, after using the bookmarks I realised that engaging them in the conversation wasn't enough to engage them in learning. I needed to involve them in planning as well. I wanted to incorporate explicit teaching of reading; I wanted students to write their own learning intentions, success criteria and reading and writing goals; I wanted them to self-assess and peer-assess in each lesson … but how? That's when I decided to design a planner with the students. A planner would allow students to use their bookmark to choose an appropriate learning intention that would be specific to their needs.

A short example of a student's planner is included in Table 8.2.

Table 8.2: *Excerpt from a student's planner*

SESSION 40–50 MIN	ACTIVITY LEARNING INTENTION SUCCESS CRITERIA	MATERIALS	SELF-ASSESSMENT	PEER ASSESSMENT
1	Act: Analyse a newspaper **Learning intention:** – Can I understand three pieces of information from a newspaper? **Success criteria:** – I can find an interesting newspaper article. – I can identify who wrote it, when it was written and for which paper.	Newspaper Laptop computer Pen English book Scissors	I rate myself 8/10. I found an interesting article, but it was a slightly above my level. I could still identify the main parts of the article.	9/10. Even though the student didn't find an article at his level, the student still achieved his success criteria.

By taking this initiative, Thomas became aware of even further ways in which he might involve his students in their own learning.

Now I had a new challenge. Students knew what they needed to do to learn and how to plan their own learning, but not how to get there. I thought, 'Wouldn't it be good if they could independently access activities that would provide evidence of their learning?' So I provided around eighty activities written in student-friendly language with step-by-step instructions that directly targeted the students' learning intentions and goals. These were open-ended, differentiated and catered for different learning styles. For example, some students visited an Art Attack online video, which ran through hundreds of different art creations that could be completed using simple school materials. Students watched and followed the instructions to create art pieces of their own and then wrote the procedure for another student. Other students then read and used those instructions to make the same product without the video. This task allowed for higher order thinking, as some students were able to suggest different ways to improve the same item or plan a design for the product. Others who enjoyed debating researched a controversial issue of their choice, and shared a 'monologue debate' where they debated the arguments of two personalities in front of the class by themselves. By filming the debate and receiving feedback from peers, the students were using self-assessment and peer-assessment strategies respectively. We were also engaged in conversations about the purposes and audiences for texts, and the links between reading, writing, speaking and listening.

The process did not stop there, but as Thomas explains it also had implications for assessment and reporting.

There was now one final piece missing in the jigsaw of planning and assessment: how to communicate outcomes to students, teachers and parents. I had the answer right in front of me. Once students had planned their activity, completed it, self-assessed, peer-assessed and then finally conferred with the teacher, we now had evidence of student learning sitting on the table for all to see and discuss. Students used this in their digital portfolios. They uploaded self-assessments and student–teacher conferences to the school website or Web 2.0 site so that parents could connect and take part in the conversations no matter where they were.

And so the cycle began again.

This approach provided Thomas with an individualised diagnostic assessment approach that established each student's entry-level achievement within the national curriculum. It gave Thomas and his students 'pre-test' assessment information, which assisted them to select appropriate classroom activities that would target specific learning outcomes for each child. As the literacy program proceeded, Thomas and his students progressively accumulated evidence of outcomes that had been met, working together to realise each student's individualised reading and writing goals.

The process that Thomas recounts illustrates the way teachers continually reflect on their teaching practice. Thomas was continually questioning, trialling and reviewing his practice and the way he went about planning for learning and teaching. He began with a suspicion that the students' learning might be enhanced if he were able to devise a strategy that made the language of the curriculum accessible to them, and through implementing this strategy he was then able to take other initiatives that gave the students even more ownership of their learning.

You might now find it useful to reread Thomas's account of his initiatives, asking yourself the following questions.

Reflection and discussion

What educational ideals seem to motivate Thomas? Do you share those ideals? How do you gauge the success of the initiatives that he has taken? Do you think that such initiatives would work in schools in which you have taught? Can you think of other ways in which students might play an active role in curriculum planning and assessment?

Gaelene's story: working with tensions and debates in literacy

We shall now consider a rather different example of planning for literacy learning and teaching, drawing on Gaelene's experience as a teacher within a middle years literacy program in a large secondary college in a coastal town in Australia. Gaelene has extensive experience as a primary school teacher, but she currently finds it professionally rewarding to work part time as the co-ordinator and teacher of students with additional needs at this school, as well as working at a university as a lecturer in curriculum and pedagogy.

When reading the following account of Gaelene's work, you might ask yourself many of the same questions that you have just asked in response to Thomas's story, but you will also be prompted to think about other issues, including how students' literacy learning can be sustained as they move from primary school to secondary school.

What is a middle years learner?

The 'middle years learner' is typically positioned between the later primary school years and the first few years of secondary schooling. In chronological years this may extend from around eight or nine years to thirteen or fourteen years. A key challenge they face relates to the transition from primary school to their secondary education, especially with respect to the literacy demands that this transition involves.

'Middle years learners' have been typically characterised by various educational stakeholders as learners who are sophisticated users of new communications media and technologies, have more exposure to popular and mass culture messages, are more heavily influenced by their peers than significant adults, are 'at-risk' of educational disengagement and under-achievement and are more demanding with respect to how the knowledge, skills and values that teachers and schools promote connect with their world.

Victoria Carrington explores middle years learners in the following text: Carrington, Victoria 2006, *Rethinking Middle Years: Early Adolescents, Schooling and Digital Culture*, Allen & Unwin, Crows Nest NSW. You might also find it interesting to read the ALEA journal, *Literacy Learning: The Middle Years* journal, which, as its name indicates, focuses on literacy issues in the middle years.

In response to such perceptions, schools approach 'the middle years' as a time where curriculum, pedagogy and assessment should be more connected to the world of adolescence, more intellectually demanding overall, developing higher-order thinking and more problem-based.

With respect to language and literacy, middle years learners are expected to read silently and with increasing speed to gain meaning from a wider range of texts, critically engage with an increasing range of multimedia and print-based texts, write independently, utilising a range of genres across various subject areas and use new and emerging forms of communication and technologies.

This, at least, is how the 'middle years' are often constructed, but you might pause to consider whether such perceptions paradoxically promote a 'one-size-fits-all' approach to the teaching and learning of literacy with such students, rather than really providing for their individual needs.

How do you feel about the 'middle years'? Do you feel that this classification really captures a distinctive phase in the development of young people?

Reflection and discussion

When reading Gaelene's story about the various strategies she uses to help students with literacy difficulties you might also consider how her pedagogy fits within this conception of the 'middle years learner'.

Throughout her teaching experiences in mainstream primary and secondary education, and now her work with students who may be deemed to be 'at-risk' or as having additional needs, Gaelene has been engaged in literacy debates, or in what one academic has styled as the 'literacy wars' (Snyder 2008). Debates over the effectiveness (or lack thereof) of this or that literacy approach have often been constructed by the media as responses to an ongoing 'literacy crisis' in Australian society, and they are often bound up with complex social and economic changes. Literacy educators themselves have been swept up in these debates, often arguing among themselves about the best approach to literacy teaching. Gaelene remembers times in the 1980s and early 1990s when heated arguments about 'process' or 'genre' approaches to teaching writing occurred between participants at conferences and professional development seminars.

If you would like to read more on these arguments, you might care to look at Ian Reid's book, *The Place of Genre in Learning*, which was published in 1984. Both *English in Australia* and the *Australian Journal of Language and Literacy* have featured articles about genre pedagogy over the past two to three decades.

Gaelene became personally involved in these debates, and they still influence her practices today, being key moments in the formation of her identity as a literacy educator. It has been argued, for example, that from the early 1970s until the mid-1980s, education was heavily influenced by 'growth pedagogy' or 'whole language', a progressive educational philosophy that emphasised the importance of 'natural' models of learning. Process approaches to teaching writing were considered by their advocates to be the best way to encourage children to express their personal 'voice' and individual points of view through writing.

> For an understanding of process approaches to the teaching of writing see Calkins (1983, 1991, 1994) and Graves (1983, 1986). The emphasis of such approaches is on negotiating with students the topics they would like to write about and the form their writing might take. Teachers encourage students to draft their work and then to seek feedback from others in order to craft the writing further.

But in the mid-1980s and 1990s a number of researchers and teachers began to identify problems with process approaches, arguing that they were not adequate to meet the needs of the groups of children who continued to experience educational disadvantage, including those from low socio-economic groups and from minority cultures with languages in addition to English.

Children have diverse cultural and linguistic resources, and some researchers argued that practices and strategies associated with whole language and process approaches to writing privileged mainstream, mostly white, middle-class children.

> For examples of such critiques of whole language and process pedagogy see Barrera (1992), Delpit (1986, 1988), Dressman (1993), Dyson (1992), Lensmire (1994, 2000), Reyes (1992) and Spiegel (1992).

Many of these studies criticised so-called progressive approaches for emphasising the particular discourse patterns, interactional styles and spoken and written language codes of predominantly white, middle-class student populations and their teachers. They argued that, in some contexts, the explicit teaching of the rules, including the conventions associated with the literacy practices of the dominant culture, is necessary in order for children from minority cultures and disadvantaged groups to experience success in reading and writing. Emphasis on individual choice in topics, purposes and forms for writing was seen to limit the range of text types that students typically used to narrative and recount (Martin & Rothery 1986). Advocates of a genre-based approach, proposed as an 'alternative' to process writing, believed that a focus on the explicit teaching of specific genres in writing would expand the children's repertoire of texts and allow non-mainstream and disadvantaged students access to the language of power (Martin 1989; Rothery & Martin 1986).

Reflection and discussion

Have you been involved in debates with colleagues about approaches to teaching English literacy? How did you resolve any differences between your approaches when planning with colleagues?

It is worthwhile to familiarise yourself with key aspects of the debates about whole language and genre approaches. (Note that many teachers drew on a combination of approaches in attempt to take a balanced approach to the teaching of literacy.) It is, after all, important to implement a pedagogy that is fully informed by research on the teaching of writing, even though you might modify what you take from such research in the light of your own teaching experience. You can access the debates about process and genre by chasing up some of the references in this chapter.

In the meantime, you might pause to consider whether in your experience some approaches to literacy teaching privilege some social groups over others. This is an issue that has always concerned literacy educators, as you can see if you revisit Chapter 2 of this book and consider the account given there of Shirley Brice Heath's work.

It seems difficult to escape the conclusion that there will always be debates and tensions within the field of literacy education, as shown by other chapters in this book. This is because literacy is complex, and people will inevitably have different views about how it should be taught. Unfortunately, while debates can be valuable, prompting teachers to think critically in an effort to improve their practice, they can also polarise, with some people adopting a 'one-size-fits-all' approach. The teaching and learning of literacy is far more complex than simply jumping on the latest pedagogical bandwagon. It is important to keep an open mind, viewing the ideas, theories and approaches that you come across as a smorgasbord from which to choose, as you consider the diverse needs of every new cohort or problem of practice that you face.

Planning for learners from diverse backgrounds in a middle years context

Can you imagine a class of children who are all exactly at the same level of development, from exactly the same socio-economic and cultural background, with exactly the same access to resources, and with exactly the same life experiences and attitudes to learning? The reality is that classrooms always comprise diverse learners, although that diversity can be wider in some settings rather than others. This is what makes planning for learning and teaching such demanding (and professionally rewarding) work. In the following story Gaelene shares with you her own challenges when catering for the needs of a diverse group of 'at-risk' literacy learners within a middle years setting.

I sit with long lists of test scores, piles of samples of writing and teacher feedback sheets, all in an effort to sift through and identify 'at-risk' students. As coordinator of additional needs students I select students in Years 7 to 9 for various Literacy Support programs based on a variety of assessments, primarily in Reading. I use scores and levels from standardised tests and on-line tests based on levels 1–10 in the national curriculum, and I ask for recommendations from English subject area teachers. I also look at past reports and transition information from primary schools, if there is any. But although these are valuable, I still feel the need to gather more data. If students are three or more year levels below their expected level, they are listed to receive small group assistance, and, in the case of Indigenous students, one-to-one tutoring. About one in five students need additional assistance of some sort. I try to select them discreetly, but the program has been running for three years now, and there's not the same stigma attached to working in Literacy Support. So I take the lists and, together with teachers, select the students we think could benefit. We look at each student's desire to achieve, degree of need, age, potential for positive improvement, attendance records and behaviour in mainstream classes. I send letters home, but in the end it is the students and the parents who make the decision whether they will participate.

Rowe, G, Daly, M,Lamont, H, Edwards, D & Mayor Cox, S 2000, *Success with Reading and Writing: Helping At-Risk Students 8–13 Years, Teacher Manual*, Dellasta, Melbourne.

We keep the groups small for intervention/support on a regular basis for several weeks, but the classes don't replace mainstream English classes. Testing in reading is the starting point, but then during classes I try to build a picture of each student as a literacy learner and their particular area of need. This isn't easy because literacy is multifaceted and hard to explain, let alone assess accurately. I use things like the BURT word test, South Australian Spelling Test, Peter's Dictation, Progressive Achievement Test – Reading (PATR) and Reading For Understanding Running Records in (Rowe, Lamont, Daly, Edwards & Mayor Cox 2000).

The English teachers are pretty happy with the withdrawal aspect of Literacy Support because they're not sure how to deal with 'these students' (as they call them) whose levels are low to mid Primary levels. They sometimes ask me: 'Shouldn't they already be literate? Why didn't they learn to read in primary school? Can't the problem be solved by preventing reading difficulties early on?'

Kids with low literacy levels sometimes display behaviour problems in class, and so they spend a lot of time in the RP (Restorative Practices) room. A good way to get out of Reading and Writing is to mess up in class. Other subject area teachers are at a loss to know how to engage such low literacy students in Science or History or Maths, and many don't think it's their job to teach students to read and write. I have given them a copy of The Four Resources Model but there's a long way to go with this.

The Four Resources Model refers to 'four roles' of the reader outlined in the following article: Freebody, P & Luke, A 1990, 'Literacies programs: debates and demands in cultural context', *Prospect*, pp. 5, 7–16. The same authors later rephrased their model as 'four practices' which include: the code-breaker, text participant, text user and text analyst (Luke, A & Freebody, P 1999). Map of possible practices: further notes on the four resources model (*Practically Primary*, vol. 4, no. 12, pp. 5–8).

Careful selection and assessment of students is important to Gaelene's practice, as is communication with teachers. At the same time, she raises questions about the perceptions of the English teachers and teachers of other discipline areas within secondary school who do not appear to be prepared to identify themselves as 'teachers of literacy'.

In her story, Gaelene mentions that the Four Resources Model can be used by educators from discipline areas other than English as a framework for the teaching of literacy. This model can assist educationalists to adopt a balanced approach to literacy education and to plan for and monitor the resources or strategies that students adopt when they are reading and writing. The model also assists teachers to plan for and monitor subject literacies (Queensland School Curriculum Council 2001).

Reflection and discussion

Why do you feel that some students continue to require additional support when they enter secondary school? You would have noted that the secondary school teachers with whom Gaelene is working seem to blame primary teachers for not ensuring that students learn to read. Do you feel that this kind of accusation is warranted? How might secondary school teachers address the needs of students who require additional support? What might primary school teachers do to help their students cope with the literacy demands associated with each subject area when they arrive at secondary school? How might secondary teachers and primary teachers work together to ensure that the literacy needs of students are met during this transition phase?

Gaelene continues with her account of the kind of preparation she feels obliged to do in order to address the needs of her students.

I plan the Year 7, 8 and 9 programs by beginning with Reading comprehension. The school has been working on improving reading engagement and comprehension for the past three years. It's part of the school's Strategic Plan. So explicit teaching of reading comprehension is a key part of Literacy Support classes. I use the comprehension processes and strategies of Snowball (2006) and Munro (2006) with the students in order to talk about reading comprehension processes like predicting, questioning, thinking aloud, using text structures and features, visualising and summarising or paraphrasing. Some students don't have, or can't remember strategies to help them solve problems when they read in order to gain meaning. We use these during shared reading, guided reading and reciprocal reading. These strategies are used in other programs and considered effective intervention/support strategies. A lot of students can't or don't want to read because they think it's about saying the words right, and so I spend time boosting their confidence by convincing them that they are reading if they can gain meaning from the text, even if they don't know all the words. Reading is a meaning-making activity, or it is nothing at all.

I use 'Hand', 'Head' and 'Heart' questions to prompt reading for meaning. The posters I have on the wall explain these as literal, inferential and evaluative/response levels of comprehension. I try to get them to read critically with the evaluative/response type questions and I mainly use newspapers for this. The local paper is good, because the text isn't too difficult, but there is a problem with suitable materials for this, as the topics don't always interest the kids. With guided silent reading (New Zealand Department of Education 1983) most can be guided to form an opinion on an issue. Guided Silent Reading asks that students read silently in response to posed questions with discussions that follow (commonly used in the middle years).

My reading of debates about genre approaches linked to diversity and disadvantage means that I am always talking about purposes, structures and text types, as I link them together and I try to use the language that's employed in some standardised tests, such as: What is the purpose of this text? Why did the author write this text? Who might read this text? Why? We begin with finding main ideas and supporting ideas in short factual DVDs and print texts. A lot of kids can't find the main ideas to begin with, but they engage with the DVDs and learn to identify facts and main ideas. Students record the main ideas on a graphic organiser and use it to retell/report in pairs. We talk constantly about purposes of reports, who writes reports and why, what makes a good report and how we go about writing reports. I do some modelled writing and they give oral reports or some might write short reports or just a paragraph.

Many of these 'at-risk' students are reluctant writers and rarely write voluntarily. They have little understanding of what makes a piece of writing 'good' and how to improve their own and other's writing. It's a struggle to get them to write anything, and so we have response journals in which teachers and students write to each other. It's like free writing, we don't correct it, it's just personal writing about interests, learning and school.

Throughout the weeks in Literacy support we work through different structures like time–order, cause–effect, problem–solution, one point of view–another point of view. We use multimodal texts, as well as texts they read and write in subjects such as Science and History. We look at cause–effect structures in their Science texts and time–order structures in History texts. Some kids make the connections and others don't. Figure 8.1 shows how it fits together.

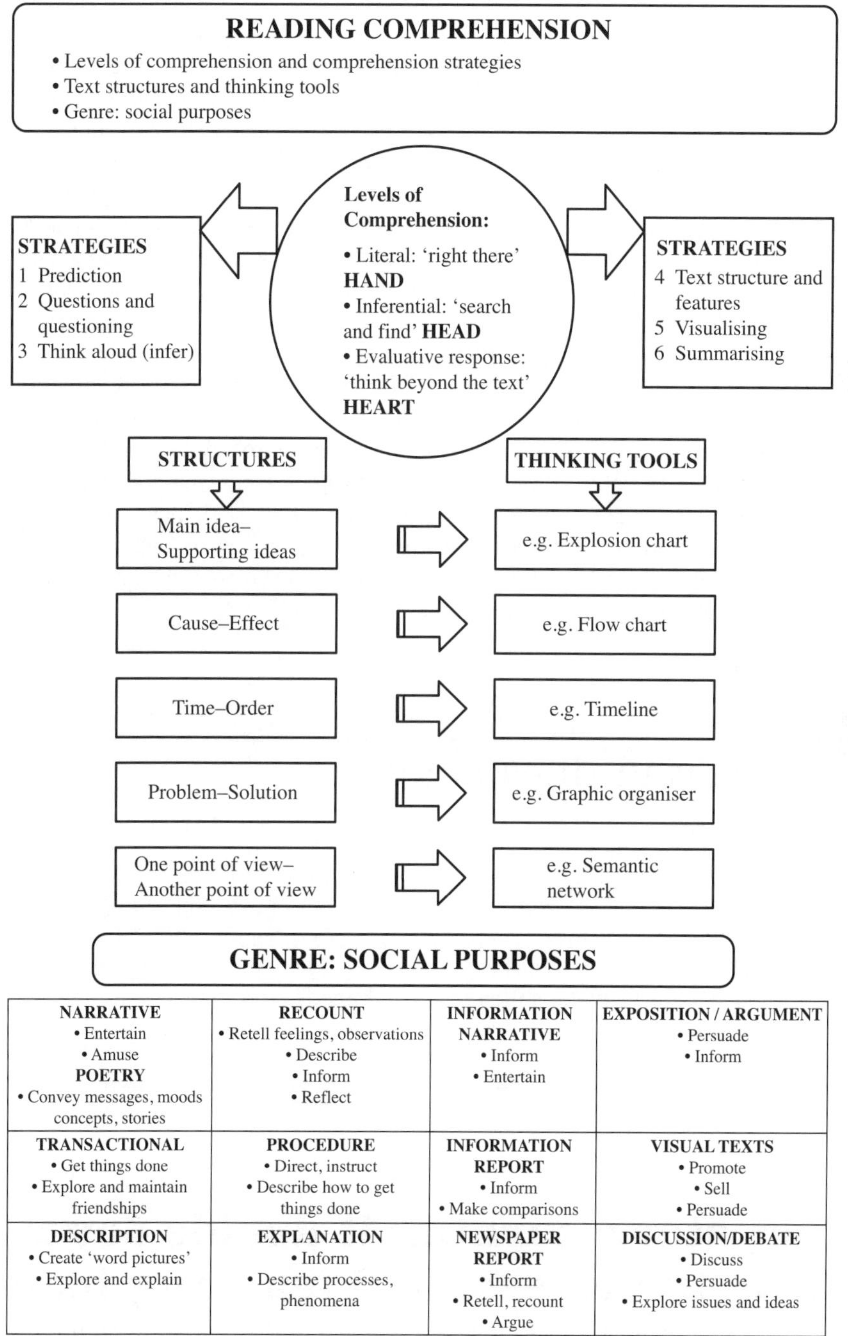

NARRATIVE	RECOUNT	INFORMATION NARRATIVE	EXPOSITION / ARGUMENT
• Entertain • Amuse **POETRY** • Convey messages, moods concepts, stories	• Retell feelings, observations • Describe • Inform • Reflect	• Inform • Entertain	• Persuade • Inform
TRANSACTIONAL • Get things done • Explore and maintain friendships	**PROCEDURE** • Direct, instruct • Describe how to get things done	**INFORMATION REPORT** • Inform • Make comparisons	**VISUAL TEXTS** • Promote • Sell • Persuade
DESCRIPTION • Create 'word pictures' • Explore and explain	**EXPLANATION** • Inform • Describe processes, phenomena	**NEWSPAPER REPORT** • Inform • Retell, recount • Argue	**DISCUSSION/DEBATE** • Discuss • Persuade • Explore issues and ideas

Fig. 8.1: *A planning template developed and used by Gaelene*

Gaelene also integrates the teaching and learning of reading, writing and speaking tasks by drawing on some aspects of genre approaches. In this respect, she experiences some tensions, as she explains in the following reflection:

> I don't really follow the curriculum cycle proposed in some genre-based teaching models (Macken 1989). We talk about the purposes and structures and features of texts as we read and view a range of texts, and link short speaking and writing tasks to the genres. I try to engage students in learning by linking tasks and experiences to their interests. So I choose content, a subject, a topic or an issue to explore as they are learning skills and concepts. At present we are exploring the natural environment and issues related to sustainability. I have heaps of great resources such as nature and travel DVDs, posters, catalogues and picture books, and *National Geographic* magazines and interactive whiteboard resources. Students pore over the fishing, hunting and surfing magazines during quiet reading and flick through the *Motorcycle Trader*, *Motor Trend* and *Classic Car* magazines any chance they get. They Google all kinds of facts about whales, crocodiles and other deadly creatures and really get into adventure movies that pit humans against the wilds of the environment. All of this gives me a context to explore some big picture ideas related to sustainability, like water conservation, alternative energies, biodiversity and climate change. This is the way I planned in upper primary year levels when I developed inquiry units of work and used strategies for integrated learning (e.g. Murdoch [1998]), so I follow this design model. It gives me a context to do some vocabulary work and spelling linked to the inquiries.

Reflection and discussion

How would you describe Gaelene's pedagogy? Can you identify specific examples where she appears to be influenced by one theoretical position rather than another? She says that 'explicit teaching of reading comprehension is a key part of Literacy Support classes'. What kind of rationale would you give for 'explicit teaching'? Why would this help students who are 'at-risk'? What is the purpose of 'free writing'? Why might this be of benefit to her students? What strategies does she appear to use in order to 'engage' students in their learning? What do you believe is necessary to facilitate student engagement? Would any of these strategies that she mentions be useful when working with high-achieving students?

Maria's story: turning it upside down: working in professional learning teams

The two previous stories about Gaelene's professional practice have opened up some of the multiple dimensions of planning for learning and teaching literacy.

No teacher plans in isolation, but his or her practice is mediated in complex ways by a wealth of considerations, not least the need to work within mandated curriculum frameworks and school policy. In Chapter 2, Rachel recalls the conflict she was experiencing between conforming with school policy and her desire for greater professional autonomy. To lessen her anxiety, one of her colleagues told Rachel to simply close her classroom door and do what she liked! Whether this is really an option is an open question – it is clear from Rachel's story that she continued to grapple with tensions in her efforts to address the needs of her students. And it is important to recognise that collaborating with others in order to plan for learning and teaching is not necessarily a bad thing. The activity of planning can generate a sense on the part of teachers of shared responsibility, not only for the welfare of students in their individual classrooms but for the welfare of students throughout the school. It can produce a sense of belonging to a professional community where everyone is working together for the benefit of all students.

Maria's story focuses on the complexities that arise when staff plan together, exploring both the challenges and the positive outcomes that can occur when staff engage in this process. It is divided into two parts: the first is a somewhat critical account of planning with one group of teachers, and the second is a more positive account, when Maria found the quality of the discussion much more satisfying. An experienced teacher who has taught in both primary and secondary school settings, she has been extensively engaged in collaborative planning. A key challenge, as she sees it, is to ensure that students remain at the centre of the planning process, when staff collaboratively take steps to ensure that they do not lose sight of their students.

As you read through the first example of planning, consider how it compares with your own experiences, especially planning that moves beyond your own classroom to involve other colleagues. This is the first part of Maria's story.

My experience of planning meetings has been one of hour-long sessions focused on packing in as much administrative information as possible. Excursions, incursions, reporting, resources, timetabling and the day-to-day business of teaching were the topics of conversation.

When units of inquiry have been reviewed it has often been a case of 'show and tell', with experienced teachers showing their breadth of knowledge and accumulated resources on the topic and less experienced teachers either feeling inadequate or madly sourcing resources that they can share. For graduate teachers or teachers new to a department, the lead-up to these meetings is often stressful and highlights their inexperience, placing the more experienced teacher in a position of authority and superiority. There is rarely engagement in reflective, collaborative discussion.

When we talk about teaching in such meetings, it is more a case of the expert teacher or a member of the leadership team passing on knowledge to those of us who are less knowledgeable. We listen attentively and leave with a checklist or formula to follow to make sure that our teaching was 'effective'. Some checklist items that I recall have included:

- Did we have all the elements of the e5 instructional model: engage, explore, explain, elaborate, evaluate? (Department of Education and Early Childhood Development 2013)

- Have we planned for whole–part–whole teaching and learning?

- Have we made use of Web 2.0 technologies in the classroom?

I can see the merit of such foci and have experienced some successes through their implementation, but over time I became concerned that these discussions were focused on the teacher with little mention of the child.

This is not uncommon practice. A study conducted into the professional development required to achieve positive student outcomes found that there was little impact on student learning when the focus remained on 'desirable teaching behaviours that should be implemented', rather than on the identification of 'a specific problem to solve or goal to achieve' (Timperley, Parr & Bertanees 2009, p. 231). This means remaining attentive to the behaviours of children in your classroom, trying to learn from your observations of their learning and the work that they produce. The focus on children can be lost in the planning process if the focus is on the implementation of a teaching template or a particular instructional model.

Wiggins & McTighe (2005) find that primary schools typically have a heavy focus on the activities that could be used in the hope that learning occurs, whereas secondary schools focus more on coverage – have we covered all the content that needs to be covered in this subject? In both cases, whether the discussion is related to the activities or to content, the focus is on what teachers intended to teach, and not on the learning that might occur or what the children might bring with them into the classroom.

However, Maria's story does not end here, with her unease about the way planning meetings tended to focus on teaching rather than learning. The second part of her story has a more positive outcome. It explores a transformation that occurred in the interactions that took place when Maria began teaching in the early years of primary school, when she became part of a new teaching team. Her team meetings during the year involved an initial change in focus that acted as a catalyst for more generative planning. Here there was a shift from a focus on teaching to a focus on learning and a move towards reflective, collaborative discussion.

More than a number: sitting in on a team meeting

At the end of a long day, we filed into the leader's classroom in dribs and drabs, talking to each other about our daily challenges, our triumphs and after-school plans, bending the ear of a sympathetic other. Prefaced with a dramatic glance down at her watch, the leader called us to attention, handing out the agenda and launching into the first item with little preamble. Having assessed all of our students on their reading skills as per our school's mandated testing schedule, we were to discuss our students' outcomes. We looked at those outcomes as an overall average reading level score and we looked at the individual outcomes of all of our students. We compared our students' outcomes with each other and with the outcomes that they received the year before. Nothing new there. This was a practice we were used to and the script was one we could have recited from previous years.

By the end of the previous year, all except one child had achieved the minimum benchmark level in reading and it appeared that we were well on the way to achieving the same outcome this year as well. We could have chosen to tick that box on our administrative checklist, pat ourselves on the back and then move on to the next agenda item, as had been our common practice. But on this occasion something transformative happened that took us in a new direction. Rather than discussing what we were going to teach next, with a cursory comment that linked back to the data we'd just looked at, we chose to dig deeper. 'But what learning has really occurred?', we asked. 'Reading a text demonstrates that a child can decode text, but what skills, strategies and understandings have they learned to use through the process?' 'How does this tell me Johnny or Jane's story so that I know what to teach next?' A reading level, a number, were summary judgements that could not answer those questions. Our leader paused for a moment, pushed her copy of the agenda aside and said, 'Let's talk about that'.

That day, we began to question intensely what we should be expecting of our students. Returning to the curriculum, we familiarised ourselves with the achievement standards from a number of levels. The curriculum indicated that at the foundational level students were expected to be able to make text-to-self connections, predict and question. The next level, level one, asked that students use text-to-self connections to explain characters and main events, and that at the next level up, level two, students are able to make text-to-text connections to inform their deeper understanding of the text. Through these professional conversations we developed a greater appreciation for where our students were heading and how the skill of reading developed in complexity and built on the skills that came before.

Through such processes teachers can come to appreciate the limitations of the data used to inform teaching. If such data do not appear to provide any valuable insights into students' learning, then teachers can jointly decide to refine those assessments or replace them with other assessments that are more diagnostic or formative in their function. Data that simply categorises students as belonging to a certain level do not necessarily show how you might scaffold them into higher learning. In addition to summative assessments, it is also necessary to implement formative assessment that provides a more nuanced picture of a child's language and learning.

As teachers we need to see purpose to our engagement in the planning process. That process should be akin to inquiring into our professional practice, addressing both our own needs and those of our students. We also need to connect with our prior knowledge and to think about how that knowledge might be transformed by what we are learning now.

> Maria and her colleagues were embarking on a cycle of collaborative inquiry that is similar to those discussed in Chapter 3. When interrogating your own practice it can be useful to consider various models of inquiry to assist you or the groups you work with to improve performance through the identification and setting of goals, self-regulation and reflection.

Above all, we need to go away from such meetings with a view to implementing new ideas and exploring new strategies that might answer some of the questions we have raised. Otherwise we run the risk of simply reverting to our previous practice the moment we leave the meeting.

A few weeks later: sitting in on another team meeting

> At the end of a long day, we filed into the leader's classroom in dribs and drabs, talking to each other about our daily challenges, our triumphs and students … yet this time it was different. This time our conversations were centred around our changes to our literacy practices. There was no glancing at watches or handing out of agendas. We knew the main topic of conversation and launched into the meeting without pausing for breath.
>
> One teacher shared how she made displays and referred to them periodically when reading a text, asking students what connections they were making and how they were interpreting what they had read, based on those connections. Asking students to reflect and interpret was part of her prior practice, but it was now more structured, scaffolded and explicit, as she was referring to the displays when asking the students to consider their interpretations. She engaged students in deep conversations, respecting their prior experiences, knowledge and reflections, respecting them as equals

rather than 'fishing' for predetermined answers. Another teacher mentioned that she often modelled this behaviour when reading aloud but had not explicitly explained the strategies she used to assist her in making those connections. This helped her to explain her 'think aloud' to the students and assisted her with her choice of language when seeking to engage them in deep conversations and to help her students to explain their own thinking. I explained that I often asked my students to predict what the text would be about, when first looking at the cover and when stopping strategically throughout a text. I integrated this focus into my prior practice by asking students to make connections to self, other texts and world, listing these on the board and then using their collective knowledge, understandings, experiences and connections to inform predictions.

This sharing of practices and resources did not feel like a 'show-and-tell' session. Everyone felt as though they could contribute, no matter how many years of experience they had. This put everyone on a level playing field, with the child squarely within focus. This also led us to reflect on how we could better gather data on our students' abilities to make more informed judgements.

This meeting generated plans for further research by the teachers into particular strategies that they could employ to meet the needs of the students. All the teachers eventually made use of those strategies, integrating them into their current practice to improve and enhance what they already considered to be relatively effective, while considering what would work best for their students. As a result of the sharing sessions and following the successes they had had in their own classroom, they were able to trial new ideas, to reflect on their practice and share those reflections with each other.

Conclusion

We began this chapter with Thomas, highlighting the need for student voices in planning, assessment and feedback so that students were empowered and became active participants in their own learning. We then moved on to Gaelene, and encouraged you to consider the diversity of the students you are teaching, and how the adoption of particular approaches or programs should always be tailored to the needs of individual students. We then invited you to sit in on team meetings with Maria. Here we encouraged you to consider whether you are planning:

- begins with the *child*
- allows for time to get to know your students
- begins with the *learning* that you want to take place
- becomes an opportunity for you to engage in further professional learning that enhances your teaching practice.

Teaching can often take place in isolation. Here we have challenged you to consider how your *planning* for learning and teaching might be developed into a process of reflective collaboration and partnerships with other teachers and more importantly – your students.

Acknowledgement

Thomas Fraser is a Year 5 teacher at Warrnambool Primary School where he has taught for five years. We thank Thomas for his help in writing this chapter.

References

Barrera, RB 1992, 'The cultural gap in literature-based literacy instruction', *Education and Urban Society*, vol. 24, no. 2, pp. 227–43.

Boushey, G & Moser, J 2009, *The CAFE Book: Engaging All Students in Daily Literacy Assessment and Instruction*, Stenhouse Publishers, Portland.

Britton, JN 1972, *Language and Learning*, Penguin Books, Harmondsworth.

Carrington, V 2006, *Rethinking Middle Years: Early Adolescents, Schooling and Digital Culture*, Allen & Unwin, Crows Nest NSW.

Christie, F Devlin, B, Freebody, P, Luke, A, Martin, JN, Threadgold, T & Walton, C 1991, *Teaching English Literacy: A Project of National Significance on the Preservice Preparation of Teachers for Teaching English Literacy*, vol. 1–3, Ministry of Employment, Education and Training, Canberra.

Delpit, LD 1986, 'Skills and other dilemmas of a progressive black educator', *Harvard Educational Review*, vol. 56, no. 4, pp. 379–85.

Delpit, LD 1988, 'The silenced dialogue: power and pedagogy in educating other people's children', *Harvard Educational Review*, vol. 58, no. 3, p. 280.

Department of Education and Early Childhood Development 2013, The e5 Instructional Model, DEECD. Retrieved 18 September 2013 from <http://www.education.vic.gov.au/school/teachers/support/Pages/e5.aspx>.

Dressman, M 1993, 'Lionizing lone wolves: the cultural romantics of literacy workshops', *Curriculum Inquiry*, vol. 23, no. 3, pp. 245–63.

Dyson, AH 1992, 'The case of the singing scientist: a performance perspective on the "stages" of school literacy', *Written Communication*, vol. 9, no. 1, pp. 3–47.

Fountas, IC & Pinnell, GS 2010, *Benchmark Assessment System*, Heinemann, Portsmouth NH.

Freebody, P & Luke, A 1990, 'Literacies programs: debates and demands in cultural context' *Prospect*, vol. 5, pp. 7–16.

Graves, DH 1983, *Writing: Teachers and Children at Work*, Heinemann Educational Books, Exeter, NH.

Graves, DH 1986, *Children Writing: Process-conference Writing*, Dove Communications, Blackburn, Vic.

Lensmire, TJ 1994, *When Children Write: Critical Re-visions of the Writing Workshop*, Teachers College Press, New York.

Lensmire, TJ 2000, *Powerful Writing/Responsible Teaching*, Teachers College Press, New York.

Lo Bianco, J & Language Australia 2001, *Australian Literacies: Informing National Policy on Literacy Education*, 2nd edn, Language Australia, Melbourne, Vic.

Luke, A & Freebody, P 1999, 'Map of possible practices: further notes on the four resources model', *Practically Primary*, vol. 4, no. 12, pp. 5–8.

Macken, M 1989, *A Genre-based Approach to Teaching Writing: Years 3–6 (4 vols)*, NSW Literacy in Education Research Network (LERN) and the NSW Directorate of Studies, NSW Department of Education, Sydney.

Martin, JR 1989, *Factual Writing: Exploring and Challenging Social Reality,* 2nd edn, Oxford University Press, Oxford.

McCormick, Calkins, L 1983, *Lessons from a Child: On the Teaching and Learning of Writing*, Heinemann Educational Books, Exeter NH.

McCormick, Calkins, L 1991, *Living Between the Lines*, Heinemann Irwin, Portsmouth, NH.

McCormick, Calkins, L 1994, *The Art of Teaching Writing*, Heinemann, Portsmouth NH.

Munro, J 2006, *Paraphrasing*, University of Melbourne.

Murdoch, K 1998, *Classroom Connections: Strategies for Integrated Learning.* Eleanor Curtain Publishing, Armadale Vic.

New Zealand Department of Education 1983, *LARIC: Guided Silent Reading*, Department of Education.

Queensland School Curriculum Council 2001, *Literacy: Position Paper*, The Council.

Reid, I & Deakin University Centre for Studies in Literary Education (eds) 1987, *The Place of Genre in Learning: Current Debates*, Centre for Studies in Literary Education, Deakin University, Waurn Ponds Vic.

Reyes, ML 1992, 'Challenging venerable assumptions: literacy instruction for linguistically different students, *Harvard Educational Review*, vol. 62, no. 4, p. 427.

Rothery, J & Martin, JR 1986, 'What a functional approach to the writing task can show teachers about "good writing"' in B Couture (ed), *Functional Approaches to Writing: Research Perspectives*, Ablex Publishing Corporation, Norwood NJ, pp. 241–65.

Rowe, G, Lamont, H, Daly, M, Edwards, D & Mayor Cox, S 2000, *Success with Reading and Writing: Helping At-risk Students 8–13 years*, Dellasta Publishing, Burwood Vic.

Snowball, D 2006, 'Comprehension for all', *Teaching Pre K-8*, vol. 36, no. 8, pp. 62–3.

Snyder, I 2008, *The Literacy Wars: Why Teaching Children to Read and Write is a Battleground in Australia*, Allen & Unwin, Crows Nest, NSW.

Spiegel, DL 1992, 'Blending whole language and direct instruction', *The Reading Teacher*, vol. 46, pp. 38–44.

Timperley, HS, Parr, JM & Bertanees, C 2009, 'Promoting professional inquiry for improved outcomes for students in New Zealand', *Professional Development in Education*, vol. 35, no. 2, pp. 227–45.

Wiggins, GP & McTighe, J 2005, *Understanding by Design*, expanded 2nd edn, Association for Supervision and Curriculum Development, Alexandria VA.

Chapter 9

Teacher and student agency in contemporary literacy classrooms

Kirsten Hutchison, Anne Cloonan and Louise Paatsch

We want our students to own their learning – how can you own your learning if you are not responsible for it?

We want our students to be engaged – how can you be engaged if someone else makes all the decisions?

We want our students to know how it feels to make mistakes, be uncomfortable and not be in control – therefore we need to put ourselves in the same situation.

We want our students to take risks and be challenged – fair enough that we do the same!

Marion, Year 5/6 teacher

This book has encouraged you to reflect on the tensions and challenges that confront you as a 21st century literacy educator and consider how your professional practice might continually evolve to meet those challenges. One challenge that has always existed, but is becoming more broadly acknowledged, is catering for the diversity of learner needs and interests present in every classroom. The flow of people around the world only intensifies the diversity of student needs and interests that educators feel obliged to address (Rizvi 2009).

Embracing diversity as 'the new normal' requires a fine-tuned understanding of students and the development of inclusive pedagogies that are sensitive to the needs of individual students. As mentioned in Chapter 2, authors such as Barbara Comber and Barbara Kamler have developed the notion of 'turnaround pedagogies' to describe teacher actions that turn around to students (2005, p. 7). Building on Luis Moll, Cathy Amantim, Deborah Neff and Norma Gonzalez's (1992) powerful metaphor of 'funds of knowledge' and Pat Thomson's (2002) notion of the 'virtual school bag', we have ourselves been challenged as literacy educators to think differently about our students and the refined and subtle work we need to do in order to enable them to connect with learning.

Becoming a language and literacy educator often involves negotiating the cultures and competing discourses that constitute schooling. This can mean accepting the way things are done at whatever school employs you. Since in all likelihood you will be on a contract, you won't feel that you are in a position to raise a dissenting view. But your standpoint as a new member of the profession means that you also bring a new pair of eyes to your work, which may enable you to challenge the 'taken for granteds' embodied in the many forms of compliance that are required of us as educators. This includes standardised testing, educational outcomes that are specified for each year level, prescribed modes of assessment and reporting, and mandated curriculum initiatives, to name a few. These cultures and discourses can often pressure teachers to maintain tight control of student learning, and to value the neat sequential development as presented in learning continua, such as outcomes statements, at the expense of appreciating the messiness of students' growth at different rates and in different directions. It's also important to appreciate when students surpass teachers' expectations as they might be formed by prescribed educational outcomes, and the difficulties in keeping pace with their knowledge and expertise in particular areas such as home languages and technological programs, 'apps' and other creative capacities.

In our quest to respond to the many pressures of our work in literacy education, there is a danger that we may habitually take up the position of authoritative expert in the classroom, at the expense of allowing ourselves to be co-learners with colleagues and students. However difficult it might be, it's necessary for us to model a capacity for exploration, improvisation and innovation to our students. How do we ensure that both students and teachers have the capacity to actively engage with literacy learning, to make decisions about the nature of this learning, to articulate challenging questions and to seek and share innovative responses? In other words, how can we create learning environments where teachers and students have 'agency' in their classrooms and hopefully embed this capacity to act thoughtfully into their lives beyond schooling?

This chapter suggests some possible answers to these questions, drawing on the experience of Marion, the teacher who has provided us with our epigraph. Although Marion is a very impressive individual, you should still feel free to engage critically in what she has done and to weigh up whether her initiatives would be feasible in the school settings in which you have worked.

Marion's commitment to student agency

Let's look back at the blog extract that begins this chapter. Marion is an experienced teacher of thirty years standing and teaches Year 5/6 with two other colleagues. This teaching team has developed a culture of challenging each other as members of a community of learners. In Marion's provocative blog extract, she acknowledges the need to take risks and to model these behaviours to the students. She also poses some challenges to her fellow teachers who regularly engage in these online dialogues about difficult questions. She outlines what she sees as key dimensions of learning: individual responsibility, the capacity to make choices and be accountable for them, the willingness to experiment, to make mistakes, as well as to take risks and seek new challenges. Ultimately, she wants to encourage her colleagues to model these learning attributes, in seeking to extend their own reach as teachers and to demonstrate to students the richness of learning by their own passionate engagement in continuing inquiry.

The qualities that Marion shows might all be seen as aspects of 'agency', which has also been described by Dana Mitra as recognisable in students' increased abilities to articulate opinions, their capacity to take up new identities, and to lead others (Mitra 2004, p. 662). Central to this idea is the linking of agency with the role of change-maker. Teachers who support and promote agency through their classroom literacy practice are very often leaders of change in the way that literacy is taught and understood.

Another way of thinking about this notion of student and teacher inspired change is the notion of 'student voice', a concept that has been present in school reform discourses over several decades. This idea of student participation in school decision-making is more than simply one of expressing opinions, but is directed towards offering students the opportunity to influence change in relation to the design, facilitation and improvement of learning (Mitra 2004).

Dana Mitra distinguishes between basic and sophisticated opportunities for student agency. Basic opportunities invite students to share opinions about potential solutions to problems. Sophisticated opportunities are built on an expectation that students engage in collaborative action with adults to improve teaching, curriculum, assessment and teacher–student relationships, and ultimately student and teacher learning (Mitra 2003). Research points to a wealth of educational benefits when students are genuinely invited to contribute to decisions about their learning. Such benefits include: improved teaching and learning, improved teacher–student relationships, increased student engagement with learning, increased student self-esteem, and a stronger sense of respect and belonging (Fielding 2001; Mitra 2003, 2004; Rudduck & Flutter 2000, 2003).

In the context of the Year 5/6 learning environment which is the focus of this chapter, Marion and her colleagues had already done a lot of work to establish supportive relationships, and they found that the introduction of netbook laptop computers had considerably enhanced the social relations of a learning community that is characterised by student agency. Both teachers and students had been repositioned as change agents, as suggested by Michael Fullan (1993), in their capacities to co-construct innovative pedagogies and practices and reshape learning for their own purposes within this new setting. The Year 5/6 learning environment is a shared space where Marion and her two colleagues work collaboratively with 85 students. The students are divided into three classes, with one member of the teaching team responsible for their own class. However, teaching is shared among the three teachers when all students come together for specific large-group lessons.

Unlike many of the teachers you have met in this book, Marion is very experienced, and she embodies what it means to be a lifelong learner. We visited her teaching space during her 30th year of teaching and participated in an ongoing conversation with her and her two colleagues around their efforts to engage students in taking responsibility for their literacy learning.

A disposition to continually be on the lookout for new challenges was a key dimension of Marion's educational philosophy and practice, as shown by the quotation from her blog that begins this chapter. This passion for continually 'raising the bar a little', to use Marion's words, was visible throughout her pedagogy, in the activities and assessment tasks she undertook with her students, in her questioning in class and group discussions and in the conversations with colleagues in the Year 5/6 team these activities engendered.

Here we look specifically at how Marion challenged herself to go beyond her previous experiences and her habitual ways of doing things to create the conditions of opportunity that enabled her students to act with more agency in their literacy learning.

We have written about other dimensions of the team's teaching and Marion's leadership elsewhere, about how she set up a netbook program in a school that missed out on Government funding (Cloonan, Hutchison & Paatsch 2014), and how the teaching team engaged eleven and twelve-year old students in analysing and creating poetry (Cloonan, Hutchison & Paatsch 2011).

As you learn more about her teaching, you might like to identify the principles that underpin it, especially with respect to the way she is able to foster a learning community. We focus on three key areas of her work: pedagogy, assessment and planning.

The challenge of 'mindsets'

As teachers, we are well aware of the impact of new literacies on our lives and the lives of our students. We are conscious of the vast potential for engaging students in literacy learning through digital technologies and of the professional challenges involved in learning and thinking about how to productively use the array of devices and modalities available as tools for meaning making (Cloonan, Hutchison & Paatsch 2011, 2014). We know literacies are constantly evolving, and new literacies challenge us to find new ways to harness the knowledge and expertise of teachers and students to promote learning.

The ever expanding new technologies that shape our worlds and our experiences of literacy might be said to be accompanied by what Colin Lankshear and Michele Knobel (2006) describe as two distinct 'mindsets'.

Mindset 1 contends that the world is essentially the same as it has always been, with economic, cultural and social systems operating as they always have, although they are now imbued with an array of sophisticated technologies. Expertise and authority are predominantly found within individuals and institutions. By contrast, Mindset 2 holds that the world is very different because of the ubiquity of digital technologies. Expertise and authority are increasingly distributed and shared. Rather than the stable 'textual order' of Mindset 1, texts now are changing as social relations take place in digital spaces. While these two mindsets may appear to be categorical and may be restrictive, their value lies in offering us a way to reflect on the huge changes that are taking place in literacy education and how we, as literacy educators, respond to these changes.

See especially Chapter 2 of Colin Lankshear and Michele Knobel (2006). For further interesting reading by these authors, you might like to have a look at Colin Lankshear and Michele Knobel (2011).

A great deal of research into the use of new technologies has argued that literacy teaching in schools needs to connect more strongly to the kinds of digital literacies students engage with in their everyday lives beyond the classroom, in order to productively draw on children's digital funds of knowledge as a resource for literacy learning (Pahl & Rowsell 2012).

Other researchers suggest that the kinds of conditions present in Mindset 2, such as collaborative learning and knowledge creation among communities of learners are essential preconditions for the possibilities of learning technologies to be fully realised. These researchers emphasise the importance of developing new pedagogies for teaching digital literacies in classrooms to support this shared learning in order to complement individualised learning and achievement. The following description of the elements of new literacy practices summarises the attributes of Mindset 2 and gives a taste of the pedagogical principles we encounter in Marion's classroom:

> See Kate Pahl and Jennifer Rowsell (2012) for an argument along these lines.

…the more a literacy practice privileges participation over publishing, distributed expertise over centralized expertise, collective intelligence over individual possessive intelligence, collaboration over individual authorship, dispersion over scarcity, sharing over ownership, experimentation over 'normalisation', innovation and evolution over stability and fixity, creative-innovative rule breaking over generic purity and policing … the more we should regard it as a 'new' literacy. (Lankshear & Knobel 2006, p. 60)

Reflection and discussion

Do you feel that digital technologies have the potential to transform learning within classroom settings? From your knowledge and experience of contemporary classrooms, what do you feel are the necessary preconditions for productively incorporating digital technologies to enhance literacy learning? How might the two 'mindsets' that Colin Lankshear and Michele Knobel describe help you reflect on the different dispositions of teachers with whom you have worked? How would you characterise your own 'mindset'?

Putting student agency at the centre of your pedagogy

Let's now turn to Marion's pedagogy. In the following account of Marion's teaching, assessment and planning of a science-based integrated unit, you might find it useful to think about the way that her practice reflects an understanding of literacy teaching as actively promoting student agency in the learning process. You might specifically explore how Marion provides opportunities for ongoing reflection on students' learning processes and encourages engagement in self and peer assessment. How does Marion encourage her students to be actively involved in their learning? How does she ensure that the students take responsibility for their own learning throughout the flow of the lessons? How does Marion maintain the students' focus on the purposes and the processes involved in their construction of new knowledge and understandings?

Earth, space and beyond: challenging literacies

Marion is introducing all the Year 5/6 students to their new fourth term integrated studies unit 'Earth, Space and Beyond'. This unit of work has been carefully planned by Marion and the two other Year 5/6 teachers. All students gather in a shared learning space for these introductory sessions. In this instance, Marion leads these sessions and begins the discussion by reminding students of the previous work they have completed, reading explanatory texts, asking them to 'look up the filing cabinet in your brains' and to talk with a partner about the features and purposes of explanatory texts. Around the room are charts summarising the structure of explanation texts and annotated samples of different kinds of explanations. The students talk animatedly for a couple of minutes and Marion then engages with them in a brief summary discussion of their knowledge of explanation texts. Students offer how such texts typically begin with a question and are often structured by subheadings, describing step-by-step processes. Marion also emphasises the importance of understanding each step in order to follow the text, 'because otherwise you get lost'. She then moves to the focus of today's lesson, asking students:

> *How do we use these texts to gather and use information? What does that mean? What are you expecting to be able to do at the end of this session?*

One student, Marnie, answers:

> *Know how to use strategies to collect, find information and then do something with it.*

Marion responds that they already know how to do this and what she intends to do in this lesson is 'to take the bar a little higher and challenge you further. We're going to look at the concept of *synthesis*', meaning the way we continually combine our knowledge and experience to reach a new understanding of the world. She asks whether anyone knows what 'synthesis' is, and when it appears that the word and the idea are new to students, she says:

T: We're going to do a demonstration of what it is. What does the sun do?

S: Provides heat, provides light.

T: Think about all the things you know about the sun. What are some of the things you know? What do you think you know? Have vaguely heard from somewhere? Who knows a lot? Who knows a little bit? You know what you know – might be a lot, maybe not much. So, synthesis is bringing together what you know about something and a whole lot of other stuff from what other people know and creating a new version of what you know. Some of this might involve changing your thinking, because something that you actually know is wrong. You might think that the Sun is 100 degrees, when it's actually one million degrees, so you might actually change your thinking when you put together all that you know, with the new things you find out. So synthesis is about putting all the new bits together. Is what you know the same as what you knew 10 years ago? No. So we're always synthesising. Where does the new information come from?

S: Reading factual books, documentaries, parents, talking with experts.

T: You've heard the word synthetic, so there's a connection between these words. Synthesis means a whole lot of different material together. Today we're going to get better at identifying what we already know, using all our reading skills to find out something new.

Marion then gives the students three minutes to form groups and record what they know about the sun. They can choose how to respond: some combine their facts by passing around one netbook and individually adding their notes or nominating a scribe, other groups write in workbooks, while some groups use the software program Audacity to make an audio recording of their conversations. At the end of the three minutes Marion asks the class, 'Who got off track?' A few hands go up. She then refocuses on the purpose of the learning and ask the students, 'What's the task?' Several voices respond that the task has been to combine what they know about the sun.

See the YouTube clip by ParticleMen (2009) <http://www.youtube.com/watch?v=3JdWISF195Y>.

Standing in front of the interactive white board, Marion reiterates to students that they have just identified their schema of what they already know and then, pointing to the screen, which has a YouTube clip 'Why does the Sun shine'? ready to play, she asks students what their expectations are of this information text and what it is likely to explain.

She reminds students that they will need to look and listen carefully, since this text combines visual and sound elements to explain the phenomenon of sunshine. What she doesn't tell them is that key information is presented in the form of a song, as she wants them to discover for themselves the challenge of internalising this information in this form, and then revisiting it when they engage in another source of information in a later lesson. She plays the first 30 seconds of the clip, before pausing it to ask a series of questions:

M: Is this the sort of explanation text you were expecting?

S: No.

M: So how did you have to change what you did with it to make sense of it? So what did you have to do to understand this as an explanation text?

S: Listen really closely because it was really fast.

M: What else would help you with it?

S: Replaying it, looking at the pictures. Having lyrics to look at.

M: We know it's a song, what else do you know about songs?

S: Patterns, rhymes.

M: Does that change the way an author conveys the information?

S: Yes.

M: We have to change the way we're taking information in. I'm going to give you the lyrics and ask you what can we learn about what makes the sun shine from the song. How is what's in here adding to what I already know. How might it challenge what I already know? [Marion projects the lyrics of the song on the interactive whiteboard.]

Why does the Sun shine?

The Sun is a mass of 'incandescent' gas.

A gigantic nuclear furnace.

Where hydrogen is built into helium,

At a temperature of millions of degrees.

M: So the trick is this is to make sure you understand what it means. For examle, what does 'incandescent' mean? So you need to clarify what the words mean.

Marion tells the students that the task is to add to their knowledge about what makes the sun shine. She asks them to write a paragraph about what they know as a group and how the information in the clip has added or challenged it. She gives each group the set of lyrics, then plays the whole clip through a couple of times. Students then collaboratively write their paragraphs, attempting to synthesise what they already know with the information presented in the YouTube clip. Marion and her two teaching colleagues move around the groups observing, taking notes for their assessment portfolios and taking part in group discussions. Again, groups negotiate the form their response will take: handwritten, typed or recorded. There is animated discussion, with some students appearing to be experts on the science, others debating and Googling the veracity of facts quoted by others or relayed in the YouTube clip.

Marion is aware that the science in the clip had been critiqued by scientists for inaccuracies and that another clip is available online from a group of scientists who provide a counter narrative addressing these inaccuracies.

You can see the associated wikis at <http://tmbw.net/wiki/Why_Does_The_Sun_Shine3F> and <http://chawedrosin.wordpress.com/2009/07/31/they-might-be-giants-sun-songs/>.

See the clip by ParticleMen (2009) at <http://www.youtube.com/watch?v=sLkGSV9WDMA&list=PL44C7ADBD6A22FF0B>

She had contemplated presenting the students with the second account, but felt that this was too much to cover in one lesson, and so she does not discuss this additional dimension with students here. In subsequent lessons that Marion leads, she presents the students with another YouTube clip called 'The Sun is a miasma of incandescent plasma', which corrects the facts presented in the previous song.

The students critique both texts drawing on contemporary understandings of scientific knowledge and find the second one has more scientific accuracy. The students go on to complete an open-ended inquiry-based investigation of a contentious topic in space science titled 'Burning questions'. They are asked to research a question and present their findings, using their choice of multimodal tools.

The notion of challenging all the Year 5/6 students is central for Marion. As we see throughout the lesson, she demands their continual engagement by asking them to identify and articulate their own prior knowledge and connect this explicitly to the focus of this lesson. All students are expected to be actively involved in this exploration. She re-introduces the new concept of 'synthesis' and again invites all students to actively participate in an experience of group synthesis of information. Students are given opportunities to articulate the metacognitive dimensions of their learning, as Marion asks them to name the strategies they use to make sense of the YouTube clip as an explanatory text and how these strategies differ between print and digital texts. She also reminds students that information presented in texts is not neutral and prompts them to maintain their critical stance in considering how the new information presented in the video might challenge their current understandings. In asking students to develop a group response about what they now know about the science of why the sun shines, she offers yet another opportunity for students to reflect on, articulate, debate and co-construct a response that draws on multiple sources of information. Knowledge is viewed as mutable, evolving, and collectively arrived at through research and dialogue.

Similarly, in the design of the 'Burning questions' inquiry learning task, Marion challenges the students to identify a big question about space that matters to them personally – literally a *burning* question. As Hannah expresses it, 'We listed some and then chose one that was what we *really* wanted to find out'. Initially, the students are encouraged to pose as many questions as they like about space in an unlimited brainstorm. They have so many questions that it is impossible to answer them all, and so they discuss what constitutes significant and answerable questions. The students then break into their smaller class groups and are asked to negotiate individually with their own class teachers about a final selection.

During these individual class sessions, Marion and the other two Year 5/6 teachers challenge the students to refine their questions, so that their answers can contribute to a deeper collective understanding of the various space-related phenomena identified by the students as significant and interesting. The students then research the answers and frame their explanations as a sequence or a process, using precise technical language.

Reflection and discussion

You might like to re-read the above account of Marion's introductory lessons and identify the teaching and learning strategies that she has employed. You will note that, like all experienced teachers, she deftly moves from whole class discussion (involving a significant amount of input from her) to small-group work. Yet the whole-group session is also very interactive, involving constant negotiation between her and the students as they take up the word 'synthesis' and try to apply it in their attempts to share their knowledge about the Sun and to extend it in significant ways. How is Marion able to use classroom talk as a vehicle for promoting a sense of student agency?

Let's now reflect further on the principles of literacy teaching and learning evident in Marion's practice throughout the integrated studies unit 'Earth, Space and Beyond', specifically with a view to the way she encourages student agency. Another cornerstone of Marion's pedagogy is the notion of 'choice'. Students are expected to exercise choice with respect to the people with whom they work, in the focus of their research investigations into a 'Burning question' they negotiate with teachers, in their selection of print and multimodal tools to document and share their learning, and in the range of resources they draw on. For example, Marion and the other Year 5/6 teachers have developed a series of masterclasses around key stages of the inquiry: framing answerable questions, writing explanatory texts, sequencing information and making meaning through visual grammar.

As part of these series of classes, students are invited to sign up for a master class of their choice. These classes provide the opportunity for students to consolidate their skills or to develop new ones. There are negotiables and non-negotiables, with some essential components and others that are optional to allow for individual preferences and passions. For example, all students are expected to include visuals in their responses. They are required to create original illustrations for their presentation, with no images copied from the internet permitted. Students make original illustrations using a variety of media, digital, photographic and drawing tools, and use Photostory, PowerPoint and Digital Stories to present their findings.

The students then present their information to their teachers and peers. Students are evaluated on their presentations, using a rubric that was co-constructed between the students and their teachers. During the development of this rubric, students were, once again, given a voice regarding content to include. There were many choices that the students made regarding how they would evaluate content, and how they would ensure consistency and clarity with the assessment, including explicit indicators for how the scientific information was communicated to answer their burning questions. These co-constructed rubrics and the process of self and peer evaluation are routinised assessment practices in these Year 5/6 classrooms and, according to the teachers, result in increased student accountability and more sophisticated responses.

Figure 9.1 is an example of the text that one student, Lisa, created and presented. In this example she used PowerPoint. You might like to consider her burning question

How did the moon form?

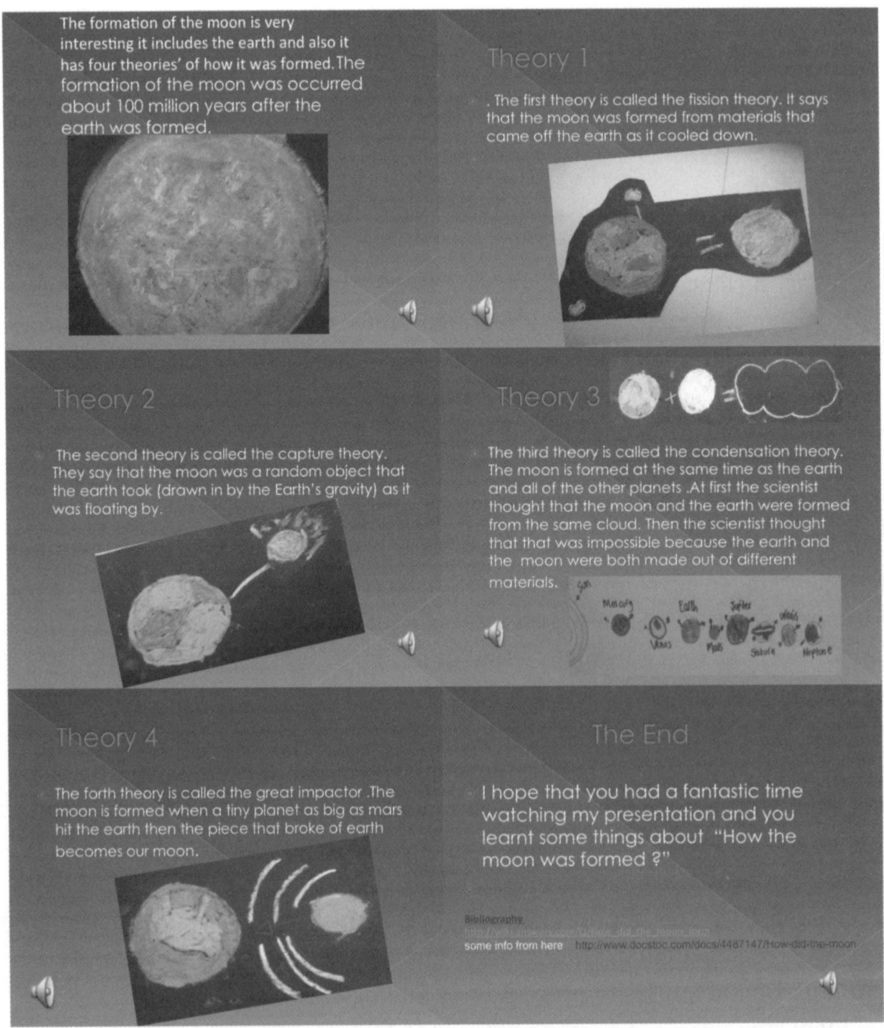

Fig. 9.1: *How did the Moon form? (<http://wiki.answers/Q/How_did_the_moon_form>)*

and how she answers it. What text types does she use to answer her question? How does the use of images support meaning in the text? Can you see any traces of the kinds of literacy pedagogies Lisa's teachers provide students in her PowerPoint presentation on her burning question: 'How did the Moon form?'

You have now seen how Marion attempts to build in a sense of student agency into the way she delivers her lessons. For Marion, student agency is integral to effective language and literacy teaching. She expects her students to actively engage in both whole-class and small-group discussion, putting their ideas into words as they engage with one another in a joint exploration of a topic that interests them. She then gives them considerable choice with respect to the way they synthesise their information and present it to others. It is also crucial that they have a sense of the importance of presenting their work to their peers, and not just to their teachers. Everything is directed towards generating knowledge that people own and which they wish to share with others. In the following sections of this chapter, the emphasis shifts slightly, as we detail Marion's efforts to engage her students in even more complex decision-making relating to the planning of their curriculum.

Further developing student agency: school planning for literacy learning

Since the introduction of the one-to-one netbook program in the Year 5/6 classes, Marion and her colleagues continually observed changes to the learning environment. While they had always thought to actively encourage collaboration and sharing, the technology prompted them to reflect on further opportunities for students to collaborate, share ideas, reflect on their learning and take greater responsibility for their own and their peers' learning. The teachers noted there was greater student agency, including: the need for increased accountability (e.g. the need to follow cyber-safety protocols); increased problem solving, independence, organisation and responsibility; increased student-to-student collaboration (e.g. peer reviewing and group work) and teacher to student collaboration (e.g. student-initiated forms of multimodal representation).

Constantly reflecting on how to increase student agency, Marion was at home late one night, writing mid-year reports on each student's achievements, when an idea came to her. She wrote a blog post entitled, 'Too much chocolate' in which she reflected on the changes she and her colleagues had made to their literacy pedagogies since the introduction of the one-to-one netbook program, particularly the impact of the netbooks on the social relations between the teaching team and the students.

As Marion thought about the teachers' imminent student-free planning day for term two big questions occurred to her: Why are we teachers doing the planning? Why aren't we asking the students what they think we should be learning?

She sent an email to her colleagues suggesting that they invite students to be involved and asking what they thought. Her colleagues were in agreement. So in the last week of term when the teachers in each area of the school are released for a day to plan together (and the students usually have a day off school), Marion and the Year 5/6 teaching team decided to work with their students to plan the term three curriculum program.

There were many uncertainties around this unprecedented approach to planning at their school. As Marion wrote in her blog (you will see that it is from this text that we have taken the epigraph for this chapter):

How many students will choose to be involved? We don't know yet.

What will it look like? We are not sure yet.

How will it go? We have no idea.

What we do know:

- *We want our students to own their learning – how can you own your learning if you are not responsible for it?*

- *We want our students to be engaged – how can you be engaged if someone else makes all the decisions?*

- *We want our students to know how it feels to make mistakes, be uncomfortable and not be in control – therefore we need to put ourselves in the same situation.*

- *We want our students to take risks and be challenged – fair enough that we do the same!*

Approximately half of the students responded to their invitation to participate in the planning day for the three Year 5/6 classes. The teachers decided to contain the students' input to two areas in the first instance: English (with a focus on writing) and their Integrated Studies topic of 'The Environment'. They gave students access to the English curriculum documents and the school's two-year Integrated Studies planner. On one-to-one laptops and large projectors, they used the microblogging software program Today's Meet to share and record their planning ideas. Planning began with a question to the students, 'what kind of English and Environmental studies learning would you like to be involved in next term?' Examples of the students' blog responses (comments followed by nicknames) can be seen below, interspersed with comments from one of the teachers in Marion's team, 'Mr M'.

Mr M: *What kind of English and Environmental work would help you learn?*

Mr M: *There's no Interschool sport, camp or excursions in Term 3.*

Mite: *People have to enjoy the work that we do in Term 3.*

Jams: *More activities to do with nature.*

Joey: *Hands-on work or going outside.*

Mite: *Some work is in groups and by yourself to get a fair share.*

Nessie: *Having more excursions to learn.*

Tara: *More hands-on work (Art and constructing).*

Maybe we can choose our favourite travel places and do a project on it.

Mr M: *I'm sure we could think of some local area excursions.*

Jams: *By activities I mean, having our own plant to look after for a certain amount of time. (Inside the school grounds!)*

Nessie*: Making a topic enjoyable.*

Larb: *You have to think about are the students going to enjoy the work.*

Kat: *Work that challenges us.*

Elec: *More projects that you get to choose your topic.*

Tara: *More passion projects.*

Mite: *Yeah because we can write something that we want to write about.*

Caik: *Find a way of getting confidence levels up.*

Joey: *Big group task.*

Tara: *Creative writing tasks.*

Busb: *Getting to choose if you want to work in a group or independently.*

Tara: *We could gain confidence levels by doing drama activities and speaking in front of a large group.*

Mite: *Doing something that the teachers have never done before.*

Vanessa: *No hard work.*

Xang: *Finding more about my computer program.*

Zald: *More challenge.*

Caik: *Thinking of doing creative work.*

Maln: *What kind of challenges?*

Vanessa: *Challenging work but not really hard.*

Zald: *More risk.*

Xang: *Use more of my computer programs for writing!*

Mite: *YES YES YES.*

Caik: *Pushing us all to our own limits.*

Marion did not participate in this discussion. Instead she read the students' responses as they appeared on the screen. She looked for patterns and tried to deeply engage with the students' suggestions. Discussions were also saved in portable document format (pdf) so that teachers could revisit the students' responses. Teachers tried not to intervene too quickly, allowing students to interact with one another and explore ideas.

The students emphasised the importance of providing choices within learning tasks and options for different working styles. They explored the notion of challenge and agreed that one student's challenge is not necessarily another's. Students wanted support to build knowledge but also wanted teachers to recognise that they like to do this in different ways (for example, some want instruction, others like to explore for themselves).

The students' use of language mirrors Marion's, reflecting her expectations and giving evidence of the transfer of responsibility for learning. The language is reflective of pedagogical principles that they found useful, including 'challenge', 'text creation' and 'choice'. Such principles are congruent with Dana Mitra's (2004) notion of sophisticated opportunities for student agency whereby the students were being offered the opportunity to influence change in relation to the planning and improvement of their own learning.

For Marion, the value of using microblogging to give students opportunities to contribute to discussions and give a voice to all students was confirmed. The Year 5/6 teachers used the blog throughout the planning day to generate a focus for their Environmental studies, to engage students with the expectations of English curriculum documents for writing, to consider the students' desires and needs for learning in writing and in Environmental Studies, and to co-generate ideas as to how learning will be organised in the coming term.

A major idea that was collaboratively generated was the planning of a Term 3 'writer's festival of comedy, film and story'. This grew from the students' desires for, 'people…to enjoy the work that we do in Term 3', designing 'a big group task' and 'creative writing tasks', while increasing choice including 'getting to choose if you want to work in a group or independently'. It also incorporated the suggestion to 'gain confidence levels by doing drama activities and speaking in front of a large group'; and 'doing something that the teachers have never done before'. Elements of choice catered for the request for 'challenging work but not really hard'. As presentations would be multimodal, there would be opportunities to 'use more … computer programs for writing.'

Students took the opportunity to reflect, and give feedback and suggestions on a range of practices, as well as their participation in curriculum planning. A heated debate on homework was noted without an immediate solution. Comments like 'the people that don't do homework shouldn't get consequences because missing out on the things that we do and learn sort of is a consequence' were acknowledged by the teachers and students but not resolved. As Marion explained at the end of the day,

> The planning is messy, the documentation is not formalised, but the ideas and understanding of where we are heading is clear.

This was a challenge for Marion, an experienced, organised and highly accomplished lead teacher. As she reflected:

> I am a control freak, I used to spend hours planning lessons that 'hit the mark', achieved my purpose, delivered content in exciting, interesting ways, that engaged my students. Now I spend hours learning, exploring and working out how to give that control back to the students and still know where they are at with their learning, where they need to go next and what I can provide to support them.

Reflection and discussion

What do you think about Marion's efforts to involve students in planning for literacy learning? What opportunities have there been for student agency in the teaching contexts in which you have worked? How Marion's ideas resonate with your experiences as a literacy teacher? How do teachers navigate between negotiating curriculum with students and delivering a prescribed curriculum, such as that set out in statements about the outcomes that students should achieve at each level of schooling?

Further to Marion's acknowledgement of her need to relinquish her control of the planning for student learning, she also acknowledges the importance of embracing students' strengths within their learning community. Recognition of these strengths, particularly in relation to students' knowledge and expertise in using technologies, may often challenge teachers to appreciate when students surpass their own level of knowledge. As Marion reflects, this may also mean a further relinquishment of control and the need to develop trust:

> I think teachers have to let go of the fact that they've got to control these IT worlds, cause they won't and you've just got to… sure you've got to put lots of protocols and usage conduct in place. But I think with that you sort of say okay, we're going to trust you and you say, well, teach us how. You know this. You know that. When this is happening … I'm always saying it to everyone, help me now. Not only to my colleagues but the students I teach. And I think actually they get a lot out of that because for some kids that's their big strength…

The change in the locus of control for responsibility for learning remains a challenge for Marion. While admitting to such anxieties, Marion sees literacy as a sociocultural practice (Street 1995) and, with meaning-making increasingly occurring in digital contexts, she engages her students in both print and digital worlds. For Marion, as a literacy teacher, the shift from page to screen as proposed by Ilana Snyder (1998) is impacting on the types of texts she engages students with and the ways in which she engages students in text analysis and creation. A major aspect of the shift is social. In line with 'Mindset 2' (Lankshear & Knobel 2006) she is attending to changing power relations, embedding expectations of student responsibility across her pedagogical, assessment and curriculum design.

She displays a teacher-as-researcher mindset, continually curious about learning and students, and models a learning persona, articulating and reflecting on her own and others' learning in an ongoing way – the uncertainties and not so successful efforts as well as the triumphs and breakthroughs. Her reflections on what it means to plan for learning challenge outcomes-based education, with its predetermined descriptions of what students will learn and in what sequence this will happen. Rather than prescribed outcomes, she now emphasises the importance of teachers and students engaging in a joint inquiry into things that they wish to know.

> I have had to do some deep thinking about what does it mean to plan with the 'end in mind'. The end for me had usually been some predetermined task and/or creation that every student worked towards achieving. I hope for my future students' sake I never fall into that trap again. The end has become … what we (students and teachers) want to know and do and we should decide together how to get there.

Marion's questioning orientation towards her own work shows that teacher professional learning, like student learning, is as an ongoing concern, evidenced in collaborative dialogue that reflects ongoing curiosity about learners and learning. It is a model for her students and colleagues. It allows for the messiness and false starts and dead-ends of learning. It rejects a step-by-step, uniform approach. As Marion remarks:

> Asking students how they want to learn, expecting them to be responsible for that, setting goals and success criteria together has led to many successes and some failures … Our most powerful learning is coming from the failures and the endless questions we are asking ourselves. How do we support all students to be independent in their learning? Does it take longer for some students to take on responsibility for their learning, their failures and successes? Do we allow students enough time to succeed before we step in? How do we measure success? How do we maintain accountability? How do we cover the curriculum? What is essential learning?

At its foundation is honest collaboration, built on trust and free exchange of opinions.

Reflection and discussion

Reflect on your own learning and the learning experiences of your students or students you have observed and worked with. How would you judge the importance of agency for language and learning? What other dimensions do you consider to be important for rich forms of language and learning to occur?

How do you, as a teacher and researcher, continue to challenge yourself to go beyond your own experiences and to foster learning communities that provide opportunities for student agency?

Conclusion

This account of one extended learning community of students, teachers and researchers has explored how a group of teachers and students, led by one very experienced teacher, endeavoured to engage students in taking responsibility for their own learning. We have witnessed how teachers challenged themselves and their students to act with greater agency. Students and teachers participated in a shared learning environment that encouraged risk-taking, collaboration, peer review, group work, and experimentation.

Marion and her colleague's ongoing reflections on teacher and student new literacy practices prompted them to explore affordances made possible by this technologically sophisticated learning environment. Students were expected to actively engage with all stages of the learning process and communicate their new understandings using innovative modes of presentation. This engagement with multiple forms of communication within the learning community led to changes in teacher–student relationships towards more collaborative, egalitarian and trusting relationships. Teachers and students demonstrated their willingness to share doubt and uncertainty in this ever-changing, fluid learning environment, and together opened up the possibility for developing innovative solutions and sophisticated opportunities for learning.

References

Cloonan, A, Hutchison, K & Paatsch, L 2011, 'Reimagining poetry: innovative literacies, national agendas and digital landscapes' in G Parr, W Sawyer & B Doecke (eds), *Creating an Australian Curriculum for English: National Agendas, Local Contexts*, Phoenix Education, Putney, NSW, pp. 81–98.

Cloonan, A, Hutchison, K & Paatsch, L 2014, 'Innovating from the inside: teacher influence on learning organisations responding to the "promisingness" of digital learning environments', *E-learning and Digital Media*, vol. 11, no. 6., (in press).

Comber, B & Kamler, B 2005, 'Designing turn-around pedagogies and contesting deficit assumptions' in B Comber & B Kamler (eds), *Turn-around Pedagogies: Literacy Interventions for At-risk Students*, PETA, Newtown, Australia.

Fielding, M 2001, 'Beyond the rhetoric of student voice: new departures or new constraints in twenty first century schooling?' *Forum*, vol. 43, no. 2, pp. 100–10.

Fullan, MG 1993, 'Why teachers must become change agents', *Educational Leadership*, vol. 50, no. 6, pp. 12–17.

Lankshear, C & Knobel, M 2006, *New Literacies: Everyday Practices and Classroom Learning*, 2nd edn, Open University Press, Maidenhead and New York.

Lankshear, C & Knobel, M 2011, *New Literacies: Everyday Practices and Classroom Learning*, 3rd edn, Open University Press, Maidenhead.

Mitra, DL 2003, 'Student voice in school reform: reframing student–teacher relationships', *McGill Journal of Education*, vol. 38, no. 2, pp. 289–304.

Mitra, DL 2004, The significance of students: can increasing "student voice" in schools lead to gains in youth development?', *Teachers College Record*, vol. 106, no. 4, pp. 651–88.

Moll, LC, Amanti, C, Neff, D & Gonzalez, N 1992, 'Funds of knowledge for teaching: using a qualitative approach to connect homes and classrooms', *Theory into Practice*, vol. 31, no. 2, p. 132.

Pahl, K & Rowsell, J 2005, *Literacy and Education: Understanding the New Literacy Studies in the Classroom*, Paul Chapman, London.

ParticleMen 2009, 'They might be giants – why does the Sun shine? (The Sun is a mass of incandescent gas)'. Retrieved 6 April 2014, <http://www.youtube.com/watch?v= 3JdWlSF 195Y>.

ParticleMen 2009, 'They might be giants – why does the Sun really shine? (The Sun is a miasma of incandescent plasma)'. Retrieved 6 April 2014 <http://www.youtube.com/watch ?v=sLkGSV9WDMA&list=PL44C7ADBD6A22FF0B>.

Rizvi, F 2009, 'Towards cosmopolitan learning', *Discourse: Studies in the Cultural Politics of Education*, vol. 30, no. 3, pp. 253–68.

Rudduck, J & Flutter, J 2000, 'Pupil participation and pupil perspective: "carving a new order of experience"', *Cambridge Journal of Education*, vol. 30, no. 1, pp. 75–89.

Snyder, I & Michael, J 1998, *Page to Screen: Taking Literacy Into the Electronic Era*, Routledge, London.

Street, B 1995, Social Literacies: Critical Approaches to Literacy in Development, Ethnography and Education, Longman, London.

Thomson, P 2002, *Schooling the Rustbelt Kids: Making the Difference in Changing Times*, Allen & Unwin, Crows Nest, NSW.

Index